Refining Familiar Contructs

Alternative Views in OB, HR, and I/O

A volume in
Research in Organizational Science

Series Editor:
Daniel J. Svyantek
Auburn University

Research in Organizational Science

Daniel J. Svyantek, Series Editor

Volume 1: A Closer Examination of Applicant Faking Behavior (2006)
edited by Richard L. Griffith and Mitchell H. Peterson

Refining Familiar Constructs

Alternative Views in OB, HR, and I/O

edited by

Daniel J. Svyantek
Auburn University

and

Elizabeth McChrystal
Accent Technologies

Information Age Publishing, Inc.
Charlotte, North Carolina • www.infoagepub.com

Library of Congress Cataloging-in-Publication Data

Industrial/Organizational and Organizational Behavior Conference (2005)
  Refining familiar constructs : alternative views in OB, HR, and I/O /
edited by Daniel J. Svyantek and Elizabeth McChrystal.
    p. cm. -- (Research in organizational science)
  Includes bibliographical references.
  ISBN 978-1-59311-619-4 (pbk.) -- ISBN 978-1-59311-620-0 (hardcover)
 1. Organizational behavior--Congresses. 2. Industrial
organization--Congresses. I. Svyantek, Daniel J. II. McChrystal, Elizabeth.
III. Title.
  HD58.7.I535 2007
  302.3'5--dc22
                                                        2007003671

ISBN 13: 978-1-59311-619-4 (pbk.)
        978-1-59311-620-0 (hardcover)
ISBN 10: 1-59311-619-5 (pbk.)
        1-59311-620-9 (hardcover)

Copyright © 2007 IAP–Information Age Publishing, Inc.

All rights reserved. No part of this publication may be reproduced, stored in a
retrieval system, or transmitted, in any form or by any means, electronic, mechanical,
photocopying, microfilming, recording or otherwise, without written permission
from the publisher.

Printed in the United States of America

**Library
University of Texas
at San Antonio**

CONTENTS

PART I: THE BEST FROM IO-OB: AN INTRODUCTION TO NEW VOICES IN THE FIELD

1. Empirical Studies Presented at the Industrial/Organizational and Organizational Behavior Conference
   Elizabeth L. McChrystal — 3

2. Hispanic Preferences in Organizational Recruiting Ads
   Viola Y. Fernandez and Barbara A. Fritzsche — 11

3. An Empirical Test of Gender-Based Differences in E-Mentoring
   Kimberly A. Smith-Jentsch, Shannon A. Scielzo, and Melissa A. Weichert — 27

4. Performance Appraisal Discomfort of Critical Incidents
   Andrew P. Kavulic, Thomas D. Carpenito, and Peter D. Villanova — 45

5. Green is the Color of This Chameleon: A Study of Pay Rate and Applicant Response Behavior
   Mitchell H. Peterson, Shawn Burkevich, Abhishek R. Gujar, and Richard L. Griffith — 57

6. Males Versus Females on Faking Behavior in Personality Testing: An Examination of Gender Differences
   Randolph Socin, Joshua A. Isaacson, and Richard L. Griffith — 75

7. Cooperation and Competition: The Effects of Team Entrainment and
   Reward Structure
   Michael Woodward, Kenneth Randall,
   Bennett Price, and Andrea Saravia 89

8. The Relationship Between Shared Leadership and
   Team Performance and Satisfaction: Task Type Matters
   Paul Pluta, Gregory Hyman,
   Ingrid Campbell, and Diana Keith 105

PART II: NEW PERSPECTIVES ON FAMILIAR CONSTRUCTS

9. New Perspectives and Research on Familiar Constructs
   Brian Perdomo, Kristin L. Cullen, and Daniel J. Svyantek 123

10. "Learning Through Listening": Conversation for
    Change in a Healthcare Provider
    David Coghlan and Claus Jacobs 129

11. The Implementation of Strategy and Organizational Reward
    Systems: An Overlooked Area in the Strategic Management of
    Human Resources
    Philip G. Benson and Terry R. Adler 151

12. Task Interdependence as a Moderator of
    Politics-Work Outcomes Relationships
    Deondra Conner, Darren Treadway, Matrecia James,
    Jason Stoner, and Wayne Hochwarter 167

13. Organizational Citizenship Behaviors: Concept Redefinition,
    Inclusion, and Reconceptualization
    Jason Harkins, Jonathan R. B. Halbesleben,
    Danielle S. Beu, and M. Ronald Buckley 189

14. Self-Concept-Job fit: Expanding the Person-Job fit Construct
    and Implications for Retention Management
    Wesley A. Scroggins and Philip G. Benson 211

15. Person-Organization Fit and Job Satisfaction: An Interactional
    Approach
    Daniel J. Svyantek, Kristin L. Cullen,
    Brian L. Perdomo, and Scott A. Goodman 233

16. Technological Determinism, Sociotechnical Systems, and
    Classical Warfare: Social Innovation During a Period of
    Technological Stasis
    Daniel J. Svyantek, Kevin T. Mahoney, and Kristin L. Cullen ... 261

17. A new Perspective on Leadership: A Review of *Resonant Leadership: Renewing Yourself and Connecting With Others Through Mindfulness, Hope, and Compassion* by Richard Boyatzis and Annie Mckee
    Loren R. Dyck   *291*

18. Leadership in the new Millennium: A Review of *Finding our way: Leadership for an Uncertain Time* by Margaret Wheatley
    David L. Luechauer and William B. Locander   *295*

About the Authors   *301*

PART I

THE BEST FROM IO-OB:
AN INTRODUCTION TO NEW VOICES IN THE FIELD

CHAPTER 1

EMPIRICAL STUDIES PRESENTED AT THE INDUSTRIAL ORGANIZATIONAL ORGANIZATIONAL BEHAVIOR CONFERENCE

Elizabeth L. McChrystal

INTRODUCTION

The Industrial Organizational Organizational Behavior (IOOB) Conference is a long standing tradition for graduate students and prominent speakers in the fields of industrial/organizational (IO) psychology, organizational behavior (OB), and human resource management (HRM). Every year different universities are selected to host the conference and provide graduate students the opportunity to present their research while networking, interacting, and learning from practitioners and academics in these respected fields. This special issue emphasizes the research presented at IOOB 2005 and enables all students, professionals, and professors the opportunity to review some of the research presented at the conference.

The objective of this special issue is to provide a forum for students to convey their empirical studies presented at IOOB 2005, and the spirit of this issue is to offer students an opportunity to experience the publication process and receive peer reviewed feedback for the first time. Therefore, the evaluation of the manuscripts, although stringent, was reviewed in light of the conference. Positive finding bias, which is typically found in most peer reviewed journals, is not present as nonsupported hypotheses are represented in the articles.

To accustom all readers with the conference and research presented, the introduction will provide a synopsis of the long standing tradition of the IOOB conference, provide an overview of the 2005 IOOB conference, and provide a brief review of the empirical studies in this special issue.

Brief Overview of the IOOB Conference

Milt Hakel is the founder of the IOOB Conference. In 1980, Ohio State University served as the first host, and unfolded a long standing tradition for graduate students in the fields of IO psychology, OB, and HRM. This tradition involves the conference being passed to different universities to serve as hosts for the annual conference. As of 2005, 26 conferences have been held by different universities with the Florida Institute of Technology hosting the last conference. George Mason University is set to host the 2006 conference. Refer to Table 1.1 to review past conference host.

The goals of the IOOB conference are to provide students (both graduate and undergraduate) with the opportunity to present their research and research ideas in a noncompetitive environment, interact with each other and create a professional network, and the opportunity to interact with and learn from prominent practitioners and academics in our respective fields. To ensure these goals are met, each host university provides several keynote speaker presentations, an array of guest speaker presentations, symposia, workshops, and student presentations in an effort to accommodate the variety of interests within IO psychology, OB, and HRM.

Brief Overview of the 2005 IOOB Conference

Since every IOOB conference has a theme, our first step in the planning process was establishing a theme that would guide us through the

Table 1.1. Past Conference Hosts

Year	Host	Year	Host
1980	The Ohio State University	1981	Michigan State University
1982	University of Maryland	1983	Illinois Institute of Technology
1984	Old Dominion University	1985	University of Akron
1986	University of Minnesota	1987	The University of Tennessee
1988	Bowling Green State University	1989	Tulane University
1990	The Ohio State University	1991	University of Missouri-St.Louis
1992	Radford University	1993	University of Waterloo & University of Guelph
1994	DePaul University	1995	University of Colorado-Denver, University of Colorado-Boulder, & Colorado State U.
1996	Bowling Green State University	1997	Radford University
1998	California School of Professional Psychology–San Diego	1999	George Mason University
2000	The University of Tennessee	2001	Penn State University
2002	University of South Florida	2003	The University of Akron
2004	The University of Tulsa	2005	Florida Institute of Technology

planning and execution of the conference. "Surfing the Waves of I/O Psychology" was the perfect theme for our conference. It provided an exceptional analogy in that the waves are responsible for shaping our local shoreline and community, the fields of IO, OB, and HRM are responsible for shaping corporate culture, climate, and practice.

The conference was held at a local beachfront hotel and conference center. The weekend long conference began on Friday with a welcoming Beach Party. Saturday was the main conference day in which the majority of the presentations, poster sessions, and special workshops took place. Table 1.2 provides a list of the 27 speakers, from both applied and academic settings that accepted our invitation and provided informative presentations and workshops. Saturday concluded with a reception that was held to recognize and honor the 2005 Lifetime Achievement Award Winner. Gerald Barrett, PhD was presented with the award and was recognized for his significant contributions to the field of IO psychology. The Sunday session began with breakfast and involved presentations, posters, and special topic workshops. The conference concluded after lunch.

One noteworthy event that was most popular for students, academics, and practitioners was the annual IOOB Jeopardy. Many different universities formed teams to compete to be the IOOB Jeopardy winner. The game was played similar to the real Jeopardy but with IO humor inserted throughout the game. The University of Minnesota-Mankato won the event and received $100 in gift certificates from Best Buy.

Table 1.2. Lifetime Achievement Award Recipient, Keynote Speakers, and Guest Speakers

Name	Affiliation	Topic
Gerald Barrett, PhD, JD	Barrett & Associates Inc.	The Intersection of the Behavioral/Social Sciences and the Law: Stereotypes & Statistics
Frank Landy, PhD	SHL Landy Jacobs, Inc.	The Pursuit of Emotional Intelligence: A cautionary tale
Edward Levine, PhD	University of South Florida	A Century of "Surfing" and Just getting Started
Don VandeWalle, PhD	Southern Methodist University	Are Leaders Born or Made: An Implicit Person Theory Model of Why the Answer Matters
Guest Speakers		
Richard Griffith, PhD	Florida Tech	Conference Opening Speakers
T. Roger Manley, PhD Wade H. Shaw, PhD	Florida Tech	Can It Be That We Are Starting to Take Partnering Seriously?: Applying Collaborative Decision Making to Private-Public Sector Joint Ventures
David Wilder, PhD	Florida Tech	Organizational Behavior management and Industrial/Organizational Psychology: Similarities and Differences
Arthur Gutman, PhD	Florida Tech	Sexual Harassment: Legal Issues and Employer Policies
Rodney McCloy, PhD	HumRRO	Innovative Selection and Classification Research for the U.S. Army
Marcy Stahl, MS	Thoughtlink	I/O Opportunities in Homeland Security Training and Exercising
John Deaton, PhD	Florida Tech	Developing and Immersive, Cultural Training System Using Virtual Non-Player Characters
Rick Frei, PhD	Philadelphia Community College	Teaching 101: A Primer for New College Professors
Chochalingam Viswesvaran, PhD	Florida International University	Assessment of Job Performance: Pitfalls to Avoid
Janet Barnes-Farrell, PhD	University of Connecticut	What can research in the fields of I/O Psychology and OB contribute to an understanding of our aging workforce?
Matthew O'Connell, PhD	Select International Inc.	120,000 candidates in 30 days: Applying technology and I/O theory to meet extreme hiring needs and still make candidates feel like they were treated fairly
William Gabrenya, PhD	Florida Tech	The Chinese Family Business: Harmony and Hierarchy in the Chinese Diaspora

Table continues on next page

Table 1.2. continued

Dale Rose, PhD	3D Group	Moving from "Efficient Survey" to "Building Effective Leaders:" Practical Answers to Difficult Questions about 360 Degree Feedback
Symposium		
Kelly Rutkowski, PhD	Hofstra University	Newly Graduated Professional Direction
Andrew English, PhD	Thoughtlink	
Elizabeth McChrystal, PhD	Florida Tech	
Kristin Stubbs, MS	Willard Brothers Construction	
Kizzy Park, MS	Florida Metropolitan University/ BrevardCommunity College	
Workshops		
Terry Oswalt, PhD	Florida Tech	Successful Strategies for Getting Your First Grant
Terri A. Scandura, PhD	University of Miami	The Never Ending Story: Item Generation and Construct Validation
Greg Northcraft, PhD	University of Illinois at Urbana-Champaign	How to get Lucky With Journals
Marshall Schminke, PhD	University of Central Florida	

Examples of Empirical Studies Presented at IOOB 2005

Students took advantage of the opportunity to present their research in presentation or poster session format with 87 accepted submissions. The research presented covered a wide array of interests across the IO, OB, and HRM fields. Students had the option to submit research in the following areas: Culture/climate/diversity, Ethics, Leadership, Legal Issues, Motivation, Organizational Development And Change, Performance Appraisal/feedback, Selection/testing, Training, Teams, Or Other (mainly compensation and technology). Research topics represented in this special issue include Culture/climate/diversity, Training And Other: Technology, Performance Appraisal/feedback, Selection/testing, Teams, And Other: Compensation.

Culture/Climate/Diversity is represented by Fernandez and Fritzsche. Their study focused on two central beliefs to the Hispanic culture (Familism and Simpatia), and suggests the content of recruiting messages can impact preemployment attitudes toward organizations that promote family-friendly policies. Results suggest that both Hispanics and non-Hispanic Whites prefer organizations high in family-friendly policies.

Training and Other: Technology is represented by Smith-Jentsch, Irving, and Weichert. Smith-Jentsch et al. investigated gender differences in computer-mediated communication (CMC) and the perception of CMC in an electronic-mentoring program. The results suggest that: (a) there are gender differences in CMC as it relates to psychosocial support and number of E-nonverbals and (b) protégé perceptions of psychosocial support was influenced by the gender of the mentor.

Performance Appraisal/Feedback is represented by Kavulic, Carpenito, and Villanova. Kavulic et al. investigated the impact of rater leniency and self-efficacy on performance appraisal ratings. The results indicate that less experienced raters focus their ratings on interpersonal factors while more experienced raters focus their attention on the administrative aspects of the performance appraisal.

Selection/Testing is represented by Peterson, Burkevich, Gujar, and Griffith and Socin, Isaacson, and Griffith. Both studies focused on the use of personality measures in selection and the applicant's ability to fake their responses in order to portray themselves in a more positive manner. The Peterson et al. study investigated pay rate on faking behavior and found that the amount of pay affected faking behaviors in the three subscales of the NEO-Five Factor Inventory (extraversion, agreeableness, and conscientiousness). On the other hand, Socin et al. investigated gender differences in faking behaviors. The results suggest that there are gender differences with males engaging in more faking behaviors than females.

Teams is represented by the Woodward, Randall, Price, and Saravia and Pluta, Hyman, Campbell, and Keith studies. Woodward et al. focused on team performance under cooperative and competitive reward structures and found that reward structure significantly impacts team performance, satisfaction, conflict, and information sharing. Pluta et al. investigated the impact that task type had on the relationship between shared leadership, team performance, and satisfaction. The results indicate that different task type impact the relationship between shared leadership, team performance, and satisfaction.

Other: Compensation is represented by Shetye, Poncheri, and Surface. Shetye et al. investigated the impact of procedural justice in a skilled based pay (SBP) system and an individual's intent to leave. The results indicate that procedural justice influences an individual's intent to leave an organization participating in SBP systems.

CONCLUSION

The eight articles presented in this special issue provide insight into the research presented at IOOB 2005. The goal of the special issue was to provide a forum to enable students to present their research, experience the publication process, and to provide all individuals the opportunity to read and review research presented at IOOB 2005.

CHAPTER 2

HISPANIC PREFERENCES IN ORGANIZATIONAL RECRUITING ADS

Viola Y. Fernandez and Barbara A. Fritzsche

The present study focuses on the content of job recruitment messages and how beliefs that are central to the Hispanic culture, simpatia and familism, and the personality trait, agreeableness, relate to preemployment attitudes about organizations. One hundred thirty-nine undergraduate students (91 Caucasians and 48 Hispanics) participated in this study. Participants completed the measures and evaluated one of four recruiting ads in which the family-friendliness of the organization's policies and the extent to which the organization encouraged cooperativeness or competitiveness were manipulated. Results suggest that, regardless of ethnic background, participants preferred an organization high in family-friendly policies. There were also differences found in the type of organization one would pursue depending on one's level of agreeableness. Implications for the design of recruiting ads, the importance of family-friendly policies in attracting applicants, and future research on Hispanics and work were discussed.

HISPANIC PREFERENCES IN ORGANIZATIONAL RECRUITING ADS

Hispanics are currently the largest minority group in the United States, and by the year 2050, nearly 25% of the U.S. population will come from a Hispanic background. In this paper, individuals are labeled "Hispanic" if they reside in the United States and trace their background either to Spain or to one of the Spanish-speaking Latin American nations. Members of this group share some common basic cultural values that make them members of a clearly identifiable group (Marin & Marin, 1991). Despite the size of the Hispanic population, relatively little research has specifically addressed how the beliefs, motivations, and customs of Hispanics influence work attitudes and behaviors (Stone-Romero et al., 2002). To attract talent and increase diversity, Stone, Salas, and Stone-Romero (2002) suggested that organizations consider the culture and work-related attitudes of Hispanics, including how cultural values impact recruiting and selection processes. Thus, in order to provide a foundation for our study, we briefly describe the relevant job attraction literature and identify two Hispanic cultural values that are expected to impact work-related attitudes and behaviors. Then, we describe the current study which examines Hispanics' and non-Hispanic Whites' job attraction as a function of cultural values and the content of job advertisements.

Even before being hired, job applicants form beliefs and attitudes about organizations. According to the attraction portion of Schneider's (1987) attraction-selection-attrition model (ASA), individuals' preferences for particular organizations are based upon their implicit estimate of the congruence of their own personal characteristics and the perceived characteristics of work organizations. Schneider suggests that personality, interests, and values are the personal characteristics that influence attraction to organizations. This idea has been supported by research on person-organization fit (Cable & Judge, 1996). Specifically, Cable and Judge found that job applicants can and do make reliable assessments of organizations' values when seeking employment. Moreover, perceptions of the congruence between job seekers' values and that of the organization predicted job choice intentions and work attitudes.

Values are enduring beliefs about preferred actions and outcomes that guide attitudes and behavior (Rokeach, 1960). Widely held values of the majority culture in the United States include, for example, rugged individualism, individuality, the nuclear family, and competition. Hispanics who strongly identify with their ethnic background tend not to espouse traditional U.S. majority values. Instead, they tend to value group achievement, the extended family, and a collectivistic orientation (Vasquez, 1994).

Two cultural values that are central to the Hispanic culture are familism and simpatia (De Las Fuentes, Baron, & Vasquez, 2003; Levine, Norenzayan, & Philbrick, 2001; Sabogal, Marin, & Otero-Sabogal, 1987). Familism is the term used to describe the belief that family is important, and it refers to an attitude of confidence and moral compromise exclusively with members of one's family group (Garzon, 2000). It is also considered to be one of the most culture-specific values of Hispanics (Sabogal et al., 1987). According to Sabogal et al., Hispanic families protect their family members against physical and emotional stressors, and they consider the needs of their families when decisions are made. Familism is found among all Hispanic groups and tends to remain personally significant independent of the number of years individuals have lived in the United States (Marin & Marin, 1991).

Simpatia, which has no equivalent in English, refers to a permanent personal quality where an individual is perceived as likeable, attractive, fun to be with, polite, agreeable, and easygoing. Someone who is *simpatico* strives for harmony in interpersonal relations (Triandis, Marin, Lisansky, & Betancourt, 1984). Simpatia emphasizes the need for behaviors that promote smooth and pleasant social relationships (Marin & Marin, 1991). Cultures that are characterized by this value, such as Spanish or Latin cultures, are defined by a concern for the well-being of others. This includes a prerogative to be friendly, polite and helpful to others (Levine, Norenzayan, & Philbrick, 2001).

Cultural values are related to personality. Personality is a configuration of cognitions, emotions, and habits activated when situations stimulate their expression (Triandis & Suh, 2002). Triandis and Suh suggest that culture shapes socialization patterns, which shape personality. The cultural value, simpatia, is related to the personality trait agreeableness. In fact, Antshel (2002) describes simpatia as valuing being agreeable. Agreeableness, like simpatia, is a dimension of interpersonal behavior and the characteristic quality of interaction. Facets of agreeableness have been identified as trust, straightforwardness, altruism, compliance, modesty, and tender-mindedness (Costa, McCrae, & Dye, 1991). Agreeable individuals are altruistic, warm, generous, trusting, and cooperative (Costa & McCrae, 1992).

Hispanics, because of their cultural values of familism and simpatia, were expected to respond more positively to organizational recruiting ads that portray the organization as family-friendly and cooperative than to ads that portray the traditional majority U.S. values of competitiveness and individualism. We expected that Hispanics would report greater organizational attractiveness, job pursuit intentions, and value congruence in response to an organization that is portrayed as family-friendly and cooperative. Organizational attractiveness refers to expressed general positive affect toward viewing an organization as a desirable entity with which to initiate some relationship (Aiman-Smith, Bauer, & Cable, 2001). Job pursuit intentions reflect an intention to take action to find out more information about an organization or to contact an organization (Aiman-Smith, Bauer, & Cable, 2001). Value congruence is the degree to which an applicant perceives his or her values matches those of the organization (Cable & Judge, 1996). These three dependent variables have been used in prior job attraction research (e.g., Aiman-Smith et al., 2001; Cable & Judge, 1996) and are consistent with predictions made by the attraction portion of the ASA model.

Specifically, we tested the following hypotheses:

Hypothesis 1: Because of the values of simpatia and familism, Hispanics were expected to rate an organization described as highly cooperative and family-friendly more positively (i.e., on organizational attractiveness, job pursuit intentions with that organization, and value congruence) than an organization described as being low in cooperativeness and having low work-family emphasis.

Hypothesis 2: Hispanics were expected to prefer the cooperative, family-friendly organization more than would non-Hispanic Whites.

Hypothesis 3: It was expected that Hispanics would score higher than non-Hispanic Whites on measures of simpatia, agreeableness, and familism. Moreover, participants who score high on simpatia, agreeableness, and familism were expected to rate more highly the high cooperative, family-friendly organization than the low cooperative, low work-family emphasis organization.

METHOD

Participants

One hundred ninety-five undergraduate students participated in this study. There were 91 Whites, 48 Hispanics, 32 African Americans, 6 Asian Americans, 3 Native Americans, and 15 people who identified themselves as other. Because this study is interested in differences between Hispanics and non-Hispanic Whites, the sample was narrowed down to participants who identified themselves as such. The final sample consisted of 139 participants (91 Whites and 48 Hispanics). Ages ranged from 17 to 48 years old ($M = 23.08$) and 74.1% of the sample was female. The majority of the participants were employed (60.4%) and single (86.3%).

Measures

Familism
The Bardis Familism Scale (Bardis, 1959); a 16-item, self-report measure was used for this study. Participants read each statement (e.g., A person should always avoid every action of which his/her family disapproves), and then rated their agreement on each item in a 5-point scale from 1 (*strongly agree*) to 5 (*strongly disagree*). The scale produced a reliability coefficient of .77 (Bardis, 1959).

Simpatia
Six simpatia items were developed. Participants read each statement (e.g., If someone says something that is not consistent with my views, I tell him/her), and then rated their agreement with each item in a 5-point scale from 1 (*strongly agree*) to 5 (*strongly agree*).

Agreeableness
The 12-item agreeableness scale of the NEO-FFI (Costa & McCrae, 1992) was used to measure agreeableness. Participants read each statement (e.g., I try to be courteous to everyone I meet), and rated them on a 5-point scale from 0 (*strongly disagree*) to 4 (*strongly agree*). The reported reliability coefficient of the scale was .86 (Costa & McCrae, 1992).

Demographic Characteristics
On a demographics sheet, participants self-identified their ethnic background, employment history, age, marital status, and sex.

Organizational Attractiveness
Organizational attractiveness was assessed using a 7-point rating scale consisting of 5 items developed by Aiman-Smith, Bayer, and Cable. Items in the scale include: "This is a company I would like to work for," and "This company cares about its employees." The reported reliability of the organizational attractiveness measure was .98 (Aiman-Smith, Bauer, & Cable, 2001).

Job Pursuit Intentions
Job pursuit intentions were assessed using a 6- item, 7-point rating scale developed by Aiman-Smith, Bayer, and Cable. Items in the scale include: "I would accept a job offer from this company," and "I would attempt to gain

an interview with this organization." The reliability estimate of the job pursuit intention mention was .91 (Aiman-Smith, Bauer, & Cable, 2001).

Value Congruence

Value congruence was assessed using a 3 item, 7-point scale (1 = *not at all* to 7 = *completely*) developed by Judge and Cable. An example of an item in the scale is: "To what degree do your values, goals, and personality 'match' or fit this organization and the current employees in this organization?" This measure produced an alpha of .80 (Judge & Cable, 1997).

Procedure

Recruiting advertisements were developed in which the independent variables, cooperativeness and work-family balance emphasis, were manipulated. High cooperativeness was operationalized as "support among employees, emphasis on shared responsibility, cooperative work environment, emphasis on teamwork." Low cooperativeness was operationalized as "emphasis on individual responsibility, competitive work environment, emphasis on individual achievement." High work-family balance emphasis was operationalized as "flexible work schedules, family-friendly benefits, on site child care, the opportunity to take work home when possible." Low work-family balance emphasis was described as "demanding work schedule, excellent benefits, on-site gym, an opportunity to work in a fast-paced, challenging environment."

A pilot test was conducted to test whether the manipulations were effective. The pilot study consisted of 21 participants. There were 15 Caucasians, 3 Hispanics, 1 African American, and 1 African American and West Indian. One participant did not complete a demographics questionnaire, so this person's data were not used. Participants read the organizational recruiting ads and rated their interest in the organization. To examine whether the manipulations were effective, 2 (family-friendliness) x 2 (cooperativeness) ANOVAs were conducted. As expected, the ads featuring a family-friendly organization ($M = 3.8$, $SD = .42$) were rated higher on family-friendliness than were the ads featuring an individually-oriented organization ($M = 1.55$, $SD = .69$), $F(1,17) = 78.863$, $p < .001$. The ads of a cooperative organization ($M = 3.78$, $SD = .44$) were rated higher on cooperativeness than were the ads of a competitive organization ($M = 2.17$, $SD = 1.11$), $F(1,17) = 15.618$, $p = .001$. Consistent with expectations, there were no other main effects or interactions. Pilot study participants also compared the ads to real recruiting ads by rating them on a 4-point scale. On average, the ads were reasonably appealing ($M = 2.76$, $SD = 1.09$) to the participants. Moreover, the ads were rated "somewhat similar" ($M =$

2.24, $SD = .62$), "somewhat typical" ($M = 1.90$, $SD = .62$), and "somewhat realistic" ($M = 2.05$, $SD = .80$) compared to real recruiting ads.

Following the pilot study, data collection began. Participants were randomly assigned to rate one of the four recruiting ads. Participants completed the individual differences scales and rated the ad. The order in which participants completed the scales and rated the ad was counterbalanced. After the study, participants received a debriefing form, and were asked if they had any questions about the study.

RESULTS

Table 2.1 presents the means, standard deviations, internal consistency estimates, and intercorrelations among the measures. The coefficient alphas for all variables were moderate to high (.76 to .92) except for the simpatia scale ($\Lambda = .61$). Simpatia correlated with agreeableness ($r = .31$, $p < .05$), and it is interesting to note that the dependent measures were highly correlated (rs ranged from .68 to .76).

Because the sample was predominantly female, sex differences were examined. Independent-samples t tests revealed no differences between males and females on agreeableness, $t(137) = -1.941, p = .466$, familism, $t(136) = .545, p = .587$, or simpatia, $t(137) = .349, p = .727$. A 2 (family-friendliness) x 2 (cooperativeness) x 2 (sex) between-subjects multivariate analysis of variance was performed on the three dependent variables: organizational attractiveness, job pursuit intentions, and value congruence. Using Wilk's criterion, the combined dependent variables were significantly affected by the sex of the participant, $F(126) = 3.037, p = .032$, partial $\eta^2 = .067$. Overall, female participants were more attracted to the

Table 2.1. Means, Standard Deviations, Internal Consistency Reliability Estimate, and Intercorrelations for Measures

Measure	M	SD	n	α	1	2	3	4	5	6
Job pursuit intentions	32.49	6.57	139	.91	—	**.76**	**.68**	.10	.04	.05
Organizational attractiveness	28.40	5.04	139	.91		—	**.77**	.09	.16	.14
Value congruence	15.03	3.80	136	.85			—	.11	.08	.08
Familism	44.07	11.27	138	.82				—	−.02	.17
Simpatia	17.50	3.24	139	.61					—	**.31**
Agreeableness	31.93	6.21	139	.79						—

Note: Correlations significant at $p < .05$ are bolded.

organizations advertised regardless of the content of the recruiting ads. No other sex-related differences were found.

Hispanic participants were expected to rate an organization described as highly cooperative and family-friendly more positively (i.e., on organizational attractiveness, job pursuit intentions with that organization, and value congruence) than an organization described as low in cooperativeness and work-family emphasis (Hypothesis 1). Moreover, Hispanics were expected to prefer the cooperative, family-friendly organization more than non-Hispanic whites (Hypothesis 2). To test these hypotheses, a 2 (family-friendliness) x 2(cooperativeness) x 2 (ethnic background) between-subjects multivariate analysis of variance was performed on three dependent variables: organizational attractiveness, job pursuit intentions, and value congruence. Using Wilk's criterion, the combined dependent variables were significantly affected by the level of family-friendliness of the organization, $F(3,126) = 2.644$, $p = .05$, partial $\eta^2 = .059$.

Because the dependent variables were highly correlated, a Roy-Bargman stepdown analysis (cited from Tabachnick & Fidell, 1996) was performed to test the impact of family-friendliness on the three dependent variables. First, a univariate ANOVA was calculated using value congruence as the dependent variable. Second, an ANCOVA was calculated to evaluate the effect of family-friendliness on organizational attractiveness after controlling for value congruence. Third, an ANCOVA was calculated using job pursuit intentions as the dependent measure after controlling for both value congruence and organizational attractiveness. Homogeneity of regression was found for each step of this analysis. A Bonferroni correction was used to control for Type I error rate. To achieve a .05 alpha level, alpha was adjusted to .017.

Value congruence was affected by level of family-friendliness $F(1,134) = 7.763$, $p = .006$, partial $\eta^2 = .055$. Participants rated the family-friendly organization as more consistent with their values ($M = 15.96$, $SD = 3.56$) than the organization that was low on family-friendliness ($M = 14.19$, $SD = 3.85$). After differences due to value congruence were entered, there was no unique contribution of organizational attractiveness, stepdown $F(1,133) = .395$, $p = .531$, partial $^2 = .003$. Moreover, no unique contribution of job pursuit intentions was found, stepdown $F(1, 132) = .087$, $p = .769$, partial $\eta^2 = .001$. Overall, participants felt that the family-friendly organization was more congruent with their values, but no differences were found between Hispanics and non-Hispanic Whites. Thus, no support for the first two hypotheses was found.

Hypothesis 3 proposed that Hispanics would score higher than non-Hispanic Whites on simpatia, familism, and agreeableness, and participants who score high on simpatia, familism, and agreeableness would rate more highly the high cooperative, family-friendly organization than the low cooperative, low work-family emphasis organization. An independent samples t test revealed no differences in familism scores between Hispanics ($M = 45.71$, $SD = 13.37$) and Whites ($M = 43.20$, $SD = 9.94$), $t(136) = -1.247$, $p = .214$. Moreover, there were no differences in simpatia scores between Hispanics ($M = 17.29$, $SD=3.05$) and Whites ($M = 17.61$, $SD = 3.35$), $t(137) = .558$, $p = .578$, nor were there differences in agreeableness scores between Hispanics ($M = 30.77$, $SD = 5.71$), and Whites ($M = 32.55$, $SD = 6.41$), $t(137) = 1.614$, $p = .109$.

Next, nine regression analyses were conducted. The dependent measures (organizational attractiveness, job pursuit intentions, and value congruence) were each regressed onto simpatia scores, family-friendliness, cooperativeness, and their interaction terms. Then, the dependent measures were each regressed onto familism scores, family-friendliness, cooperativeness, and their interaction terms. Finally, the dependent measures were each regressed onto agreeableness scores, family-friendliness, cooperativeness, and their interaction terms. For these analyses, family-friendliness and cooperativeness were dummy coded, whereas the continuous variables, simpatia, familism, and agreeableness, were centered at their means (Aiken & West, 1991).

None of the regression equations involving simpatia or familism were significant. For agreeableness, the overall regression using Job Pursuit as the dependent measure was significant, $F(7, 131) = 2.911$, $p = .007$, $R^2 = .135$ (see Table 2.2). Agreeableness was negatively related to job pursuit intentions, $\beta = -2.509$, $t = -3.116$, $p = .002$. Moreover, there were two significant two-way interactions and a significant three-way interaction (see Figures 2.1 and 2.2). The interaction between agreeableness and family-friendliness was significant, $\beta = 2.03$, $t = 2.456$, $p = .015$, and the interaction between agreeableness and cooperativeness was significant,

Table 2.2. Results of Regression Analyses of Job Pursuit Intentions on Agreeableness, Family-Friendliness, Cooperativeness, and Their Interactions ($N = 139$)

Variable	B	SE B	β	t	p
Centered agreeableness	−2.660	.854	−2.509	−3.116	.002
Family–friendliness	3.352	3.489	.255	−3.961	.338
Cooperativeness	2.547	3.637	.193	.700	.485
Centered agreeableness by family–friendliness	1.352	.551	2.030	2.456	.015
Centered agreeableness by cooperativeness	1.648	.594	2.386	2.772	.006
Family–friendliness by cooperativeness	−1.058	2.289	−.194	−.462	.645
Centered agreeableness by family–friendliness by cooperativeness	−.775	.365	−1.863	−2.121	.036

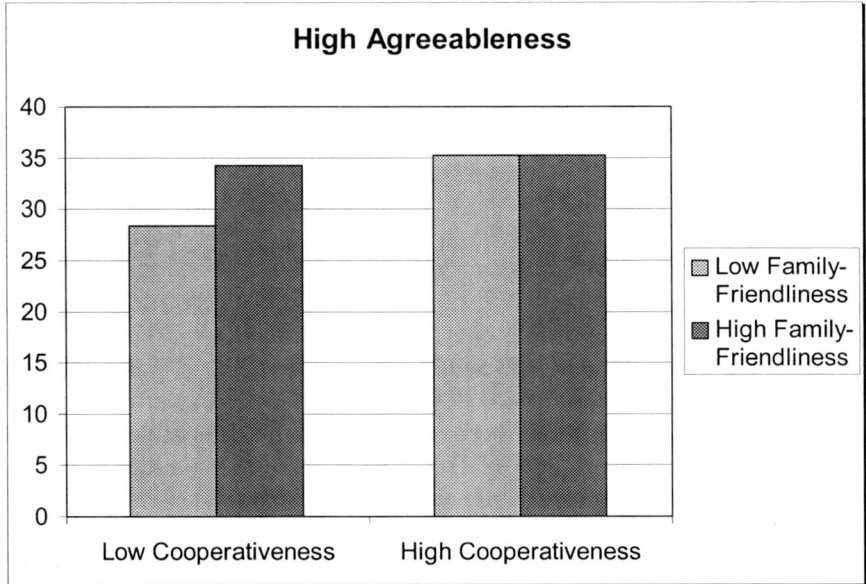

Figure 2.1. Job pursuit intentions of individuals scoring high on agreeableness when family-friendliness and cooperativeness of the organization were manipulated.

$\beta = 2.386$, $t = 2.772$, $p = .006$. However, these two-way interactions must be interpreted in light of the significant interaction between agreeableness, family-friendliness, and cooperativeness.

Participants with a high agreeableness score were least likely to pursue an organization which was low in both cooperativeness and family-friendly policies. They were most likely to pursue an organization high in cooperativeness, regardless of level of family-friendly policies. Unlike highly agreeable participants, participants with a low agreeableness score were most likely to pursue the organization that was low in both cooperativeness and in family-friendliness. When the organization was high in cooperativeness, they were more likely to pursue the highly family-friendly organization than the low family-friendly organization. Thus, partial support for Hypothesis 3 was found.

DISCUSSION

The increase of Hispanics in the workforce has important implications for organizations including the way organizations are managed (Stone-Romero et al., 2002). However, relatively little research has specifically

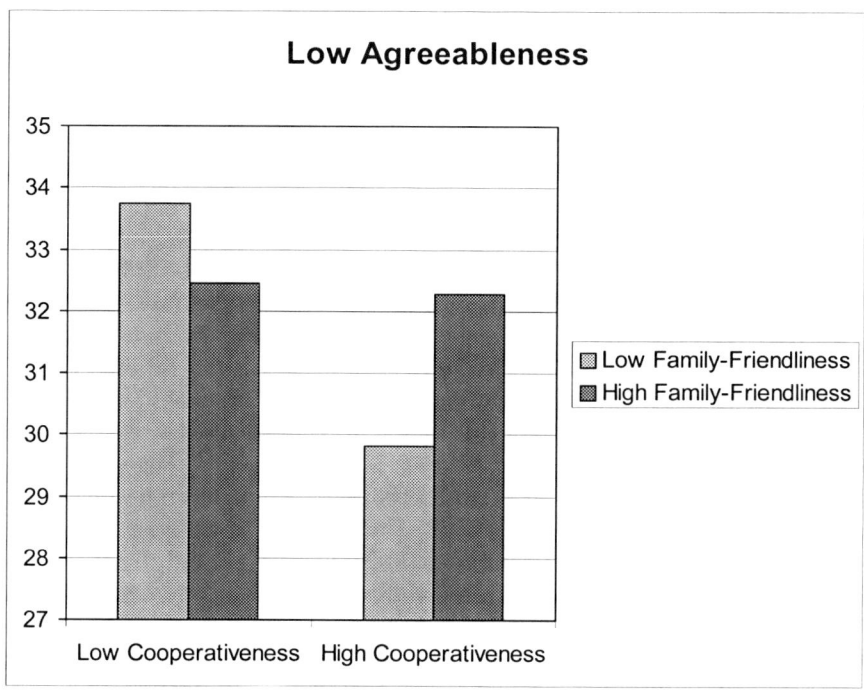

Figure 2.2. Job pursuit intentions of individuals scoring low on agreeableness when family-friendliness and cooperativeness of the organization were manipulated.

addressed how the beliefs, motivations, and customs of Hispanics influence work attitudes and behaviors (Stone-Romero et al., 2002). The present study empirically examined how two values that are important to the Hispanic culture relate to perceptions of organizational attractiveness, value congruence, and job pursuit intentions when job ads varied in value-related ways.

Our results suggest that, regardless of ethnic background, having family-friendly policies appears to be important to this predominantly young and single sample of college students. Research has already shown that work-family benefit availability and supportive work family culture were positively related to affective commitment and negatively related to work-family conflict and intentions to leave the organization (Thompson, Beauvais, & Lyness, 1999). This study adds to the literature on work and family issues by suggesting that offering family-friendly policies may help organizations attract new employees.

Surprisingly, there were no significant differences between non-Hispanic Whites and Hispanics on familism, simpatia, or agreeableness. One possible reason for this finding is that the Hispanic college students who participated may have been acculturated into U.S. culture. As a minority group, Hispanics are exposed to the mainstream cultural patterns of the United States and modifications in their values, norms, attitudes, and behaviors may be expected to occur because of this contact. This process of changes in behavior and values by individuals has been labeled acculturation (Gordon, 1964). As individuals become exposed to a new culture and learn the values, expectancies, norms, and attitudes of the members of the new cultural group, changes may be produced in the earlier values and attitudes as well as in the level of acceptance of new ones. Acculturation could be expected therefore to reinforce, modify, or change the values that individuals hold from their original culture (Marin, 1993). Acculturation may have played a role in this study. One would expect that if Hispanic participants were acculturated, their responses would be more similar to those of non-Hispanic Whites.

An interesting finding of this study was the relationship between agreeableness and job pursuit intentions. Participants who scored high on agreeableness preferred an organization high in cooperativeness and family-friendly policies; those lowest in agreeableness preferred the organization low in cooperativeness and low in family-friendly policies. This is consistent with prior research on agreeableness, as agreeableness has been shown to be positively related to cooperation (Zuckerman, Kuhlman, Joireman, & Teta, 1993). This finding is also consistent with our hypothesis and Schneider's (1987) attraction-selection-attrition model. According to the ASA model, applicants are attracted to, and stay in organizations with cultures that are compatible with their personality; and will leave an organization when they feel their personality no longer "matches" that of the organization (Schneider, 1987).

Although the agreeableness results suggest that organizations should tailor their ads to the applicants they hope to attract, this practice can be taken too far. Recruiting ads should be realistic job previews (Wanous, 1993). In other words, it is important to not use misleading information or "catch phrases" in order to attract people. Once the applicants become employees and discover that the organization does not really value families, for example, negative consequences can result. For example, employees may be dissatisfied, unproductive, leave the organization, or sabotage the organization because they were misled.

Several limitations are associated with this study. The relatively small sample of Hispanics used may be partially responsible for not finding an effect of ethnic background. A related limitation is the wording of the ethnic background question on the demographics sheet. Individuals were asked to describe themselves as: African American, Asian American, Caucasian, Native American, Hispanic, or Other. Marin and Marin (1991) suggest that confusion about categories can be minimized by adding "or Latino" to the Hispanic category. Marin and Marin also suggest that although the meaning of "Hispanic" may be clear to social scientists, labels used by scientists may be different from labels used "on the street." In a study done by Heindselman (2002), among participants who were highly ethnically identified with Latino culture, overall Anglo orientation scores increased over time, while overall Latino orientation scores decreased. This may suggest that some Hispanics may be identifying more with Anglo culture and therefore, identifying themselves as such. Finally, another limitation is that this study draws inferences from multiple levels. We measured cultural values, a group level variable, and analyzed it as if it was an individual-level variable.

Future research should develop different ways of asking ethnicity questions in order to avoid confusion for the participants. Specifically, future research should include multiple assessments of ethnicity and an acculturation measure. In addition, a larger and more representative sample of Hispanics should be sought. Moreover, because women were more likely than men to prefer the organization, regardless of the specific content of the ad, future research should use gender neutral job ads and obtain a more balanced sample of men and women. Finally, future research should consider applying structural equation modeling as a framework to make comparisons across individual- and group-level variables.

In conclusion, as the largest minority group in the country, Hispanics are an important part of the workforce, yet this study is one of only a few studies that have examined their work attitudes and preferences. We encourage future research on the relationship between culture, ethnic background, and job attraction.

REFERENCES

Aiken, L., & West, S. (1991). *Multiple regression: Testing and interpreting interactions.* Thousand Oaks, CA: Sage.

Aiman-Smith, L., Bauer, T., & Cable, D. (2001). Are you attracted? Do you intend to pursue? A recruiting policy-capturing study. *Journal of Business and Psychology, 16,* 219-237.

Antshel, K. M. (2002). Integrating culture as a means of improving treatment adherence in the Latino population. *Psychology, Health, and Medicine, 7,* 435-449.

Bardis, P. D. (1959). A familism scale. *Marriage and Family Living, 21,* 340-341.

Cable, D., & Judge, T. (1996). Person-organization fit, job choice decisions, and organizational entry. *Organizational Behavior and Human Decision Processes, 3,* 294-311.

Costa, P. T., Jr., McCrae, R. R., & Dye, D. A. (1991). Facet scales for agreeableness and conscientiousness: A revision of the NEO personality inventory. *Personality & Individual Differences, 12,* 887-898.

Costa, P. T., Jr., & McCrae, R. R. (1992). *Revised NEO personality inventory (NEO PI-R) and NEO five-factor inventory (NEO-FFI).* Odessa, FL: Psychological Assessment Resources.

De Las Fuentes, C., Baron, A., Jr., & Vasquez, M. J. T. (2003). Teaching latino psychology. In P. Bronstein & K. Quina (Eds.), *Teaching gender and multicultural awareness: Resources for the psychology classroom.* Washington, DC: American Psychological Association.

Garzon, A. (2000). Cultural change and familism. *Psicothema, 12,* 45-54.

Gordon, M. M. (1964). *Assimilation in American life: The role of race, religion, and national origins.* New York: Oxford University.

Judge, T., & Cable, D. (1997). Applicant personality, organizational culture, and organization attraction. *Personnel Psychology, 50,* 359-392.

Heindselman, T. L. (2002). Acculturation and ethnic identity: Issues in theory and measurement among Latino populations. *Dissertation Abstracts International, 62,* 4266.

Levine, R. V., Norenzayan, A., & Philbrick, K. (2001). Cross-cultural differences in helping strangers. *Journal of Cross-Cultural Psychology, 32,* 543-560.

Marin, G. (1993). Influence of acculturaion on familiaism and self identification among Hispanics. In M. E. Bernal & G. Knight (Eds.), *Ethnic identity: Formation and transmission among Hispanic and other minorities. SUNY series, United States Hispanic Studies* (pp. 181-196). Albany, NY: State University of New York Press.

Marin, G., & Marin, B.V. (1991). *Research with Hispanic populations.* Newbury Park, CA: Sage.

Rokeach, M. (1960). *The open and closed mind.* Oxford, England: Basic Books.

Sabogal, F., Marin, G., & Otero-Sabogal, R. (1987). Hispanic familism and acculturation: What changes and what doesn't? *Hispanic Journal of Behavioral Sciences, 9,* 397-412.

Schneider, B. (1987). The people make the place. *Personnel Psychology, 40,* 437-454.

Stone, D., Salas, E., & Stone-Romero, E. (2002). *Human resources strategies for attracting and retaining Hispanic Americans in multicultural organization.* Unpublished manuscript.

Stone-Romero, E. F., Aguinis, H., Blancero, D., Ramos, R., Salas, E., Sanchez, J., et al. (2002, April). *Hispanic Americans and human resources practices.* Panel discussion at the annual meeting of the Society for Industrial/Organizational Psychology, Toronto, Ontario, Canada.

Tabachnick, B., & Fidell, L. (1996). *Using multivariate statistics* (3rd ed.). New York: College Publishers.

Thompson, C. A., Beauvais, L .L., & Lyness, K. S. (1999). When work family benefits are not enough: The influence of work-family culture on benefit utilization, organizational attachment, and work-family conflict. *Journal of Vocational Behavior, 54,* 392-415.

Triandis, H., Marin, H., Lisansky, J., & Betancourt, H. (1984). Simpatia as a cultural script for Hispanics. *Journal of Personality and Social Psychology, 47,* 1363-1375.

Triandis, H., & Suh, E. (2002). Cultural influences on personality. *Annual Review of Psychology, 53,* 133-160.

Vasquez, M. J. T. (1994). Latinas. In L. Comas-Diaz & B. Greene (Eds.), *Women of color: Integrating ethnic and gender identities in psychotherapy* (pp. 114-138). New York: Guilford.

Wanous, J. P. (1993). Newcomer orientation programs that facilitate organizational entry. In H. Schueler & J. Farr (Eds.), *Personnel selection and assessment: Individual and organizational perspectives* (pp. 125-139). Hillsdale, NJ: Erlbaum.

Zuckerman, M., Kuhlman, D., Joireman, J., & Teta, P. (1993). A comparison of three structural models of personality: The big three, the big five, and the alternative five. *Journal of Personality and Social Psychology, 65,* 757-768.

CHAPTER 3

AN EMPIRICAL TEST OF GENDER-BASED DIFFERENCES IN E-MENTORING

**Kimberly A. Smith-Jentsch,
Shannon A. Scielzo, and Melissa A. Weichert**

Organizational functions that have traditionally occurred face-to-face are now increasingly occurring through computer-mediated communication (CMC). However, little empirical research has specified how CMC affects interpersonal relations and whether this varies for different types of individuals. The present study investigated gender-related differences in CMC and on perceptions of that communication in the context of an electronic-mentoring program. Results indicated that female mentors communicated a greater amount of psychosocial support (PS) and used a greater number of E-nonverbals than male mentors. However, both male and female mentors used a greater number of E-nonverbals when communicating with opposite-gender protégés. Finally, results suggested that protégé perceptions of the PS they received was biased by gender-related expectations. Specifically, protégés reported receiving greater PS from female mentors than from males even after accounting for coded PS, and coded PS was only a significant predictor of perceived PS for those with male mentors.

AN EMPIRICAL TEST OF GENDER-BASED DIFFERENCES IN E-MENTORING

With the progression of the technological age, organizational functions that have traditionally occurred utilizing face-to-face communications are now occurring through computer mediums, thus creating new obstacles for organizations to overcome (Drew & Bensley, 2001; Rowley, 1999). For example, organizations are increasingly allowing employees to work from home (Stinson, 2000), and employing teams whose members are physically distributed. It has been argued that these changes have dramatically changed the way that managers interact with their employees (Drew & Bensley, 2001). Unfortunately, research on the impact of computer-mediated communication has not kept up with its use in organizations. For instance, Ensher, Heun, and Blanchard (2003) noted that the practice of online mentoring has grown exponentially in recent years. However, poor research designs and other methodological flaws are rampant in the little research that has been conducted to test such programs. Thus, many questions regarding best approaches and ethics of such programs remain unanswered (Ensher et al., 2003). The present study was designed to advance our knowledge in this regard. Specifically, we investigated the impact of mentor gender on E-mentoring communication and on protégé perceptions of that communication.

Mentor Gender and Computer-Mediated Communication

Ensher et al. (2003) proposed a typology of E-mentoring relationships. The first represents a situation whereby mentors and protégés primarily interact face-to-face, however supplement that interaction with occasional computer-mediated communication (CMC). The second includes situations whereby the mentor and protégé communicate primarily through CMC with occasional face-to-face meetings or phone conversations. The third, referred to as CMC-only, includes those situations whereby mentors and protégés' only mode of communication is through CMC. The effects of CMC on the overall success of such relationships should be greatest for relationships in this last category. Thus, as one of the first empirical studies to investigate E-mentoring processes and outcomes, we chose to focus our attention on a context that can be categorized as CMC-only.

Ensher et al. (2003) noted that CMC is often described as a cold medium; one in which it is difficult to develop strong interpersonal bonds. Given this challenge, she suggested that the quality of E-mentoring relationships will be dependent in part on mentors' ability to communicate empathy, trust, and acceptance of their protégé adequately in writing. Individual differences in this ability are likely to moderate the effectiveness of mentoring relationships conducted through electronic means. Given well-documented gender differences in orientation toward intimacy and the expression of emotion, (Chodorow, 1999; Hook, Gerstein, Detterich, & Gridley, 2003), the present study investigated differences between male and female mentors in the psychosocial support they conveyed in an E-mentoring context.

Psychosocial Support

Psychosocial Support (PS) has been identified as one of the primary functions served by a mentor. This would include things such as providing acceptance, role modeling, confirmation, empathy and counseling (Kram & Isabella, 1985). These behaviors, in turn, have been associated with a number of positive mentoring outcomes such as increased mentoring relationship satisfaction, increased job-satisfaction, increased career-satisfaction, and increased intentions to remain with the same company (Allen, Eby, Poteet, Lentz, & Lima, 2004). Results from prior research investigating gender differences in the provision of PS have been mixed. Female mentors have been shown to provide greater psychosocial support in some studies (e.g., Burke & Mckeen, 1996) and not others (e.g., Ensher & Murphy, 1997). Moreover, at least one study has found that male protégés with female mentors reported receiving less of certain aspects of PS (i.e., acceptance) than any other gender composition (Ragins & Cotton, 1999).

One possible explanation for this is that female mentors with male protégés may fear that their attempts at providing PS will be misinterpreted as having romantic undertones (Burke, McKeen, & McKenna, 1994; Clawson & Kram, 1984; Noe, 1988). The anonymity and privacy afforded in computer-mediated conversations should decrease concerns regarding misinterpretations of PS as having romantic intent. Thus, unlike in a face-to-face situation, female E-mentors may not feel the need to suppress their natural inclination toward developing the psychosocial aspects of a relationship regardless of the gender of their protégé. No prior published research has empirically tested the impact of mentor gender on PS in an E-mentoring relationship. However, females have been shown to give more emotional support and to communicate more honestly than men in other types of CMC (Whitty, 2002). Thus, we expected that regardless of protégé gender, females would be more comfortable with and skilled at communicating messages that are psychosocial in nature than would male mentors in a CMC-only context.

(H1) Females E-mentors will communicate a greater amount of PS than will male E-mentors.

E-Nonverbals

Computer-mediated communication does not allow communicators to see smiles and body language, or to hear tone of voice. Such nonverbal cues are often communicated without conscious thought in face-to-face situations. However, in CMC, the sender must consciously convey those same emotions in writing. Females should be more likely than males to self-monitor the emotional content of their written communication and more motivated to ensure that the emotional content of their message is apparent.

Consistent with this notion, prior studies have found that chat users with female screen names made greater use of "Emoticons," or typed symbols designed to insinuate emotion (e.g., ':)' or ':(',) than did users with male screen names (e.g., Marvin, 1995; Wolf, 2000). Moreover, Wolf reported that males who interacted with females tended to use more emoticons than did males interacting with males. Wolf interpreted this finding as meaning that males mirrored females' more emotionally-conscious communication style when communicating with them online. However, the design of this study left open at least one alternative explanation.

In order to obtain sufficient numbers of dyads representing each gender composition, Wolf sampled Internet newsgroups that varied substantially in topic. For example, male-male communication was obtained from a football newsgroup, whereas male-female communication was obtained from a newsgroup for depression. One cannot ignore the likelihood that the males who chose to participate in the depression newsgroup differed significantly from those who chose to participate in the football newsgroup in ways related to emotional expression. Thus, differences in the use of emoticons between males communicating with males and males communicating with females may have had more to do with the topic they were discussing than it did with who they were discussing it with.

In the present study, all dyads were randomly assigned to each other and communicated with one another for the same purpose (i.e., formal peer-mentoring). Thus, our design provided a more controlled test of the impact of gender composition on CMC. Moreover, we sought to extend prior research on emoticon usage by investigating additional ways in which E-mentors may compensate for the lack of nonverbal cues. Specifically, we assessed the use of written descriptions of auditory sounds (e.g., whew, sigh) and facial expressions (e.g., smile), the use of font changes (e.g., bolding, italics, color); and the use of excessive punctuation (e.g.,

!!!!) in addition to traditional emoticons (e.g., ☺). We will refer to these collectively as "E-nonverbals." On the basis of prior theory and research we put forth the following hypotheses regarding mentor gender and the use of E-nonverbals.

(H2) Female E-mentors will make greater use of E-nonverbals than will male E-mentors.

(H3) Males E-mentors will use a greater number of E-nonverbals toward female protégés than they will toward male protégés.

Protégé Perceptions of Psychosocial Support

Numerous studies have documented the fact that individuals' perceptions of objective job characteristics and/or coworker behaviors are colored by their unique frames-of-reference (e.g., O'Reilly, Parlette & Bloom, 1980; Smith-Jentsch, Salas, & Brannick, 2001). Likewise, protégé-reports of the PS they receive from their mentors should be affected by their unique expectations, values, and needs. Using a policy-capturing design, Sanchez, Smith-Jentsch, Lorenzet, Lopez, and Bencaz (2005), found that both males and females systematically reported greater expectations of receiving PS from female mentors than from male mentors. This finding was based on ratings assigned to profiles of "paper mentors" presented to individuals who were interested in participating in a formal peer-mentoring program. Thus, it would appear that, even prior to an initial meeting with one's mentor, protégés may form expectations of him/her on the basis of limited demographic information (e.g., gender). Those expectations, in turn, are likely to affect protégés' attention to, interpretation and recall of mentor behaviors when asked to report on the quality of that relationship. Thus, gender-related expectations may bias protégé ratings of the PS they receive from their mentors and this may be even more likely to occur within the context of a CMC-only relationship.

According to Eysenck and Keane, 1990, *ambiguous stimuli*, stimuli that have multiple possible interpretations, "are especially likely to be encoded in accordance with people's expectations" (Ormrod, 1999, p. 227). Ambiguous information or comments will be incorporated as confirming the "expectation" rather than being discarded or classified as ambiguous. It is therefore possible that confirmatory biases lead protégés to give female, but not male, E-mentors credit for behaviors that do not clearly fit the definition of PS when assessing the PS they received. This should lead protégés to over-estimate the amount of PS they receive from a female mentor. As evidence of such a bias, one would expect mentor gender to moderate the relationship between objectively coded PS provided and protégé perceptions of PS received. Thus, the following hypotheses were offered:

(H4) Protégés will perceive that female E-mentors provide them with greater PS than male E-mentors, even after controlling for coded PS provided.

(H5) Coded PS will be less predictive of protégé perceptions of PS provided by female mentors than it will be of that provided by male mentors.

METHOD

Participants

Fifty-one undergraduate freshmen (31 female and 20 male) were each randomly assigned to one junior or senior "mentor" (30 female and 21 male) as part of a formal peer-mentoring program designed to reduce attrition at a large southeastern university. Mentors' mean age was 21.43 years, whereas protégés mean age was 18.20 years. Mentors were required to have a minimum grade point average of 3.0. The gender composition of the mentoring dyads consisted of a total of 6 male mentor–male protégé dyads, 15 male mentor–female protégé dyads, 14 female mentor–male protégé dyads, and 16 female mentor–female protégé dyads.

Preprogram Measures

Demographic Data

Both mentors and protégés were asked to report their age, gender, and race/ethnicity.

Protégé Expectations

In order to assess protégé expectations of receiving PS through the formal mentoring program, we adapted a 14-item scale that was developed by Allen, McManus, and Russell (1999) to assess mentoring functions received. Specifically, the items were reworded to reflect protégés' expectation of receiving PS prior to meeting their assigned mentor. An example from this measure would be "I expect my mentor to share personal experiences as a different perspective to my problems." Participants responded on a 6-point Likert-type scale (1 "strongly disagree" to 6 "strongly agree"). An alpha coefficient of .80 was obtained for this scale.

Coded Variables

Psychosocial Support

Prior to coding, all indicators of gender were removed from the transcripts to prevent contamination of the data from possible gender biases. For example, pronouns that may have disclosed gender were changed to he/she, and first names were changed to Socrates for mentors, and Plato for protégés, and boyfriend or girlfriends were changed to "significant other."

Two coders were trained to identify passages from the transcripts that qualified as psychosocial support (PS) as operationally defined by the items in the preprogram expectations scales. For example, if a mentor were to say "Last time I had that experience, I cried for a while then decided to go out with some friends to get over it," this would be an example of sharing a personal experience as a different perspective to the protégés problems.

The two raters independently coded transcripts of the chat sessions. First, raters identified each passage in a transcript that qualified as PS. Then each word accounting for PS was summed for each transcript. Specifically, each word of PS was counted and totaled for each transcript. Inter-rater reliability of the word counts representing PS was estimated based on 100 transcripts that were coded by both raters ($r = .77$). Word counts for coded PS provided were summed across the three E-mentoring sessions for each mentor-protégé dyad. This variable was used in all subsequent analyses.

E-Nonverbals

Two undergraduate research assistants were trained to review all session transcripts for the use of four types of E-nonverbals. The first type of e-nonverbal included the use of symbols, commonly referred to as "emoticons," such as happy ☺ and sad ☹ faces. The second category included words used to indicate noises, gestures, or facial expressions such as "swoosh," LOL (laughing out loud), and "smile." The third category included the use of excessive punctuation, such as "!!!!!" and the fourth category included font changes such as **bolding**, *italics*, or underlining to accentuate words. Frequency counts assigned by the two raters were highly correlated ($r = .99$). Thus, the two raters' scores were averaged to produce a single score for each of the three mentoring sessions. Finally, E-nonverbal scores for the 3 weeks were summed for each mentor to arrive at an overall indicator of E-nonverbals that was used in all subsequent analyses.

Dialogue Changes

E-nonverbals, particularly emoticons, are frequently used at the end of a sentence or passage. Thus, we included a measure of dialogue changes as a potential covariate for our analysis of E-nonverbal usage. Transcripts were simply reviewed for the number of times the dialogue changed from mentor to protégé or visa versa. Coefficient alpha computed on dialogue changes across the three mentoring sessions indicated that mentor-protégé dyads were highly consistent on this variable (.93). Dialogue changes were then averaged across the three chat sessions for each mentor-protégé dyad.

Post-Program Measure

Protégé-Reported PS Received

Protégé perceptions of the PS they received from their mentors were assessed using the measure developed by Allen, McManus, and Russell (1999). As previously discussed, these items mirrored those used to assess preprogram expectations. For example, instead of "I expect my mentor to share his/her personal history with me" the item would read "My mentor shared his/her personal history with me." Participants responded to the items utilizing the same 6-point Likert-type scale (1–strongly disagree to 6–strongly agree). An alpha coefficient of .87 was obtained for this scale.

Procedure

All participants attended an orientation session that detailed proper equipment usage and rules/regulations for chat sessions. At this time, protégés provided demographic information, as well as completing the program expectations scale. Protégés were then randomly assigned to a mentor. All participants were told that their first three meetings must be conducted via electronic chat from our experimental laboratory, once a week for 15 minutes over the span of 3 weeks. Participants were asked not to exchange contact information or to meet with one another outside of these initial three sessions in order to ensure that at this point their relationships would develop solely through CMC. Following these initial three sessions, protégés were asked to report the degree to which they had received PS from their mentors. Participants were then debriefed and were free to continue their peer-mentoring relationships outside the experimental setting.

Table 3.1. Intercorrelations Among Study Variables

Variables	M	SD	1	2	3	4	5	6	7
Preprogram Measures									
1. Mentor gender (MG) (Male = 1, Female = 2)	—	—	—						
2. Protégé gender (PG) (Male = 1, Female = 2)	—	—	-.14	—					
3. Protégé expectations of psychosocial support	4.36	.58	.17	.11	-.80				
4. Coded psychosocial support (Word count)	14.84	17.34	.24*	.12	.00	-.77			
5. Dialogue changes	197.80	95.47	.04	-.11	.13	-.11	-.93		
6. E-nonverbals	4.50	5.60	.18	-.13	.08	.08	.37*	-.87	
Post-Program Measure									
7. Protégé-reported psychosocial support received	3.98	.91	.30**	-.01	.37**	.40**	.40**	.03	-.87

Note: *p < .05, one-tailed **p < .05 two-tailed.

RESULTS

Correlations Among Study Variables

Table 3.1 presents means, standard deviations, and correlations among all study variables. As shown in Table 3.1, protégé-reported PS was positively correlated with preprogram expectations of receiving PS, coded PS, and the average number of dialogue changes per session. The use of E-nonverbals was positively correlated with the number of dialogue changes but not with coded or perceived PS provided.

Descriptive Statistics for Study Variables

The total number of mentors and protégés by gender are displayed in Table 3.2. In addition, mean scores and standard deviations for each of the study variables across mentor gender and dyad gender composition are provided.

Gender Differences in E-Mentoring

As shown in Table 3.1, mentor gender was significantly correlated with coded PS ($r = .24$, $p < .05$, one-tailed). Specifically, female mentors spent more time during their chat sessions making statements involving PS than did male mentors, in support of Hypothesis 1. Although we did not hypothesize main or interaction effects of protégé gender in combination with mentor gender on coded PS, we did explore whether such effects existed. Specifically, a moderated multiple regression analysis was conducted whereby coded PS was regressed on mentor gender, protégé gender, and their interaction. This equation was not found to be significant ($F(3, 47) = 1.470$, $p = .24$).

Next, multiple regression analysis was used to examine the impact of gender composition on the use of E-nonverbals. As shown in Table 3.3, the average number of E-nonverbals per session used by mentors was regressed on mentor gender, protégé gender, dialogue changes, and the interaction between mentor and protégé gender using simultaneous multiple regression. A significant overall model emerged $F(4, 28) = 2.952$, $p < .05$. In support of Hypothesis 2, female mentors used a greater number of E-nonverbals overall than did male mentors ($\beta = .27$, $p < .01$). In addition, a significant interaction between mentor and protégé gender was found ($\beta = .49$, $p < .05$). Specifically, both male and female mentors used a greater number of E-nonverbals if they were assigned to an opposite-

Table 3.2. Descriptive Statistics for Mentor Gender and Dyad Composition for all Study Variables

	Males		Females	
Mentor gender	21		30	
Protégé gender	20		31	

	Male Mentors		Female Mentors	
	M	SD	M	SD
1. Protégé expectations of psychosocial support	4.24	.65	4.44	.53
2. Coded psychosocial support (Word count)	29,571	39.02	55.00	57.78
3. Dialogue changes	64.389	21.69	66.87	37.11
4. E-nonverbals	3.37	3.79	5.36	6.61
5. Protégé-reported psychosocial support received	3.68	.83	4.01	.79

	Male Mentor/Male Protégé		Male Mentor/Female Protégé		Female Mentor/Male Protégé		Female Mentor/Female Protégé	
	M	SD	M	SD	M	SD	M	SD
1. Protégé expectations of psychosocial support	4.26	28.69	4.22	.65	4.28	.56	4.55	.50
2. Coded psychosocial support (Word count)	20.33	28.25	33.27	42.89	43.77	64.62	63.59	52.31
3. Dialogue changes	68.83	24.85	62.17	21.39	70.07	25.63	63.67	47.21
4. E-nonverbals	2.60	2.97	3.64	4.11	4.39	6.27	7.86	7.29
5. Protégé-reported psychosocial support received	3.57	.86	3.68	.74	4.19	.98	4.20	.95

Table 3.3. Summary of Multiple Regression Analysis for Variables Predicting Mentor's Use of E-Nonverbals

	Variable	B	SE B	β
1.	Mentor gender (MG)	−14.05	6.00	1.42**
2.	Protégé gender (PG)	−10.54	5.41	.98*
3.	Dialogue changes	.02	.01	.39**
4.	MG x PG	−7.77	3.41	−1.78**

Note: $N = 33$. Adjusted $R^2 = .196$. *$p < .05$ one-tailed. **$p < .05$ two-tailed.

gender protégé. Thus, Hypothesis 3, which stated that male mentors would use a greater number of E-nonverbals toward female protégés than they would toward male protégés was supported.

Predictors of Protégé-Reported Psychosocial Support

Next, protégé-reported PS received was regressed on mentor gender, preprogram expectations of receiving PS, coded PS, and the interaction of mentor gender and coded PS. Using simultaneous multiple regression, a significant overall model emerged, $F(4, 46) = 6.156, p < .01$, adjusted $R^2 = .292$. As shown in Table 3.4, mentor gender ($\beta = .32, p < .05$), coded PS ($\beta = 1.27, p < 05$), and expectations of receiving PS ($\beta = .37, p < .05$) were each unique predictors of protégé-reported PS. Additionally, the interaction of mentor gender and coded PS ($\beta = -.98, p < 05$) was also a unique predictor. Specifically, mentors who provided greater coded PS were perceived to give more PS. As predicted, mentor gender accounted for unique variance in perceptions of PS beyond that accounted for by coded PS. Specifically, in support of Hypothesis 4, female mentors were perceived to give greater PS. Finally, a significant interaction between mentor gender and coded PS was found ($\beta = -.983, p < .01$). As illustrated in Figure 3.1, coded PS was a significantly better predictor of per-

Table 3.4. Summary of Multiple Regression Analysis for Variables Predicting Protégés' Perceptions of Psychosocial Support Received From Their Mentors

	Variable	B	SE B	β
1.	Coded psychosocial support (Word count) (CPS)	.60	.25	1.27**
2.	Expectation of receiving psychosocial support	5.24	1.73	.37**
3.	Mentor gender (MG)	5.32	2.61	.32**
4.	CPS x MG	−.24	.14	−.98**

Note: $N = 51$. Adjusted $R^2 = .292$. *$p < .05$, one-tailed. **$p < .05$, two-tailed.

ceived PS for protégés with male mentors than it was for protégés with female mentors.

DISCUSSION

The present study is among the first to empirically investigate factors contributing to the success of online mentoring relationships. Specifically, we examined the influence of mentor and protégé gender on mentor communication and on protégé perceptions of that communication in the context of a formal peer-mentoring program. Results indicated that, when compared to male mentors, female mentors spent more of their chat sessions making statements of psychosocial support (PS). In addition, female mentors made greater use of what we have termed "E-nonverbals" overall than did male mentors. These E-nonverbals included the use of emoticons, text-written sounds, gestures, and facial expressions as well as excessive punctuation and font changes for emphasis. As predicted, male mentors used E-nonverbals more frequently when communicating with female mentors. Unexpectedly, however, females also used greater E-nonverbals when communicating with opposite-gender protégés than they did when communicating with same-gender protégés. Finally, consistent with our hypotheses, females were perceived to give greater PS even after accounting for coded PS. And, coded PS was a significantly better predictor of perceived PS when the mentor was male than when the mentor was female.

Theoretical Implications

These results have a number of theoretical implications. First, the fact that females were perceived to have given greater PS both by their protégés and by our coders supports the notion that they are better able and more willing than males to communicate psychosocial messages online. Second, our findings provide evidence that electronic communication may in fact reduce inhibitions associated with cross-gender mentoring relationships. By all accounts (objective coders, protégé perceptions) mentors did not provide less PS to opposite-gender protégés as they have been shown to in previous studies of face-to-face relationships (e.g., Burke, McKeen, & McKenna, 1990). Moreover, mentors were actually *more* apt to use E-nonverbals to augment their messages to opposite-gender protégés.

Third, the fact that coded PS was a weaker predictor of perceived PS for those with a female mentor than for those with a male mentor suggests that protégés may hold gender-based expectations that affect the manner in which they interpret and/or recall their experiences. We argue that, when in doubt, protégés were more likely to classify an ambiguous communication as PS if it was sent from a female mentor than if it was sent from a male mentor. In a CMC-only relationship there is likely to be far greater ambiguity in this regard than in a face-to-face relationship and thus fertile ground for confirmation biases to operate.

Finally, consistent with prior research (Wolf, 2000), male mentors in the present study used a greater number of E-nonverbals when interacting with a female protégé. It was hypothesized that this would occur because male mentors would mirror the more emotionally-conscious communication style of a female protégés. However, this does not explain why, unexpectedly, female mentors used a greater number of E-nonverbals when interacting with a male protégé than when interacting with a female protégé. It may be that, in a mixed-gender relationship, gender-based expectations were more salient to females, leading them to adopt a more stereotypical feminine communication style. Alternatively, given that our participants were college students, it is possible that the increased level of E-nonverbals used toward an opposite-gender protégé was simply a form of flirtation. Additional research is needed to explore these notions further using organizational participants. Nevertheless, it is important to note that E-nonverbals were not associated with protégé perceptions of the PS that they received. It may be that, for some protégés, the use of excessive E-nonverbals came across as insincere. For others less experienced with CMC, some of the E-nonverbals may have been misunderstood or confusing. Thus, E-nonverbal usage may actually interact with individual differences on the part of the receiver to determine their impact. Future studies should continue to explore the impact of E-nonverbals on both affective and cognitive relationship outcomes.

Study Limitations and Future Directions

The experimental control employed in the present study makes it unique in comparison to most research into computer-mediated communication in general and E-mentoring specifically. Notably, the objectives for the online chat sessions were identical across dyads that differed in gender composition. Additionally, participants were randomly assigned to one another, the frequency and duration of sessions were controlled, and transcripts were coded by condition-blind raters. These features enable causal inferences to be made. However, the strengths of this study in terms of internal validity come with associated weaknesses in terms of external validity. For instance, data were not collected in an organizational environment, participants had fairly limited interaction with one another, and there were no real consequences associated with their performance. The findings from our study do provide, however, a basis from which to posit gender-based effects on computer-mediated communication in the workplace in future studies; particularly in the context of online mentoring.

Practical Implications

As computer-mediated communication continues to replace many forms of face-to-face interaction in the workplace, it will become increasingly important to understand the implications of this practice. There are likely to be both advantages and disadvantages of employing computer-mediated communication. For instance, our findings imply that such communication may help to reduce certain barriers to interaction among employees of mixed gender. In addition, special preparation or instruction could be given to those who are less able or willing to perform certain roles (e.g., mentor) solely through the computer. In sum, organizations can benefit in many ways from knowing when and for whom computer-mediated communication is likely to hinder or facilitate the attainment of organizational goals.

Conclusion

In the present study, mentor gender was found to have a causal impact on both objectively scored communication as well as protégé interpretations of that communication. Female E-mentors were perceived to be more effective at providing PS than were male E-mentors regardless of protégé gender. Our data suggest that this was likely due to both objective differences in mentor communication and confirmatory biases associated with gender that were held by protégés.

REFERENCES

Allen, T. D., Eby, L. T., Poteet, M. L., Lentz, E., & Lima, L. (2004). Career benefits associated with mentoring for protégés: A meta-analysis. *Journal of Applied Psychology, 89*(1), 127-136.

Allen, T. D., McManus, S. E., & Russell, J. E. A. (1999). Newcomer socialization and stress: Formal Peer relationships as a source of support. *Journal of Vocational Behavior, 54*, 453- 470.

Burke, R. J., & McKeen, C. A. (1996). Gender effects in mentoring relationships. *Journal of Social Behavior, 11*(5), 91-104.

Burke, R. J., McKeen, C. A., & McKenna, C. (1990). Sex differences and cross-sex effects on mentoring: Some preliminary data. *Psychological Reports, 67*, 1011-1023.

Burke, R. J., McKeen, C. A., & McKenna, C. (1994). Benefits of mentoring in organizations. *Journal of Managerial Psychology, 9*(3), 23-32.

Chodorow, N. J. (1999). *The power of feeling: Personal meaning in psychoanalysis, gender, and culture.* New Haven, CT: Yale University Press.

Clawson, J. G., & Kram, K. E. (1984). Managing cross-gender mentoring. *Business Horizons, 27*, 22-31.

Drew, G., & Bensley, L. (2001). Managerial effectiveness for a new millennium in the global education sector. *Higher Education in Europe, 26*(1), 61-68.

Ensher, E. A., Heun, C., & Blanchard, A. (2003). Online mentoring and computer mediated communication: New directions in research. *Journal of Vocational Behavior, 63*, 264-288.

Ensher, E. A., & Murphy, S. E. (1997). Effects of race, gender, perceived similarity, and contact on mentor relationships. *Journal of Vocational Behavior, 50*(3), 460-481.

Hook, M. K., Gerstein, H., Detterich, L., & Gridley, B. (2003). How close are we? Measuring intimacy and examining gender differences. *Journal of Counseling and Development, 81*(4), 462-472.

Kram, K. E., & Isabella, L. A. (1985). Mentoring alternatives: The role of peer relationships in career development. *Academy of Management Journal, 28*, 110-132.

Sanchez, A., Smith-Jentsch, K.A., Lorenzet, S., Lopez, G., & Bencaz. (2005, April). *The impact of gender and race on protégé expectations of potential mentors: A policy capturing study.* Paper presented at the annual 20th meeting of the Society for Industrial and Organizational Psychology, Los Angeles, CA.

Marvin, L. (1995). Spoof, spam, lurk, and lag: Aesthetics of text-based virtual realities. *Journal of Computer-Mediated Communication, 1*(2). Retrieved from http://www.asusc.org/jcmc/vol1/issue2/marvin.html

Noe, R. A. (1988). Women and mentoring: A review and research agenda. *Academy of Management Review, 13*, 65-78.

Ormrod, J. E. (1999). *Human learning* (3rd ed.). Upper Saddle River, NJ: Prentice Hall.

O'Reilly, C. A., Parlette, G. N., & Bloom, J. R. (1980). Perceptual measures of task characteristics: The biasing effects of differing frames of reference and job attitudes. *Academy of Management Journal, 23*, 131-181.

Ragins, B. R., & Cotton, J. L. (1999). Mentor functions and outcomes: A comparison of men and women in formal and informal mentoring relationships. *Journal of Applied Psychology, 84*(4), 529-550.

Rowley, J. (1999). Computer mediated communication—Is it good for organizations. *Industrial and Commercial Training, 31*(2), 72-74.

Sanchez, A., Smith-Jentsch, K. A., Lorenzet, S., Lopez, G., & Bencaz, N. (2005, April). *Expectations in mentoring: How race and gender influence pre-relationship expectations.* Presentation at the 20th annual society for Industrial Organizational Behavior Conference, Los Angeles, CA.

Smith-Jentsch, K. A., Salas, E., & Brannick, M. T. (2001). To transfer or not to transfer? Investigating the combined effects of trainee characteristics, team leader support, and team climate. *Journal of Applied Psychology, 86*(2), 279-292.

Stinson, S. (2000). Office cubicles get smaller as more workers telecommute. *New Orleans City Business, 21*(17), 27-28.

Whitty, M. T. (2002). Liar, liar! An examination of how open, supportive and honest people are in chat rooms. *Computers in Human Behavior, 18*(4), 343-352.

Wolf, A. (2000). Emotional expression online: Gender differences in emoticon use. *CyberPsychology & Behavior, 3*(5), 827-833.

CHAPTER 4

PERFORMANCE APPRAISAL DISCOMFORT OF CRITICAL INCIDENTS

Andrew P. Kavulic, Thomas D. Carpenito, and Peter D. Villanova

> This study investigated the predictability of rater leniency from scores on an instrument designed to measure rater discomfort with performance appraisal situations (PADS). Subject critical incidents were also collected as a tool to measure self-efficacy of raters. This data was collected through the use of a mailed questionnaire that included the short PADS, long PADS, and instructional space for including up to four critical incidents. Most concerns in the appraisal process involved a focus on interpersonal aspects of the appraisal process by less experienced raters, while more experienced raters were more concerned with the administrative aspects of appraisal.

Performance appraisals are a widely used behavioral maintenance mechanism, occurring in roughly 90% of organizations (Coens & Jenkins, 2000). Where as the notion underlying performance appraisals posits that desired employee behaviors are to be reinforced through administrative rewards such as merit increases, promotions, and job stability, Longnecker, Sims, and Gioia (1987) found that individuals at the top of the hierarchical food chain are not always concerned with performance rating accuracy. Executives do recognize the inherent benefits of performance appraisals in organizational settings, but combat the possibility of negative consequences arising from assigning undesirable ratings to subordinates, for instance, by intentionally elevating ratings (leniency) (Longnecker et al., 1987). The current research is a replication and extension of earlier studies (Bernardin & Villanova, 2005; and Villanova, Bernardin, Dahmus, & Sims, 1993) that was interested in filling the knowledge gap in rater sources of leniency, and why certain managers are more likely to rate in a lenient fashion. We hypothesize that the ratings of raters scoring higher on the PADS would evidence greater leniency than those who scored lower on the PADS. Furthermore, we hypothesize from previous research that differences in sex will not account for differences in rater self-efficacy, but instead managerial experience will reflect greater disparity in the types of critical incident responses. Self-efficacy can be inferred from the types of managerial responses, and the critical incident taxonomy should allow the researchers to make this distinction.

This study implements the PADS questionnaire for the purpose of predicting rater leniency tendencies in the sample. Upon its development (Bernardin, 1989; Villanova & Bernardin, 1990), it was reasoned that the PADS would report higher discomfort from raters that avoid potentially aversive situations by inflating ratings of subordinate performance. More specifically, as described by Bernardin (1989), the preference by workers to maintain a level of job compatibility concerning the characteristics and actual demands on the job represent a precursor to discomfort. Withdrawal and lower levels of job involvement are manifested within on-the-job behaviors that are inherently incompatible with worker preference. Villanova et al. (1993) explored the possibility of predicting rater leniency by means of a 20-item measure, the Performance Appraisal Discomfort Scale (PADS). The PADS tool measures self report appraisal discomfort by raters immediately after completing a performance appraisal. The researchers administered the PADS 3 times throughout the study to one 178 undergraduate students as part of a class assignment in which the students worked together to complete group assignments. Responses to the PADS tool were then summed to derive a total overall discomfort score in appraisal situations. Due to lower levels of compatibility with performance monitoring and ability to offer feedback, higher scores indicated higher levels of rater discomfort. Through the multiple application of the PADS tool, the researchers suggested that rater leniency is stable and predictable. Furthermore, rater leniency can be predicted through the completion of the PADS.

A collection of critical incidents can be used to determine individual preferences in managers, specifically, the manifestation of leniency. It was hypothesized (Komaki, Slotnick, & Jensen, 1986) that an Operant Supervisory Taxonomy and Index (OSTI) can help explain differences in supervisory behavior, particularly in behavioral antecedents of supervisors and how it influences performance monitors of work and nonwork related behaviors. Along a similar vein, Komaki (1986) demonstrated how highly effective managers were more particular in collection of appraisal information than less-effective managers. It can be inferred from this finding that effective managers recognize the demands of collecting appraisal information on their employees (antecedent), translating to more structured, specific methods of data collection (behavior), and yielding lower levels of leniency in appraisals (consequent).

To better understand how self-efficacy influences rater leniency, Bernardin and Villanova (2005) investigated the effects of rater training on leniency. In the context of performance management, the researchers refer to the raters' beliefs that they may "orchestrate performance in the course of fulfilling their role obligation as it pertains to performance management" (p. 62). Consistent with Bandura's (1997) definition of self-efficacy, self-efficacious raters believe they are capable of carrying out a performance appraisal that may have significant influence on their future relationships with ratees. In order to become a more self-effacious rater, managers may have developed methods to provide justification for their ratings according to a standard, or perhaps they perceive themselves as more capable of socially engaging a ratee that will lead to successful resolution of potential conflict. In this study, the researchers collected critical incident responses from upper level managers who had experience completing performance appraisals. The two researchers then independently coded 121 critical incident responses describing instances of difficulty in carrying out their role requirements during the appraisal process and established four primary categories of responses. Of these four responses, two were chiefly concerned with administrative aspects of the appraisal process, such as company policy, format of the scale, rating dimensions, or procedures involving appraisal. The other two categories represented interaction with the ratee during the appraisal process. The researchers found that more experienced raters (> 50 months experience as a manager) reported fewer instances of discomfort in the interpersonal category, and conversely reported a proportionately higher rate of instances of administrative discomfort during the appraisal process. For a more descriptive examination of the four-dimensional critical incident taxonomy, refer to the Appendix.

This research represents a synergy of prior development and testing using the PADS and a four-dimensional analysis of open-ended responses of critical incidents. According to Bernardin and Villanova (2005) and Komacki (1986), rating leniency manifested in critical incident responses can be categorized, if present, along process, subjectivity, discussion, and improvement suggestion groupings. In turn, process and subjectivity responses can be collapsed into an "Administrative" group that will be more representative of experienced, effective managers, and discussion and suggesting improvement responses will appear more frequently with less experienced managers.

METHOD

Subjects

One hundred sixty managers participated in this study (92 males, 68 females). All participants at the time of data collection were employed in a managerial role and were the direct report for subordinates ($X = 33.61$, $SD = 53.86$). The mean age of these managers is 38.07 with a SD of 12.27 and the mean experience is 10.60 years with a SD of 9.22 years.

Procedure

Data collection was performed through the use of a questionnaire that was distributed to managers throughout the southeast by undergraduate and graduate students at Appalachian State University. Through this distribution, the researchers gathered 160 responses. The questionnaire included the Performance Appraisal Discomfort Scale (PADS) which includes the long and short questionnaire, critical incident report, and descriptive data about the subject.

Measures

The short PADS questionnaire was meant to reflect the level of leniency in rating by each respondent, which was measured using a 5-point Likert scale. Respondents were asked to rate their discomfort in (1) the appraisal of others, (2) encouraging employees to monitor their own performance, (3) informing employees about performance, (4) asking employees about their reaction to appraisal, and (5) justifying and defending the ratings. The responses for the short PADS was then summed to create a total score for each subject, where higher scores denote a higher level of leniency due to the rating and feedback process. Individual subject scores were also tabulated by taking the mean of all five responses on the short PADS tool to determine overall discomfort. The 20-item PADS questionnaire is used to measure discomfort levels for employee appraisal, and are categorized into four distinct types of questions: provision of negative feedback, solicitation of feedback, encouragement of performance monitoring, and justification and/or defense of ratings. Subjects responded for each situation using a 5-point scale where 1 represented "no discomfort" and 5 represented "high discomfort." Summation of all 20 responses was then calculated for each subject to determine an overall discomfort score, where high scores represented more discomfort experienced by the subject due performance monitoring and feedback with their employees.

Open-ended critical incident responses were also collected in which participants were asked to describe, in their own words, aspects of the performance appraisal process that they found difficult to perform. "Process" responses include statements that reflect a difficulty to implement the appraisal within the format of the organization. "Subjectivity" responses are statements that concern the rater's difficulty to remain unbiased. "Discussion" responses are statements that reflect the rater's challenge of conveying to the ratee why they rated the way they did. "Suggesting Improvement" responses are statements that reflect the rater's discomfort while trying to explain how the ratee could perform better. The researchers then classified each open-ended response within the four-dimension taxonomy and performed a test of interrater reliability in which a random sample of 35 participant responses were selected and reclassified. Of the 85 critical incidents in the interrater test sample, there was a discrepancy in 14 classifications, yielding a reliability measure of 83.53% found between two separate researchers.

RESULTS

Analyses of this data began with the computation of short and long PADS scores for each participant, and correlations were explored between these two tools, as well as any differences that may be accountable in PADS scores due to the gender of the participant. The factor structure of the PADS was then investigated using a principle component analysis. Additional inferential statistics were performed on critical incident responses

Table 4.1. PADS Questionnaire Summation

	Mean	Standard Deviation
Short PADS Sum	10.04	4.18
Short PADS Men	1.86	0.34
Short PADS Women	2.21	0.51
Long PADS Sum	37.99	19.34

using a collapsed two-dimensional summary score measuring the effect of gender and experience on response type. Using an Independent sample t-test, men ($M = 1.86$) reported significantly less discomfort than women ($M = 2.21$) on the short PADS ($t(158) = -2.71, p = .008$). Scores on the short PADS and long PADS were found to be highly correlated ($r(160) = .40$) by participants, suggesting PADS scores are predictive or rater leniency within the confines of this study. Furthermore, this supports our hypothesis that higher scores on the PADS would reflect higher levels of leniency during the appraisal process.

Principal Components Analyses of PADS

The Kaiser Meyer Olkin measure of sampling adequacy reported at 0.90, with a Bartlett's Test of Sphericity of $p < .0001$. The Scree plot indicated that 58.50% of variance was explained by the first four factors (Table 4.2). Using a Varimax rotation with Kaiser normalization, the simplest solution converged in seven iterations and replicated original findings of the four situational demands determined in previous research (Villanova et al., 1993).

The minimum eigenvalue criterion (mineigen) and scree plots were used to identify the principal components which emerged from this analysis. The data was deemed suitable for factor analysis by the aforementioned Kaiser-Meyer-Olkin measure of sampling adequacy (MSA) and the results of Bartlett's test of sphericity. No items were deleted due to cross loadings onto different factors. While a confirmatory factor analysis could have been used to test the specific hypotheses from previous research, a principal components analysis was utilized to examine any possibility of a different factor structure.

Upon interpretation of the critical incidents, "process" and "subjectivity" were collapsed into an "Administrative" response column, and "discussion" and "suggesting improvement" were collapsed into an "Interpersonal" response column. See Table 4.3 for a complete listing of critical incident responses by category.

An independent sample t-test revealed that there was no significant difference between men ($M = 0.88$) and women ($M = 0.75$) in the number of administrative responses made $t(158) = 0.87, p = .39$, nor in the number of interpersonal responses made by men ($M = 1.33$) or women ($M = 1.24$) $t(158) = 0.53, p = .60$. The independent sample t test of administrative responses showed a significant difference between high experienced managers ($M = 1.80$) and low experienced managers ($M = .88$) $t(158) = 1.46, p = .04$. The independent sample t test for interpersonal responses did not produce a significant difference for high experi-

Table 4.2. Principal Components of PADS

	Rotated Factors			
	I	II	III	IV
Provision of Negative Feedback				
Tell employee performance can improve	55			
Inform employee work is "satisfactory"	72			
Communicate intolerance of long breaks	69			
Interview ineffective employee	66			
Recommend employee discharge	58			
Demand employee correct work problems	45			
Tell male employee to improve	61			
Respond to employee upset with rating	52			
Tell female employee to improve	62			
Warn ineffective employee of discharge	66			
Solicitation of Feedback				
Let subordinate talk during interview		58		
Allow employee to give his/her view		73		
Interview effective employee		75		
Give satisfactory rating to employee		51		
Encourage Performance Monitoring				
Admonish employee late behavior			68	
Ask for comments about rating			74	
Discuss job performance with employee			38	
Encourage employee to evaluate own work			58	
Justify/Defend Ratings				
Accused of favoritism				73
Challenged to justify ratings				68
Eigenvalue	7.70	1.78	1.19	1.03
% of Variance	38.51%	8.92%	5.95%	5.13%

Extraction Method: Principal Component Analysis.
Rotation Method: Varimax with Kaiser Normalization.
a. Rotation converged in 7 iterations.

Table 4.3. Frequency of Critical Incidents by Category, sex, and Rating Experience

	Administrative Responses				Interpersonal Responses					
	Process		Discussion		Suggest Improvement		Subjectivity		Total	
Sample Characteristics	#	%	#	%	#	%	#	%	#	%
Total Sample	57	16.86	75	22.19	155	45.86	51	15.09	338	100
Sex										
Male	33	57.89	48	64.00	90	58.06	32	62.75	203	100
Female	24	42.11	27	36.00	65	41.94	19	37.25	135	100
Experience										
High (> 50mo)	28	49.12	54	72.00	105	67.31	34	68.00	221	100
Low (<50 mo)	29	50.88	21	28.00	51	32.69	16	32.00	117	100

enced managers ($M = 1.16$) and low experienced managers ($M = 1.36$) $t(158) = -0.55, p = .26$. This supports our second hypothesis that managerial experience levels will help dictate the types of responses given through collection of appraisal discomfort critical incidents.

DISCUSSION

In conclusion, this study supports the original findings of earlier PADS development and testing, showing rater leniency is a stable phenomenon within performance appraisal research. While acidulously unavoidable in the appraisal process, leniency can be more accurately accounted for and taken into consideration when appraisal scores are tabulated. Furthermore, experience levels account for differences in the type of incident composed by respondents. Experienced raters displayed differences in the type of critical incident responses, leaning toward responses more administrative in nature, rather than an interpersonal response. This finding supports the notion that less experienced raters with lower levels of self-efficacy are concerned with control over the interpersonal aspect of appraisal, and thus exert more energy trying to control this aspect of the managerial process. Conversely, experienced raters' lack of significantly different levels of response in the interpersonal Critical Incident dimension suggests that they have developed strategies to handle these situations, while focusing their frustration on administrative characteristics of the appraisal process that may be beyond their immediate control. This finding is congruent with previous self-efficacy research (Bernardin & Villanova, 2005) that modeled results found after an appraisal training intervention took place. In these instances, less focus is placed on the interaction with ratees through experience, and instead is shifted toward responses about the system in general.

While this may be one possible explanation of our results, we cannot rule out the possibility that less experienced raters have fewer experiences to draw from, and these incidents are more readily available for report. Also, interpersonal experiences, particularly negative experiences, may be more important to novice raters in regard to their subordinates and their beliefs about their capacity as a supervisor. Nevertheless, novice raters may still be learning these roles as a supervisor, and grapple with interpersonal issues that veteran raters have learned how to handle. As far as the self-efficacy of more experienced raters, they appear to show higher levels of mastery in their interpersonal skills in appraisal, and focus more on the subjective aspects of the rating process.

One obvious limitation to this study is the sample size used in the Principal Components analysis. Difficulty gathering this information from respondents is the primary cause of a small sample size. Furthermore, Comrey and Lee (1992) would state that as a general rule of thumb, our sample size could be characterized as fair, regardless of the number of items on the PADS tool. When considering that the PADS tool only has 20 items, another rule of thumb could be utilized that states we would need five times the total number of items. Regardless, a similar factor structure to previous research was offered as a solution, thus assuring researchers of the fidelity of the data and factor structure.

This study will add to the ever-growing research base in performance appraisal rater leniency literature. Like a vast majority of these studies, rater leniency is viewed as a single event in time, and is not considered on a longitudinal basis. This research is not different in that respect, as it only examines discomfort scores at one time and critical incidents that were collected from the respondents at a single given time. Future research endeavors should consider how experienced raters got to the point of concerning themselves more with aspects of the appraisal process, in the context of how leniency may have shifted as their personal viewpoints in appraisal shift. This research is built upon the idea of experienced raters and nonexperienced raters performing a certain way, given their abilities. Longitudinal data is readily available for performance appraisals, and future examination of leniency by rater is necessary in this field of research.

Appendix: Sample Responses for Each of the Four Dimensions Identified in the Answers to Open-Ended Questions

Process	*Subjectivity*
"It is difficult to judge people without a set of quantitative standards, therefore I am uncomfortable creating my own."	"I find it difficult to overlook personal feelings in the evaluation process when the employee's personal life may be in conflict with their professional life."
"I find it difficult to have to make a performance review fit what my boss had predetermined the budget to be."	"It is difficult to avoid personal biases when rating employees."
Discussion	*Suggesting Improvement*
"I find it difficult to inform poor performers of bad performance when they are in denial that they have problems."	"It is difficult to suggest ways to improve performance when subordinates are much older than you."
"It is difficult to inform employees that their work was below average when they actually were pleased with their contribution."	"I find it difficult to suggest ways of improvement to people who do not have the right job fit. In such cases, people do not want to listen to any suggestions you might offer to improve their performance."

Administrative dimension consists of process + subjectivity row.
Interpersonal dimension consists of discussion + suggesting improvement row.

REFERENCES

Bandura, A. (1997). *Self-efficacy: The exercise of control.* New York: Freeman.

Bernadin, H. J. (1989). Innovative approaches to personnel selection and performance appraisal. *Journal of Management Systems, 1,* 25-36.

Bernardin, H. J., & Villanova, P. D. (2005). Research streams in rater self-efficacy. *Group & Organization Management, 30,* 61-88.

Coens, T., & Jenkins, M. (2000). *Abolishing performance appraisals.* San Francisco: Berrett-Koehler.

Comrey, A. L., & Lee, H. B. (1992). *A first course in factor analysis* (2nd ed.). Los Angeles: Hillsdale.

Kaiser, H. F. (1974). An index of factorial simplicity. *Psychometrika, 39,* 31-36.

Komaki, J. L. (1986). Toward effective supervision: An operant analysis and comparison of managers at work. *Journal of Applied Psychology, 71*(2), 270-279.

Komaki, J. L., Zlotnick, S., & Jensen, M. (1986). Development of an operant-based taxonomy and observational index of supervisory behavior. *Journal of Applied Psychology, 71*(2), 260-269.

Longnecker, C. O., Sims, H. P., Jr., & Gioia, D. A. (1987). Behind the mask: The politics of employee appraisal. *The Academy of Management Executive, 1,* 183-193.

Villanova, P. D., & Bernardin, H. J. (1990). Work behavior correlates of interviewer job compatibility. *Journal of Business and Psychology, 5,* 179-195.

Villanova, P. D., Bernardin, H. J., Dahmus, S. A., & Sims, R. L. (1993) Rater leniency and performance appraisal discomfort. *Educational and Psychological Measurement, 53,* 789-799.

CHAPTER 5

GREEN IS THE COLOR OF THIS CHAMELEON

A Study of Pay Rate and Applicant Response Behavior

Mitchell H. Peterson, Shawn Burkevich,
Abhishek R. Gujar, and Richard L. Griffith

Given the increasing popularity of using personality measures in personnel selection, it is important for researchers and practitioners to remain aware of issues surrounding applicants' responses to these measures. Previous research has indicated that personality measures are susceptible to response distortion on the part of applicants who are attempting to portray themselves in a positive light. There are numerous situational factors that may impact the propensity of applicants to engage in response distortion (faking). Job desirability may be one factor that can impact faking behavior. The present study will examine the relationship between hourly pay rate and response distortion on a personality measure through the implementation of a unique research design that allows for examination of faking behavior in an applicant setting. In this study, hourly pay rate was used as a proxy for job desirability, and job desirability was assumed to increase as pay increased. Results indicated that amount of pay did affect faking behavior for the NEO-FFI subscales of extraversion, agreeableness, and conscientiousness.

In the last 2 decades, personality measures have gained prominence as a selection method capable of screening out undesirable job candidates, and as top down selection tools that are often used in multitest batteries. The emergence of a refined five factor model of personality (McCrae & Costa, 1985) has allowed for more focused research on the utility of personality measures in a selection setting. The factors associated with this model (as outlined and defined by Barrick & Mount, 1991) are: neuroticism, extraversion, openness to experience, agreeableness, and conscientiousness. Neuroticism refers to the tendency to exhibit traits such as anxiousness, anger, worry, and insecurity. The dimension of extraversion is a collection of traits including talkativeness, sociability, and assertiveness. Openness to experience may be one of the least clearly defined factors, and is composed of predispositions toward being imaginative, curious, and cultured. Agreeableness is a tendency to exhibit cooperativeness, courtesy, and tolerance. The final factor, conscientiousness, is reflective of behaviors such as carefulness, dependability, and attention to detail.

One of the main unresolved issues surrounding the use of personality measures is that the accuracy of these self-report measures is dependent upon truthful responding. However, it is often not in the best interests of the job applicant to respond in any manner that would reveal their shortcomings. Additionally, the job applicant may be motivated to misrepresent him/herself for a variety of reasons including elements of the job description such as monetary incentives. However, personality measures like the NEO-Five Factor Inventory (NEO-FFI) (Costa & McCrae, 1992) are designed with the assumption that examinees are only motivated to represent themselves accurately. These conflicting goals have the potential to compromise the ability of noncognitive measures to predict job performance, and subsequently may select in those job candidates they are designed to screen out.

Previous research findings (Douglas, McDaniel, & Snell, 1996; Zickar & Drasgow, 1996) caution the use of personality measures due to the negative impact of socially desirable responding (faking) on predictive inferences. Additional research (Barrick & Mount, 1996; Ones & Viswesvaran, 1998) has reported a negligible impact on the predictive inferences drawn from noncognitive measures. While the impact of faking has yet to be determined, research efforts in the area of applicant faking behavior have continued to expand. One line of investigation arising out of this research arena is concerned with the determinants of faking behavior. According to a model by McFarland and Ryan (2000), situational and motivational factors are just a couple of the factors that may play a role in determining faking behavior.

The current study investigates one possible source of motivation to fake a personality measure; initial hourly pay rate. We hypothesize that increases in starting pay will increase job desirability and thus increase the amount of faking behavior observed in applicant responses. We begin with a review of relevant research regarding the determinants of job desirability and response distortion, or faking, as it is predominately referred to in the research literature. We will then present a methodology for measuring faking behavior (Griffith et al., 2004), along with the findings of our research which manipulated the starting pay of an entry level customer service position in order to determine the effects of a motivational variable on applicant faking. We will then close with a brief discussion of the implications associated with this empirical investigation.

APPLICANT FAKING BEHAVIOR

Previous research suggests that applicant faking on personality or noncognitive measures used for employment selection is a pervasive problem (Douglas et al., 1996; Luther & Thornton, 1999; Zickar & Drasgow, 1996). Faked responses on these noncognitive tests may affect the rank ordering of the respondents, which can impact both top-down and cut-off selection decision models (Douglas et al., 1996). Several studies have suggested that different validity coefficients may be obtained when noncognitive tests are administered to groups in a research setting where participants are expected to answer honestly, as opposed to an applicant condition in which individuals may be motivated to inflate their responses (Douglas et al., 1996; Frei, Snell, McDaniel, & Griffith, 1998; Leuke, Snell, & Illingworth, 2002, Zickar & Drasgow, 1996).

Previous research has also suggested that applicant faking, or response distortion, has minimal negative influences on the criterion-related validity of measures of the Big Five factors of personality that are used to make selection decisions in an employment setting (Barrick & Mount, 1996; Christiansen, Goffin, Johnston, & Rothstein, 1994; Hough, Eaton, Dunnette, Kamp, & McCloy, 1990; Ones & Viswesvaran, 1998; Ones, Viswesvaran, & Reiss, 1996). Other researchers propose criterion-related validity may actually be improved when response distortion is statistically corrected (Rosse, Stecher, Miller, & Levin, 1998).

Lack of generalizability has been a major criticism of the studies that report negligible negative impacts associated with the presence of faking behavior. These studies have used nonapplicant or incumbent data in which the tested individuals may have little or no motivation to fake as compared to real job applicants. Contextual factors and the motivation to fake must be considered; otherwise they may swing the balance of the analysis outcome (Douglas et al., 1996). Stark, Chernyshenko, Chen, Lee, and Drazgow (2001) suggest that personality measures used in the selection setting have reduced utility due to situational faking that is associated with an applicant setting. In addition, previous research (Mueller-Hanson, Heggestad, & Thornton, 2003) suggests that criterion-related prediction error is higher in the top one-third of a group of individuals given the employment incentive to fake on a noncognitive measure as compared to the lower third. The control group, which was provided with no incentive to fake, was found to have similar prediction error between the lower and upper thirds (Mueller-Hanson et al., 2003).

Studies which posit that faking has minimal negative effects on the criterion-related validity of personality measures often use scores on social desirability, or lie scales, as proxy measures for actual amounts of applicant faking. This is a second major limitation because although social desirability may be a component of applicant faking, but there are likely to be larger contributors in the explanation of faking variance (Griffith et al., 2004). Fernandez-Ballesteros and Zamarron (1996) argue that faking and social desirability are distinct concepts. They define faking as overt lying, or a conscious attempt to distort responses specific to contextual factors. On the other hand, they argue that social desirability is not a conscious effort, not context specific, and can be better described as a trait.

Previous research has demonstrated that there are reliable mean level differences between applicant scores on a personality measure and incumbent scores, with applicant scores typically being higher (Stokes, Hogan, & Snell 1993). However, these studies examine the faking phenomenon at a group level. To understand the mechanics of faking, it is necessary to examine faking at an individual level. Snell and McDaniel (1998) state that when the mean score of a group of fakers is higher than the mean score of a group of applicants, it cannot be inferred that all applicants have faked; rather some of the applicants engaged in overt faking whereas others did not. This level of analysis has implications for the assessment of validity because it is unlikely that all members of the applicant group have faked. However, the ones who engaged in overt faking and succeeded, would elevate their rank order, and potentially compromise validity.

In an applicant setting, individuals may answer in a fashion that does not reflect their true level of the trait that is being assessed, in order to increase their chances of being hired. The methodology applied in the present study allows for a unique conceptualization and measurement of faking behavior. Faking will be determined by the degree of change that occurs for participants completing the same measure of personality across two administrations; in an applicant setting, as well as a non-applicant setting with instructions to respond honestly (see Figure 5.1).

This faking behavior may be influenced by a number of factors. Applicants must possess the ability to understand what the scale is measuring, and determine the "correct" response. In addition, the applicant must be motivated to alter their true scores. One possible source of motivation to fake could be the degree to which a person wants or needs the job that they are applying for.

Job Desirability

Recruitment and selection strategies are, in large part, designed to increase the desirability of a job. The rationale behind this is that the more desirable a job becomes, the greater number of applicants will be recruited for openings, and as a result more stringent selection standards can be applied to the selection of personnel. The aforementioned scenario is one that organizations strive for when they are selecting employees. This logic has been supported by psychological research (Taylor & Collins, 2000) investigating recruitment strategies. Additionally, job desirability is often a product of a competitive labor market and recruitment strategies adapted to the availability of qualified applicants (Ryan & Tippins, 2004). In this competitive environment starting pay and signing

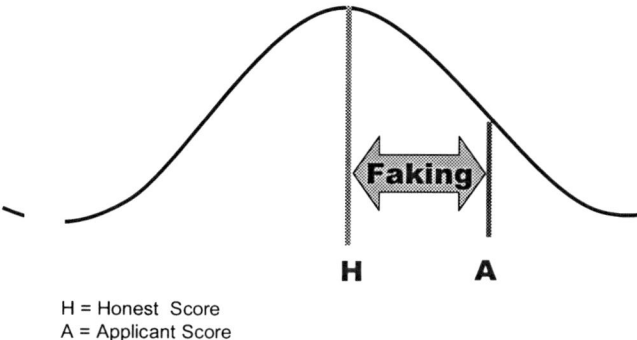

Figure 5.1. A graphical representation of applicant faking behavior.

bonuses become negatively skewed in an attempt to increase job desirability. This recruitment strategy was shown by Wells (2001) to have significant effect on hiring rates, as his results revealed significant increases at one dollar intervals on individual acceptance of a job offer across sex and job type. In another study of the effect of starting pay and signing bonuses, Winter and Logsdon (2004) found significant differences between the desirability rating of a nursing job based upon a six dollar per hour pay increase, and significant differences between those offered a signing bonus of 10,000 dollars and those who did not. A study by Wotruba, Thomas, Simpson, and Reed-Draznik (1989) asked college students to rate the relative importance of numerous factors that they would take into consideration when deciding whether or not to pursue a job offer. The most important factor was "Opportunities for Advancement," while "Job Incentives" ranked 11th and "Starting Salary" ranked 16th out of 42 possible factors related to the job desirability of a sales position. Although pay was rated as only moderately important to applicants, many of the factors that outranked pay were characteristic of higher level jobs, rather than an entry level customer service position like the one featured in the present study. Therefore, these rankings were interpreted as general support for a linkage between pay and job desirability.

Additional research has indicated that starting salary or pay level is an important factor in determining applicant attraction to an organization (Bretz & Judge, 1998; Cable & Judge, 1994; Gerhart & Milkovich, 1990). These studies show the significant impact of starting pay and appear to support recruitment strategies that manipulate starting pay to increase job desirability. However, can an increase in job desirability have an undesirable effect on the selection environment when non-cognitive measures are used?

Although situational factors have been proposed to influence applicant faking, the relationship between pay rates as a proxy for job desirability and faking has yet to be empirically tested. Based on previous literature on pay and job desirability (Bretz & Judge, 1998; Cable & Judge, 1994; Gerhart & Milkovich, 1990; Wotruba et al., 1989) and research that suggests situational variables, such as job desirability, may impact applicant faking behavior (Griffith et al., 2004; McFarland & Ryan, 2000), the present study will set out to test a proposed positive relationship between hourly pay rate and amount of faking.

Hypotheses

> H1: Starting pay will form a significant relationship with faking behavior on a work frame-of-reference personality inventory.

H2: Increases in starting pay will increase the amount of faking observed on a work frame-of-reference personality inventory, such that the amounts of faking observed will be highest in the $26 pay rate condition, followed by the $12 pay rate condition, and lowest in the $6.15 condition.

METHOD

Participants

The participants in the present study were 108 undergraduate students enrolled in psychology courses at a university and community college in the southeastern United States. The sample was comprised of 54% females and 46% males, with ages ranging from 18 to 61. The mean age for males was 21.47, while the mean age for females was 23.45. The participants were offered extra-credit for the course that they were enrolled in at the time, in exchange for their voluntary participation in the study. In terms of employment status, 63% of the sample reported being currently employed, 36% were not currently employed, and 1% did not respond to the question about current employment situation.

Measures

The personality measure that was used in the present study was a revised version of the NEO-FFI, which is a shortened version of the NEO-Personality Inventory-Revised (NEO-PI-R) (Costa & McCrae, 1992). The NEO-FFI is composed of 60 items (12 for each construct) that assess the five personality constructs of neuroticism, extraversion, openness, agreeableness, and conscientiousness. Costa and McCrae (1992) reported estimates of internal consistency of .86, .77, .73, .68, and .81 for the respective factor scales. The revision that was used in this study involved changing the wording of the questions on the NEO-FFI to obtain a work-related frame of reference. This same method of revision was used in the study by Griffith et al. (2004), and was based on the rephrasing method of Schmit, Ryan, Stierwalt, and Powell (1995). Essentially, the items were rewritten so that the participants would think about each item within the context of their behavior at work. For example, an item from the conscientiousness scale that typically reads "I keep my belongings neat and clean," would be changed to read "At work, I keep my belongings neat and clean." It is important to note, however, in concordance with the study by Griffith et al. (2004), seven of the openness to experience items were not reworded because their content would have been difficult to relate to the workplace. For example, the item "Poetry has little or no effect on me" could not be rewritten to reflect a work context; therefore this item was left in its original form as it appears on the NEO-FFI.

In addition to the personality measure, each participant completed a job application form that aided in our pursuit of simulating a true applicant setting. The application asked participants for biographical information (name, address, phone number, GPA, etc.) and previous employer contact information. In addition, the application also asked participants if they were interested in the job, if they had ever worked (or were currently working) as a customer service representative, and whether they were familiar with the tasks associated with customer service jobs.

Procedure

Prior to participation in the study, the participants were informed by their instructor that they would have the opportunity to participate in a research study as a chance to earn extra-credit for the course. The research took place during a scheduled class period for a variety of introductory psychology classes. Because of the nature of the study and the hypotheses that the experimenters wished to test, deception was incorporated into the design of the study.

The experimenters arrived at the participants' psychology classes posing as consultants for a university based consulting firm. The participants were informed that in addition to participating in the research study, they were being given the opportunity to apply for customer service positions that were available at the consulting firm. The participants were given a packet of surveys, with a job description attached to the cover. The participants were asked to examine the job description as one of the experimenters discussed the nature of the job. Each participant received the same job description form, with the exception of the starting pay that was listed on the job description. Participants were given a job description indicating a starting wage of \$26 per hour ($n = 34$), \$12 per hour ($n = 32$), or \$6.15 per hour ($n = 40$). After reading the job description, the participants were told to open their packet and take out the job application form.

After completing the job application, the participants completed the NEO-FFI. The experimenter informed the participants that this would be the final measure that needed to be completed in order to apply for the customer service position. After all participants had completed this measure, the experimenters informed the participants that there was no job available. The participants were informed that all of the information that they had provided with regards to demographics and employer contact information would be used for research purposes only, and that their employer would not be informed of their application for the job.

After being debriefed, the participants were asked to complete the NEO-FFI again, but with additional instructions. The additional instructions asked the participants to complete the measure honestly, and to provide the most accurate representation of their answers to the items that they could provide. The participants were again informed that their completion of the measure was purely for research purposes, and that there would be no implications associated with answering the items in an honest fashion. Upon completion of this measure, the participants were informed that they would be receiving their extra-credit points, and thanked for their patience and participation.

Analyses

In order to determine the amount of faking on the scales of the NEO-FFI, a change score was calculated. The amount of faking for each of the five NEO-FFI scales was calculated for each participant by subtracting his/her score from the condition with instructions to respond honestly, from his/her score in the applicant condition. A higher score (or in the case of Neuroticism, a lower score) in the applicant condition would indicate that the participant had elevated their responses.

To test Hypothesis 1, a bi-variate correlation analysis was conducted in order to determine whether a relationship existed between pay rate and the amount of faking on the five scales of the NEO-FFI. The test of Hypothesis 2 involved a multivariate analysis of variance (MANOVA) to determine whether there was an overall effect for level of pay on the amount of faking observed on the NEO-FFI. This was followed by a series of One-Way ANOVAs to determine whether there were mean level differences between the three pay rates in terms of the amount of faking that applicants engaged in, considering each scale separately.

RESULTS

Descriptive Statistics

Means and standard deviations for the amount of applicant faking on each of the NEO-FFI subscales for each pay rate condition are presented in Table 5.1. In addition, scale reliabilities for the NEO-FFI scales are presented for the applicant and honest conditions in Table 5.2 and Table

5.3 respectively. As expected, the means of applicant response distortion on the NEO FFI subscales are in the positive direction suggesting faking behavior. This finding is concurrent with previous research (e.g. Douglas et al., 1996), which suggests that participants can elevate their scores on a personality inventory if they choose to do so.

The results of the correlational analysis (see Table 5.4) indicate that there were significant relationships between amount of pay and amount of faking on the scales of Neuroticism ($r = -.19$, $p < .05$), Extraversion ($r = .23$, $p < .05$), Openness ($r = .25$, $p < .05$), Agreeableness ($r = .26$, $p < .01$), and Conscientiousness ($r = .25$, $p < .01$). These results support Hypothesis 1 as they indicate a relationship between amount of pay and amount of applicant faking on the 5 scales of the NEO-FFI.

Based on Wilks' multivariate criterion, the results of the MANOVA indicated that there was no main effect present for level of pay on the amount of faking observed on the NEO-FFI ($\lambda = .85$; $p < .08$). Due to the fact that the results from the MANOVA approached significance, as well as the distinctness of each construct assessed by the NEO-FFI, a series of One-Way ANOVA's were conducted to determine whether the hypothesized effects of the amount of pay offered to participants were present in any of the five subscales.

ANOVA results (see Table 5.5) suggest significant differences in amount of faking for different pay levels on scales of extraversion, $F(2, 105) = 3.82$, $p < .05$, agreeableness, $F(2, 105) = 7.29$, $p < .01$, and conscientiousness, $F(2, 105) = 5.48$, $p < .01$. Marginally significant results were obtained for the ANOVAs comparing the amount of faking across pay conditions for the scales of neuroticism, $F(2, 105) = 2.45$, $p < .09$, and openness to experience $F(2, 105) = 2.86$, $p < .06$. Given the fact that these results approached significance at the $p < .05$ level, it is likely that a larger sample may provide the requisite statistical power to achieve significance.

Table 5.1. Descriptive Statistics for Amount of Faking on the NEO-FFI Scales

	Pay Rate					
	$6.15(n = 41)		$12.00(n = 33)		$26.00(n = 34)	
Scale	Mean	SD	Mean	SD	Mean	SD
Neuroticism	−.88	5.45	−.52	4.94	−3.64	8.47
Extraversion	.73	3.63	.24	3.48	3.17	6.52
Openness	.17	3.11	.12	3.03	2.24	6.02
Agreeableness	2.09	4.31	−.37	2.64	5.67	10.30
Conscientiousness	1.86	5.58	.25	3.71	5.31	8.96

Table 5.2. NEO-FFI Scale Reliabilities for Applicant Condition

	Pay Rate		
Scale	$6.15(n = 41)$	$12.00(n = 33)$	$26.00(n = 34)$
Neuroticism	.61	.76	.78
Extraversion	.64	.55	.76
Openness	.66	.52	.41
Agreeableness	.80	.77	.70
Conscientiousness	.78	.89	.75

Note: Table values indicate internal consistency as measured by Cronbach's Alpha.

Table 5.3. NEO-FFI Scale Reliabilities for Honest Condition

	Pay Rate		
Scale	$6.15(n = 41)$	$12.00(n = 33)$	$26.00(n = 34)$
Neuroticism	.78	.74	.90
Extraversion	.66	.68	.86
Openness	.69	.64	.70
Agreeableness	.82	.80	.91
Conscientiousness	.79	.89	.93

Note: Table values indicate internal consistency as measured by Cronbach's Alpha.

Table 5.4. Intercorrelations Among Study Variables

	1	2	3	4	5	6
1. Pay Rate						
2. Amount of faking on neuroticism	−19*					
3. Amount on faking on extraversion	.23*	−.53**				
4. Amount of faking on openness	.25*	−.34**	.32**			
5. Amount of faking on agreeableness	.26**	−.60**	.58**	.41**		
6. Amount of faking of conscientiousness	.25**	−.65**	.62**	.42**	.74**	

$*p < .05.$ $**p < .01.$

Post hoc analysis results for the scales of extraversion, agreeableness, and conscientiousness yielded a similar pattern across the three constructs. Participants exhibited a significant enhancement of responses on the three scales for the $26.00 pay level when compared to the $12.00 pay

Table 5.5. Analysis of Variance for Amount of Faking on the NEO-FFI

Scale	SS	df	MS	F	p
Neuroticism					
Between	202.05	2	101.03	2.45	.092
Within	4,335.99	105	41.30		
Total	4,538.05	107			
Extraversion					
Between	168.68	2	84.34	3.81	.025*
Within	2,319.82	105	22.09		
Total	2,488.50	107			
Openness					
Between	102.08	2	51.04	2.86	.062
Within	1,877.25	105	17.88		
Total	1,979.34	107			
Agreeableness					
Between	620.13	2	310.06	7.29	.001**
Within	4,469.03	105	42.56		
Total	5,089.15	107			
Conscientiousness					
Between	452.16	2	226.08	5.46	.005**
Within	4,335.97	105	41.30		
Total	4,788.13	107			

*$p < .05$. **$p < .01$.

level. However, the $6.15 pay level was not significantly different from the other two conditions. This finding provides mixed support for Hypothesis 2. Although participants in the $26 condition faked more than participants in the $12 condition, the $6.15 condition was not significantly different from either of the aforementioned groups in terms of amount of faking.

DISCUSSION

The results of the present study indicate that pay rate may play a role in determining the amount of response distortion that individuals engage in while completing a personality measure under simulated applicant conditions. Although these data did not provide unequivocal support for our hypotheses, there was partial support. Amount of pay exhibited significant positive relationships with each of the NEO-FFI subscales. Additionally, levels of faking were the higher in the $26 pay rate condition than in the $12 pay rate condition for the NEO-FFI subscales of extraversion, agreeableness, and conscientiousness. However, somewhat surprisingly, the participants in the $6.15 condition did not fake significantly more or less than either the $12 or $26 conditions on these three scales. The differences between the pay rate conditions in the amount of faking on the scales of neuroticism and openness to experience approached significance, but failed to meet the $p < .05$ criteria. The marginally significant results achieved from the MANOVA were likely a result of the fact that the differences between the pay rates on the two aforementioned scales only approached significance and the $p < .05$ level. From a practical standpoint, however, it is likely to be more important to consider each scale as a separate entity when examining the amounts of faking behavior present. In a selection setting, it is unlikely that a composite score from the NEO-FFI as a whole would be used to make hiring decisions. A more likely scenario would involve using scores from the personality constructs that were most relevant to the job in question.

One possible explanation for the mixed findings is that there could be a rather complex set of influences that play a role in determining how a certain pay rate appears to the potential applicants. In the case of the sample used in this study (undergraduate students), $12 per hour may seem a little too good to be true, but not good enough to warrant misrepresenting oneself. In contrast, because $26 per hour would be considered an exceptionally high wage for an undergraduate, participants may feel that it is worth distorting their responses to try and attain the job. Finally, undergraduate students may feel that most of the people in their cohort have a good chance at landing a job that pays $6.15 per hour, which could lead to response distortion in order to separate oneself from all of the other potentially qualified applicants.

Limitations and Future Research

There are a few limitations associated with the present study that are worth noting. First, a larger sample may allow for more clarity when interpreting the differences between the three pay rate conditions. In addition, this study did not include a manipulation check to assess whether the participants believed they were applying for an actual job. However, in the study by Griffith et al. (2004), a manipulation check indicated that nearly 75% of the participants believed that they were applying for a real job. Given the fact that the present study was conducted using a very similar methodology and sample of participants, it is reasonable to assume that a manipulation check would have yielded similar results. Furthermore, individuals who do not believe the manipulation are likely to have less motivation to elevate their responses. Given this, any negative effects associated with the small proportion of participants who do not believe the manipulation are likely to be manifested in the form of a slight underestimation of the amount of faking that can occur in a true applicant sample.

Another limitation of our research can be found in our methodology. In this study we attempted to establish a recruiter-applicant relationship in a classroom during normal class time with extra credit as a competing incentive to participate in the study. This presents a potential confound of our ability to measure the impact of job desirability on faking because many of our participants may have assumed the applicant role only as a means to earn extra credit only, especially if they were not currently seeking employment. In future studies, it would enable the recruiter-applicant relationship to only sample participants who are interested primarily in employment, and to conduct these studies outside the normal class time. Again, this limitation may limit the amounts of faking behavior observed on the NEO-FFI.

Future research examining situational factors that may impact applicant faking behavior will likely have a wide array of situational variables to investigate. More research needs to focus on determining whether direct relationships exist between situational variables and levels of response distortion. Furthermore, additional research could examine the phenomenon of faking across different types of jobs, as well as a wider range of pay rates. Based on the results of this study, it would appear that situational variables do play some sort of a role in determining applicant faking behaviors. The task before researchers is to determine what this role is, and what situational variables deserve the most consideration when examining applicant faking behavior.

Conclusion

Overall, this study presents moderate evidence for a relationship between one element of job desirability, starting pay, and response distortion on a noncognitive measure in an applicant setting. This relationship is important for the understanding of faking behavior in general, but more specifically this relationship advises the recruiter-applicant relationship of possible validity decay in personality measures under highly desirable job conditions. Our results suggest that personnel selection for high paying positions can be informed by noncognitive measures, but the results of those measures should endure increased scrutiny on par with initial pay increases.

AUTHOR'S NOTE

Correspondence concerning this paper should be addressed to: Mitchell H. Peterson, Department of Psychology Florida Institute of Technology Melbourne, FL 32901 mpeterso@fit.edu

REFERENCES

Barrick, M. R., & Mount, M. K. (1991). The Big Five personality dimensions and job performance: A meta-analysis. *Personnel Psychology, 44*, 1-26.
Barrick, M. R., & Mount, M. K. (1996). Effects of impression management and self-deception on the predictive validity of personality constructs. *Journal of Applied Psychology, 81*, 261-272.
Bretz, R. D., & Judge, T. A. (1998). Realistic job previews: A test of the adverse self-selection hypothesis. *Journal of Applied Psychology, 83*, 330-337.
Cable, D. M., & Judge, T. A. (1994). Pay preferences and job search decisions: A person-organization fit perspective. *Personnel Psychology, 47*, 317-348.
Christiansen, N. D., Goffin, R. D., Johnston, N. G., & Rothstein, M. G. (1994). Correcting the 16PF for faking: Effects on the criterion-related validity and individual hiring decisions. *Personnel Psychology, 47*, 847-860.
Costa, P. T., & McCrae, R. R. (1992). *Revised NEO Personality Inventory (NEO PI-R) and NEO Five-Factor Inventory (NEO-FFI) Professional Manual*. Odessa, FL: Psychological Assessment Resources.
Douglas, E. F., McDaniel, M. A., & Snell, A. F. (1996, August). *The validity of noncognitive measures decays when applicants fake*. Paper presented at the annual meeting of the Academy of Management, Cincinnati, OH.
Fernandez-Ballesteros, F., & Zamarron, M. D. (1996). New findings on social desirability and faking. *Psychological Reports, 79*, 612-614.
Frei, R. L., Snell, A. F., McDaniel, M. A., & Griffith, R. L. (1998, April). *Using a within subjects design to identify differences between social desirability and faking*. Paper presented at the 13th annual conference of the Society for Industrial and Organizational Psychology, Dallas TX.
Gerhart, B., & Milkovich, G. T. (1990). Organizational differences in managerial compensation and financial performance. *Academy of Management Journal, 33*, 663-691.
Griffith, R. L., English, A., Yoshita, Y., Gujar, A., Monnot, M., Malm, T., et al. (2004, April). Individual differences and applicant faking behavior: One of these applicants is not like the other. In N. D. Christiansen (Chair), *Beyond social desirability in research on applicant response distortion*. Symposium conducted at the 19th annual conference for the Society for Industrial and Organizational Psychology, Chicago, IL.

Hough, L. M., Eaton, N. K., Dunnette, M. D., Kamp, J. D., & McCloy, R. A. (1990). Criterion-related validities of personality constructs and the effect of response distortion on those validities. *Journal of Applied Psychology, 75*, 581-595.

Leuke, S. B., Snell, A. F., & Illingworth, A. J. (2002, April). *The effect of different types of fakers on reliability coefficients.* Poster session presented at the 17th annual meeting of the Society for Industrial and Organizational Psychology, Toronto, Ontario, Canada.

Luther, N. J., & Thornton, G. C. III (1999). Does faking on employment tests matter? *Employment Testing Law and Policy Reporter, 8*, 129-138.

McCrae, R. R., & Costa, P. T. (1985). Updating Norman's "adequate taxonomy": Intelligence and personality dimensions in natural language and in questionnaires. *Journal of Personality and Social Psychology, 49*, 710-721.

McFarland, L. A., & Ryan, A. M. (2000). Variance in faking across noncognitive measures. *Journal of Applied Psychology, 85*, 812-821.

Mueller-Hanson, R., Heggestad, E. D., & Thornton, G. C. (2003). Faking and selection: Considering the use of personality from select-in and select-out perspectives. *Journal of Applied Psychology, 88*, 348-355.

Ones, D. S., & Viswesvaran, C. (1998). The effects of social desirability and faking on personality and integrity assessment for personnel selection. *Human Performance, 11*(2/3), 245-269.

Ones, D. S., Viswesvaran, C., & Reiss, A. D. (1996). Role of social desirability in personality testing for personnel selection: The red herring. *Journal of Applied Psychology, 81*, 660-679.

Rosse, J. G., Stecher, M. D., Miller, J. L., & Levin, R. A. (1998). The impact of response distortion on preemloyment personality testing and hiring decisions. *Journal of Applied Psychology, 83*(4), 634-644.

Ryan, A. M., & Tippins, N. T. (2004). Attracting and selecting: What psychological research tells us. *Human Resource Management, 43*, 305-318.

Schmit, M. J., Ryan, A. M., Stierwalt, S. L., & Powell, A. B. (1995). Frame-of-reference effects on personality scale scores and criterion-related validity. *Journal of Applied Psychology, 80*, 607-620.

Snell, A. F., & McDaniel, M. A. (1998, April). *Faking: Getting data to answer the right questions.* Paper presented at the annual meeting of the Society for Industrial and Organizational Psychology, Dallas, TX.

Stark, S., Chernyshenko, O. S., Chan, K., Lee, W, C., & Drasgow, F. (2001). Effects of the testing situation on item responding: Cause for concern. *Journal of Applied Psychology, 86*, 943-953.

Stokes, G. S., Hogan, J. E., & Snell, A. (1993). Comparability of incumbent and applicant samples for the development of biodata keys: The influence of social desirability. *Personnel Psychology, 46*, 739-762.

Taylor, M. S., & Collins, C. J. (2000). Organizational recruitment: Enhancing the intersection of research and practice. In C. L. Cooper & E. A. Locke (Eds.), *Industrial and organizational psychology: Linking theory with practice* (pp. 304-330). Oxford, England: Blackwell.

Wells, T. (2001). *Opportunities, preferences, and outcomes: The matching of people to jobs*. Paper presented at the 96th annual meeting of the American Sociological Association, Anaheim, CA.

Winter, P. A., & Logsdon, M. R. (2004). Recruiting health information faculty: The effects of monetary recruitment incentives. *Community College Journal of Research and Practice, 28,* 455-466.

Wotruba, T. R., Simpson, E. K., & Reed-Draznik, J. L. (1989). The recruiting interview as perceived by college student applicants for sales positions. *The Journal of Personal Selling and Sales Management, 9,* 13-24.

Zickar, M. J., & Drasgow, F. (1996). Detecting faking on a personality instrument using appropriateness measurement. *Applied Psychological Measurement, 20,* 71-87.

CHAPTER 6

MALES VERSUS FEMALES ON FAKING BEHAVIOR IN PERSONALITY TESTING

An Examination of Gender Differences

Randolph Socin, Joshua A. Isaacson, and Richard L. Griffith

The use of noncognitive measures in selection has been contested on the basis of applicants' ability to fake their responses. In order to improve these useful tools, research identifying variables associated with applicant faking behavior is needed. This study examined the gender/faking relationship on personality measures. Previous literature in the area of academic dishonesty suggests that males may have more liberal attitudes than females toward cheating on tests (Whitley, Nelson, & Jones, 1999), but that actual behavior may not differ. Based on these findings, we hypothesized that gender would not be related to the amount of applicant faking in a personnel selection setting. Our results suggest that in fact gender differences do occur in applicant faking with a higher percentage of males engaging in applicant faking behavior. Differences were also found in the amount of applicant faking with males having significantly higher means levels.

Increased utilization of personality inventories has recently ensued within the selection context stemming from the recognition that personality constructs can be categorized into a descriptive taxonomy referred to as the five-factor model (FFM) (Barrick & Mount, 1991; Digman, 1990). The contribution of the FFM has guided research and application of personality in a common fashion, increasing consensus and generalizability across researchers and fields of study, occupations, and cultures (Barrick & Mount, 1991; Salgado, 1997; Tett, Jackson, & Rothstein, 1991). Furthermore, prior research contended that personality measures contain desirable characteristics, such as producing and low adverse impact (Hough & Oswald, 2000). In addition, these measures have been suggested to be useful in promoting social justice, and may increase organizational productivity when used in preemployment screening (Hogan, Hogan, & Roberts, 1996). Most notably in relation to selection, previous examinations have demonstrated the value of personality as a predictor of job performance and other work-related behaviors (Barrick & Mount, 1996; Tett et al., 1991).

Although the use of noncognitive measures in selection has demonstrated promise, debate within the literature remains as to their vulnerability to faking by respondents (Douglas, McDaniel, & Snell, 1996; Rosse, Stecher, Miller, & Levin, 1998). Faking has been described by terms such as frankness, social desirability, claiming unlikely virtues, denying common faults and unpopular attitudes, exaggerating personal strengths, good impression, self-enhancement, and response distortion (Ones, Viswesvaran, & Reiss, 1996). Although these terms are often used interchangeably, they may have important conceptual differences. While many of these constructs may influence faking behavior, the term faking focuses more on the outcome of behavior, that is, an exaggeration in a positive direction.

While a large amount of research on faking behavior has been conducted, little consensus exists regarding the nature of its determinants. Although noncognitive measures have been a useful tool in industrial and organizational psychology, they still produce rather low to moderate validities, and improvement in our research and practice in this area is warranted. Accordingly, identifying and narrowing down the potential variables associated with applicant faking behavior and developing cogent theoretical models is a necessary step toward improving noncognitive selection systems.

The current variable of interest, gender, is extensively investigated within the ethics and academic cheating literature, although not as prevalent in the area of faking, despite the similarities between the two. Research has supported the proposition of gender differences in academic cheating, and these differences may also appear in an applicant setting. Thus, we posited that applicant faking may simply be an extension of cheating in an academic setting, and that the dynamics of academic cheating may generalize to the applicant faking phenomenon. The focus of this study was to integrate and apply prior findings from the academic dishonesty literature with present faking research, to determine if gender will influence faking on personality measures.

FAKING BEHAVIOR ON PERSONALITY INSTRUMENTS

Most researchers agree that applicants have the ability to fake their responses in a more favorable manner when instructed to do so (Hough, Eaton, Dunette, Kamp, & McClough, 1990; Viswesvaran & Ones, 1999; Zickar & Robie, 1999), although some argue that this behavior is rare in the actual selection context (Hough et al., 1990). Thus, it has been proposed that faking is not a pervasive problem, and should not be controlled for in selection settings (Ones, Viswesvaran, & Reiss, 1996).

Empirical support suggesting that faking behavior is rare in operational settings was provided by a study conducted by Hough et al. (1990). The authors examined the levels of a social desirability (SD) scale using a large military sample, finding little evidence to suggest faking was present. Caution should be taken when interpreting these results. While the construct of SD and faking behavior are often referred to as synonyms, they are not interchangeable. Thus, the usefulness of SD scales as a proxy for applicant faking has been called into question (Christiansen, Goffin, Johnston, & Rothstein, 1994; Griffith, Rutkowski, Gujar, Yoshita, & Steelman, 2005). Furthermore, although a large military sample was used, participants completed the personality inventory after they had been sworn in, thus degrading the generalizability of the results to a realistic applicant condition.

In contrast, previous research exists suggesting that some applicants actually engage in faking behavior (Barrick & Mount, 1996; Griffith, Snell, Frei, McDaniel, & Yoshiya, 2000; Schmit & Ryan, 1993; Stokes, Hogan, & Snell, 1993). For example, Griffith et al. (2000) provided evidence that a significant number of applicants distorted their responses on a measure of conscientiousness in an applicant setting. In this study, 55% of respondents elevated their scores by ½ standard deviation or more when applying for a job. As a result, a significant amount of fakers were able to raise their scores into the hiring range. Further, significant changes were found in the rank ordering of applicants due to faking. Additional evidence was attained by Becker and Colquitt (1992) using a job applicant-incumbent response research design. Results illustrated that an applicant sample scored approximately two-thirds of a standard deviation higher than the incumbent group, indicating that applicants were thus likely to fake. Therefore, based on these findings, faking may potentially be a pervasive problem for selection specialists.

Several explanations have been proposed which provide a rationale for why applicants may display faking behavior. First, demand characteristics of the situation may be attributed to a respondent's desire to enhance one's self image on a personality inventory. Thus, in a highly motivational and impression demanding context such as an employment setting, candidates may attempt to exhibit a positive self-representation through means of inflating attractive qualities and demonstrate attributes of a prototypic employee (Rosse, Stecher, Miller, & Levin, 1998). Indication of this may be established through research which found that applicants' scores are higher on personality measures than those of their job incumbent counterparts (White & Moss, 1995). Second, the content of personality inventories is prone to be highly transparent. Trait descriptors have a tendency to be value laden, making social desirability of endorsing items easy to distinguish (Alliger, Lilienfeld, & Mitchell, 1995). Last, the belief of nonverifiability of responses may reinforce faking behavior. Hence, when respondents believe that actual abilities cannot be verified, they tend to overstate their capabilities (Fiske & Taylor, 1991). Personality inventories used in employment selection may provide applicants the opportunity to fake their responses in order to present themselves as being more desirable than they actually are.

Gender, Academic Dishonesty, Ethics, and Faking Behavior

Academic testing and employment selection environments are similar in that they both provide the opportunity and motivation to be dishonest in order to accomplish a significant goal. Thus, as the demographic variable of gender is virtually absent within the research area relating to faking behavior, literature involving cheating behavior in academia and ethical beliefs/behaviors was utilized as a surrogate. Due to the similarities between these areas, they may provide another framework to facilitate the understanding of faking behavior within the selection context, and the role that gender may play in this environment.

Within the research fields of academic cheating and ethical attitudes/behavior, gender difference is a topic that is highly debated. On one side of the argument, support was found that males possess more positive attitudes toward cheating (Whitley, Nelson, & Jones, 1999). Furthermore, it has been found that men obtain lower scores on ethics scales (Glover, Bumpus, Logan, & Ciesla, 1997; Mason & Mudrack, 1996) as compared to females.

In contrast, these results are not definitive, as males may be more likely than females to report cheating behavior (Cochran, Wood, Sellers, Wilkerson, & Chamlin, 1998; Tibbetts & Myers, 1999; Ward & Tittle, 1993). Thus, the willingness of male subjects to be open about their attitudes in comparative studies may provide an obscuring factor in the actual trait levels in women. Even if this may not be true, others have found no ethical differences between males and females (Dubinsky & Levy, 1985; Fritzsche, 1988; Kidwell, Stevens, & Bethke, 1987; Singhapakdi & Vitell, 1990). In addition, several studies report no significant differences in actual cheating *behavior* between genders (Whitley, Nelson, & Jones, 1999; Wiley, 1998).

Although prior research in cheating and ethical attitudes/behavior is somewhat inconclusive, a large body of research has suggested that there are no significant gender differences in actual dishonest behavior in an academic setting (Cochran et al., 1998; Tibbetts & Myers, 1999; Ward & Tittle, 1993). Extending this rationale to the applicant setting, no gender differences would be expected in actual amounts of applicant faking behavior. Accordingly, our hypotheses are as follows:

Hypothesis 1: There will be no significant difference in the amount of applicant faking between males and females.

Hypothesis 2: There will be no significant difference in the percentage of applicants identified as fakers between males and females.

METHOD

Participants

A sample of 284 undergraduate students from several large southeastern universities participated in this study. Of these, 165 (58.10%) were women and 119 (41.90%) were men, with a mean age of 24.51 and 23.28 respectively. All participants were given extra-credit for their involvement, and treated in accordance with APA guidelines.

Materials

Summated Conscientiousness Scale (SCS). A dimension of personality delineated within the five-factor model, conscientiousness, was assessed using the SCS. This measure is composed of 20 [work-related conscientiousness] items that are rated on a 7-point Likert scale. An example of an item on this scale would be "I complete work projects from start to finish." An internal consistency reliability has been previously estimated ($\alpha = 0.84$), and has a correlation of $r = 0.75$, $p < .05$ with the NEO-PI-R conscientiousness scale (Griffith et al., 2000). Conscientiousness has been shown to be a robust predictor of job performance over a variety of work setting, which is the rationale behind the utilization of this scale (Barrick & Mount, 1991; Tett et al., 1991).

Design and Procedure

Researches have argued that laboratory faking behavior study designs are not adequate to assess true applicant behavior due to the use of nonrealistic experimental environments (Hough, 1997). Thus, to replicate a true applicant condition, deception was used for this study. Acting as consultants for a local university-based consulting firm, the experimenters offered a false employment opportunity for a student position as a customer service representative. We expected this to induce an applicant-type response on the measures, as participants will be motivated to present themselves in a positive fashion that will increase their chances of obtaining the (false) position (Rosse, Stecher, Miller, & Levin, 1998).

In addition to an employment opportunity, participants were informed that they will be participating in a research study to receive extra-credit, and consent was given to proceed. A job description was then provided and participants were instructed to complete materials in the applicant packets provided, which contained a job application and the SCS (Summated Conscientiousness Scale). Following the applicant condition, participants were debriefed, being informed there is no job opportunity, and that all information obtained will be used for research purposes only. Afterward, the SCS was administered under an honest condition, directing participants to answer all items as truthfully as possible, and being reminded that their cooperation will result in extra-credit points.

Manipulation Check

To ensure that the manipulation was successful, a brief survey was randomly collected from a sub-sample of 64 participants. This survey solicited "Did you believe that you were applying for a real job during this experiment?" This resulted in 75% of the participants believing they were applying for a real job, suggesting the manipulation was effective.

In addition, the application also contained an item to measure the manipulation's effect. On a 5-point Likert scale, participants were asked to rate their interest in the job, from 1 (no interest) to 5 (very interested). 79.9% of the participants rated their interest a 2 or greater (Mean = 3.43, Median = 4, Mode = 5, SD = 1.51). Additional support for the applicant manipulation was found upon examining the means across applicant and honest conditions. Table 6.1 delineates the mean levels, as the applicant condition produced higher scores than the honest condition.

RESULTS

Analysis

To statistically examine the gender/faking relationship within our sample, analyses were conducted to determine if both: (a) the amount of faking differs between males and females, and (b) the percentage of male and female fakers differ. As a true score on the SCS is impossible to obtain and must be inferred, the honest scores were used as a baseline comparison score. To determine the amount of faking, the honest scores were subtracted from the applicant scores, producing an estimate of applicant faking (Griffith et al., 2005). With the use of an ANOVA, group differences were assessed, with the mean amount of faking on the SCS for each gender being compared. To determine the number of fakers, a confidence interval around the mean honest score on the SCS was obtained using the Standard Error of Measurement (SEM) x (1.96) confidence interval around the baseline score. Scores lying beyond this interval were considered to be faked by participants who distorted their responses (with 95% certainty). A chi-square analysis was conducted, to assess the differences in frequencies of faking between groups.

Addressing Hypothesis 1, change scores were computed to determine the amount of applicant faking present in the deception condition. To accomplish this, each participant's composite honest score was subtracted from their composite applicant score. A descriptive analysis for the applicant and honest condition was conducted, as outlined in Table 6.1. Item

Table 6.1. Descriptive Statistics for Applicant and Honest Conditions

Condition	Mean	SD	Alpha
Applicant	122.66	10.67	.86
Honest	117.15	15.24	.91

reliability was estimated for both the honest and applicant conditions (α = .91 and α = .86, respectively) to determine the dependability of the difference scores. A .70 alpha level is sufficient to produce a reliable measure (Nunnally, 1978), thus, the obtained alpha level for each scale suggests the difference scores are stable. Based on the mean difference scores from each gender, an ANOVA was executed to establish if the amount of applicant faking differs between males and females [$F(1, 282) = 4.72; p = .03$]. In consequence, Hypothesis 1 was not supported, as there were significant differences between groups. This indicates that the magnitude of faking is higher for males than for females within our sample (Table 6.2).

In reference to Hypothesis 2, a confidence interval around the mean honest score on the SCS was obtained using the SEM [$(4.57) \times (1.96) = 8.96$]. Scores larger than this confidence interval are considered to be from participants who have distorted their responses (with 95% certainty). 42.02% (n=50) of males were considered fakers, while 21.21% ($n = 35$) of females were considered fakers. A chi-square analysis was conducted, to assess the differences in frequencies of faking between genders ($\chi^2 = 14.27, p < .001$). Thus, Hypothesis 2 was not supported, as there were significant differences between the frequencies of fakers between groups. Accordingly, there are a significantly higher percentage of male fakers than female fakers within our sample.

DISCUSSION

Due to the lack of research that assesses the gender/faking issue in the employment selection setting, our hypotheses were based on cheating and ethical behavior in academia. Seeing that there are conflicting results on the role of gender within these examinations (i.e., Cochran et al., 1998; Dubinsky & Levy, 1985; Fritzche, 1988; Glover et al., 1997; Kidwell et al., 1987; Mason & Mudrack, 1996; Singhapakdi & Vitell, 1990; Tibbets & Myers, 1999; Ward & Tittle, 1993; Whitley et al., 1999), it is understandable that our hypotheses were not supported. While the academic dishonesty literature suggested little gender differences in actual cheating *behavior*, dif-

Table 6.2. **Amount of Faking by Gender**

	Males	*Females*
N	119	165
Applicant	120.16	124.45
Honest	112.90	120.22
Amount of faking	7.26	4.23

ferences have been found in *attitudes* toward cheating. The studies examining actual behavior have been criticized for relying on self report behavior (Cochran et al., 1998; Tibbets & Myers, 1999; Ward & Tittle, 1993) so the distinction in actual cheating behavior may not be so clear. In this study, we found clear gender differences in both the percentage of applicant fakers and the amount of applicant faking. Our data suggested that males both are more likely to fake personality measures during the selection process, and have higher overall amounts of applicant faking.

Although scholastic and applicant contexts both provide the opportunity to engage in dishonest behavior and involve highly motivational environments to achieve a goal, differences may exist in terms of the consequences of negative behaviors. For example, individuals in an academic setting may be more cautious toward cheating as opposed to those in the selection environment, due to prior investment such as sunk cost (Staw & Ross, 1986). Thus, individuals in school have "capital" to loose (i.e., credits and professional relationships obtained); while in contrast, those in an applicant setting only stand to not obtain a goal. Furthermore, those who cheat or act unethically in school may find this as an ultimate roadblock in their educational goals, as they may be "blackballed," making it extremely hard to find other sources of goal attainment. In contrast, those who fake on selection measures may just move on to the next hiring opportunity, and no one will be the wiser.

The concept of consequences is supported through the "warning" literature, which suggests that a reduction of faking behavior on selection measures will incur when applicants are cautioned against self-misrepresentation (Hough, Eaton, Dunnette, Kamp, & McCloy, 1990). In a common selection context (with no warning), applicants may perceive a low degree of verifiability of responses, and thus a low valence of repercussions as a result of faking. In contrast, if an applicant is under the impression that results may be verified (possibly through performance data), faking is reduced stemming from the belief that negative action may take place due to discrepancies (faking versus actual level of traits or performance).

Limitations and Future Research

As is the nature of any research, there are several limitations with the current study that should be noted. First, although this research methodology clearly has advantages and enables researchers to collect information in an applicant like setting, it is still not a true applicant setting. The manipulation solely depends on the ability of the researcher to deceive the participants. This simulated applicant setting could also elicit negative reactions to the deception and participants may provide inaccurate data. However, the manipulation check results were positive; this suggests that participants did believe they were applying for a job, and furthermore, students were awarded extra-credit, so there is currently no reason to assume they would provide faulty information. Additionally, the use of an honest instructional set has been criticized due to the possibility of unconscious bias when instructed to respond honestly. One such bias, self deceptive enhancement, would suggest that individuals may self report lower levels of an undesirable behavior (Paulhus, 1991). Last, using academic dishonesty literature as a surrogate is a cogent and rational model to borrow from, however there is no evidence suggesting that these phenomena are linked. From a practical perspective, additional research investigating the similarities between academic dishonesty and faking would be useful for understanding the variables that lead to these phenomena.

Overall, some important implications for future research may be gained from the obtained outcomes. Understanding gender differences in faking behavior may add increased clarity of the selection context. First and foremost, gender differences may have serious implications in terms of adverse impact in selection, as men may have an unmerited advantage in gaining employment especially in occupations that are already dominated by men (i.e., Law enforcement). Employment laws are put forth to prevent unfair practices, and without considering these gender differences in faking behavior, organizations may be exposing themselves to legal liability, in addition to possessing a less diverse workforce. Ryan, Ployhart, and Friedel (1998) found evidence for adverse impact against females in a police applicant sample, though the majority of evidence in this area suggests that personality instruments result in low adverse impact between genders (Hogan & Hogan, 1995; Hough & Oswald, 2000; Ones & Anderson, 2002; Sandal & Endresen, 2002). These results are unclear, as faking may provide an obscuring factor in validity coefficients (see Douglas et al., 1996; Zickar, Rosse, & Levin, 1996), which these studies did not consider. Thus, it is possible that adverse impact may occur when considering faking behavior differences. More research is warranted in order to identify the impact gender has on the validity, utility, and legal implications of noncognitive selection measures.

Further, considering gender differences will assist in shaping a comprehensive theoretical model of faking behavior in the selection environment. The current results bring forth the question of which traits vary between sexes; what makes males and females different? For example, prior research suggests that there may be personality differences between genders (Feingold, 1994; Hall, 1984; Maccoby & Jacklin, 1974; Ones & Viswesvaran, 1998). This may be attributed to biological (Eysenck, 1992;

Zuckerman, 1991), sociocultural (Eagly, 1987; Eagly & Wood, 1991), or bio-social differences (Feingold, 1994). As additional research is required in order to narrow down antecedent faking characteristics and solidify prior research and theory, these results may provide a foundation and direction for future research.

CONCLUSION

The current results indicate that the magnitude of applicant faking behavior is larger in males. In addition, males display faking behavior more than females (i.e., higher percentage or frequency). Thus, the aforementioned outcomes may imply that males and females possess different characteristics or traits which may contribute to discrepancy in faking behavior. This is suggested by a multitude of disciplines, which have found significant gender differences in attitudes (Bettencourt & Miller, 1996; Clouse, 1973; Lindgren, Youngs, McDonald, Klenow, & Schriner, 1987), ethical perceptions (Franke, Crown, & Spake, 1997), deviance (Robbins & Martin, 1993), and factors of social control and rational choice (Tibbetts & Herz, 1996). Although gender itself may not directly contribute to faking behavior, it may provide an avenue to facilitate explanation of antecedents of faking, cheating, and ethical behavior. Thus, identifying these variables may therefore aid in the improvement of selection instruments and add clarity to faking behavior within the selection environment, as well as cheating/ethical behavior in an academic setting.

AUTHOR'S NOTE

Correspondence concerning this article should be addressed to: Randolph Socin, Department of Psychology Florida Institute of Technology, Melbourne, FL 32901.

REFERENCES

Alliger, G. M., Lilienfield, S. O., & Mitchell, K. E. (1995). The susceptibility of overt and covert integrity tests to coaching and faking. *Psychological Science, 7*, 32-39.

Barrick, M. R., & Mount, M. K. (1991). The Big Five personality dimensions and job performance: A meta-analysis. *Personnel Psychology, 44*, 1-26.

Barrick, M. R., & Mount, M. K. (1996). Effects of impression management and self-deception on the predictive validity of personality constructs. *Journal of Applied Psychology, 81*, 261-272.

Becker, T. E., & Colquitt, A. L. (1992). Potential versus actual faking of bio-data form: An analysis along several dimensions of item type. *Personnel Psychology, 45*, 389-406.
Bettencourt, B. A., & Miller, N. (1996). Gender differences in aggression as a function of provocation: A meta-analysis. *Psychological Bulletin, 119*, 422-447.
Christiansen, N. D., Goffin, R. D., Johnston, N. G., & Rothstein, M. G. (1994). Correcting the 16PF for faking: Effects on the criterion-related validity and individual hiring decisions. *Personnel Psychology, 47*, 847-860.
Clouse, B. (1973). Attitudes of college students as a function of sex, politics, and religion. *Journal of College Student Personnel, 14*, 260-264.
Cochran, J. K., Wood P. B., Sellers, C. S., Wilkerson, W., & Chamlin, M. B. (1998). Academic dishonesty and low self-control: An empirical test of a general theory of crime. *Deviant Behavior, 19*, 227-255.
Digman, J. M. (1990). Personality structure: Emergence of the Five-factor model. *Annual Review of Psychology, 41*, 417-440.
Douglas, E. F., McDaniel, M. A., & Snell, A. E. (1996, August). *The validity of noncognitive measures decays when applicants fake.* Paper presented at the annual meeting of the Academy of Management, Cincinnati, OH.
Dubinsky, A. J., Levy, M. (1985). Ethics in retailing: Perceptions of retail salespeople. *Journal of the Academy of Marketing Science, 13*, 1-16.
Eagly, A. H. (1987). *Sex differences in social behavior: A social role interpretation.* Hillsdale, NJ: Erlbaum.
Eagly, A. H., & Wood, W. (1991). Explaining sex differences in social behavior: A meta-analytic perspective. *Personality and Social Psychology Bulletin, 17*, 306-315.
Eysenck, H. J. (1992). Four ways five factors are not basic. *Personality and Individual Differences, 13*, 667-673.
Feingold, A. (1994). Gender differences in personality: A meta-analysis. *Psychological Bulletin, 116*, 429-456.
Fiske, S. T., & Taylor, S. E. (1991). *Social cognition* (2nd Ed.). New York: McGraw-Hill.
Franke, G. R., Crown, D. F., & Spake, D. F. (1997). Gender differences in ethical perceptions of business practices: A social role theory perspective. *Journal of Applied Psychology, 82*, 920-934.
Fritzsche, D. J. (1988). An examination of marketing ethics: Role of the decision maker, consequences on the decision, management position, and sex of the respondent. *Journal of Macromarketing, 8*(2), 29-39.
Glover, S. H., Bumpus, M. A., Logan, J. E., & Ciesla, J. R. (1997). Re-examining the influence of individual values on ethical decision making. *Journal of Business Ethics, 16*, 1319.
Griffith, R. L., Chmielowski, T., Snell, A. F., Frei, R. L., & McDaniel, M. A. & Yoshiya, Y. (2000, April). *Does faking matter? An examination of rank order changes in applicant data.* Symposium presented at the 15th annual meeting of the Society of Industrial and Organizational Psychologists. New Orleans, LA.
Griffith, R., Rutkowski, K. A., Gujar, A., Yoshita, Y., & Steelman, L. A. (2005). *Modeling applicant faking: New methods to examine an old problem.* Manuscript submitted for publication.

Hall, J. A. (1984). *Nonverbal sex differences: Communication accuracy and expressive style*. Baltimore, MD: John Hopkins University Press.
Hogan, R, & Hogan, J. (1995). *Hogan Personality Inventory Manual* (2nd ed.). Tulsa, OK: Hogan Assessment Systems.
Hogan, R., Hogan, J., & Roberts, B. (1996). Personality measurement and employment decisions: Questions and answers. *American Psychologist, 51*, 469-477.
Hough, L. M. (1997). The millennium for personality psychology: New horizons or good old daze. *Annual Review of Psychology, 47*(2), 233-261.
Hough, L. M., Eaton, N. K., Dunnette, M. D., Kamp, J. D., & McCloy, R. A. (1990). Criterion-related validities of personality constructs and the effect of response distortion on those validities. *Journal of Applied Psychology Monograph, 75*(5), 581-595.
Hough, L. M., & Oswald, F. L. (2000). Personnel selection: Looking toward the future—Remembering the past. *Annual Review of Psychology, 51*, 631-664.
Kidwell, J. M., Stevens, R. E., & Bethke, A. L. (1987). Differences in ethical perceptions between male and female managers: Myth or reality? *Journal of Business Ethics, 6*, 489-493.
Lindgren, H. E., Youngs, G. A., McDonald, T. D., Klenow, D. J., & Schriner, E. C. (1987). The impact of gender on gambling attitudes and behavior. *Journal of Gambling Behavior, 3*, 155-167.
Mason, E., & Mudrack, P. (1996). Gender and ethical orientation: A test of gender and occupational socialization theories. *Journal of Business Ethics, 15*, 599-604.
Maccoby, E. E., & Jacklin, C. N. (1974). *The psychology of sex differences*. Stanford, CA: Stanford University Press.
Nunnally, J. C. (1978). *Psychometric theory* (2nd ed.). New York: McGraw-Hill.
Ones, D., & Anderson, N. (2002). Gender and ethnic group differences on personality scales in selection: Some Brittish data. *Journal of Occupational and Organizational Psychology, 75*(3), 255-276.
Ones, D. S., & Viswesvaran, C. (1998). Gender, age, and race differences on overt integrity tests: Analyses across four large-scale applicant data sets. *Journal of Applied Psychology, 83*, 35-42.
Ones, D. S., Viswesvaran, C., & Reiss, A. D. (1996). Role of social desirability in personality testing for personnel selection: The red herring. *Journal of Applied Psychology, 81*, 660-679.
Paulhus, D. L. (1991). Measurement and control of response bias. In J. P. Robinson, P. R. Shaver, & L. S. Wrightsman (Eds.), *Measures of personality and social psychological attitudes* (pp.17-59). New York: Academic Press.
Robbins, C. A., & Martin, S. S. (1993). Gender, styles of deviance, and drinking problems. *Journal of Health and Social Behavior, 34*, 302-321.
Rosse, J. G., Stecher, M. D., Miller, J. L., & Levin, R. A. (1998). The impact of response distortion on pre-employment personality testing and hiring decisions. *Journal of Applied Psychology, 83*, 634-644.
Ryan, A. M., Ployhart, R. E., & Friedel, L. A. (1998). Using personality testing to reduce adverse impact. *Journal of Applied Psychology, 83*, 298.
Salgado, J. F. (1997). The five factor model of personality and job performance in the European Community. *Journal of Applied Psychology, 82*, 30-43.

Sandal, G. M., & Endresen, I. M. (2002). The sensitivity of the CPI good impression scale for detecting "faking good" among Norwegian students and job applicants. *International Journal of Selection and Assessment, 10,* 304-311.

Schmit, M. J., & Ryan, A. M. (1993). The Big Five in personnel selection: Factor structure in applicant and non-applicant populations. *Journal of Applied Psychology, 78*(6), 966-974.

Singhapakdi, A., & Vitell, S. J. (1990). Marketing ethics: Factors influencing perceptions of ethical problems and alternatives. *Journal of Macromarketing, 10,* 4-18.

Staw, B. M., & Ross, J. (1986). Behavior in escalation situations: Antecedents, prototypes, and solutions. In T. G. Cummings & B. M. Staw (Eds.), *Research in organizational behavior* (pp. 39-78). Greenwich, CT: JAI Press.

Stokes, G. S., Hogan, J. E., & Snell, A. (1993). Comparability of incumbent and applicant samples for the development of biodata keys: The influence of social desirability. *Personnel Psychology, 46,* 739-762.

Tett, R. P., Jackson, D. N., & Rothstein, M. (1991). Personality measures as predictors of job performance: A meta-analytic review. *Personnel Psychology, 44,* 703-742.

Tibbetts, S. G., & Herz, D. C. (1996). Gender differences in factors of social control and rational choice. *Deviant Behavior, 17,* 183-208.

Tibbetts, S. G. & Myers, D. (1999). Low self-control, rational choice, and student test cheating. *American Journal of Criminal Justice, 23,* 179-200.

Viswesvaran, C., & Ones, D. S. (1999). Meta-analysis of fakability estimates: Implications for personality measurement. *Educational and Psychological Measurement, 59,* 197-210.

Ward, D. A., & Tittle, C. R. (1993). Deterrence or labeling: The effects of informal sanctions. *Deviant Behavior, 14,* 43-64.

White, L. A., & Moss, M. C. (1995, May). *Factors influencing concurrent versus predictive validities of personality constructs: Impact of response distortion and item job content.* Paper presented at the 10th annual meeting of the Society of Industrial and Organizational Psychology, Orlando, FL

Whitley, B. E., Nelson, A. B., & Jones, C. J. (1999). Gender differences in cheating attitudes and classroom cheating behavior: A meta-analysis. *Sex Roles: A Journal of Research, 657*-677.

Wiley, C. (1998). Reexamining perceived ethics issues and ethics roles among employment managers. *Journal of Business Ethics, 17*(2), 147.

Zickar, M. J., & Robie, C. (1999). Modeling faking good on personality items: An item-level analysis. *Journal of Applied Psychology, 84(4),* 551-563.

Zickar, M., Rosse, J., & Levin, R. (1996, April). *Modeling the effects of faking on personality instruments.* Paper presented at the 11th annual meeting of the Society for Industrial and Organizational Psychology, San Diego, CA.

Zuckerman, M. (1991). *Psychobiology of personality.* Cambridge, MA: Cambridge University Press.

CHAPTER 7

COOPERATION AND COMPETITION

The Effects of Team Entrainment and Reward Structure

Michael Woodward, Kenneth Randall, Bennett Price, and Andrea Saravia

In the last several years, there has been a great deal of interest in the use of teams within organizations (Alper, Tjosvold, & Law, 1998; Johnson, Hollenbeck, Humphrey, Ilgen, & Jundt, 2004; Wageman & Baker, 1997). Just as culture and values differ across organizations, so does the design of work teams. Often, organizations will create cross-functional teams comprised of individuals from a variety of departments, locations, or functions in order to tackle complex problems requiring a multidisciplinary approach. Another common scenario is for organizations to partner with other companies to fill gaps in expertise and enhance their market capabilities. When organizations create teams, the individual members bring not only their unique expertise to the table, but they also carry with them their individual past experiences and expectations with respect to reward structures. The current study seeks to examine the effects of these past experiences and expectations through an empirical investigation. The study focuses on the impact of reward structure on task performance and how the prior exposure of individual team members affects a team's ability to complete a simple task.

REINFORCEMENT AND ENTRAINMENT

Patterns of behavior in individuals and groups can be impacted by the nature of how that behavior is reinforced. Operant conditioning or reinforcement theory states that behavior is influenced by the consequences associated with it. Behaviors that elicit positive consequences are strengthened and reinforced. In organizational settings behavior often translates to both task work and performance, whereas consequences or positive outcomes are often only associated with rewards. A meta-analysis conducted by Jenkins, Mitra, Gupta, and Shaw (1998) found a significant relationship between performance (defined as quantity) and financial incentives. Jenkins et al. argue that this relationship lends credibility to the application of reinforcement theory in organizational settings.

Behaviors that are consistently reinforced will likely be repeated, and will often take on somewhat of a recurring pattern. The rhythmic nature of these patterns is often referred to as entrainment. The term entrainment generally refers to a "process by which one internal (or endogenous) rhythmic process is captured and modified by another (endogenous or exogenous) rhythmic process" (Kelly, 1988, p. 89). Entrainment occurs when patterns of behavior that are initially established as a result of an external force are maintained over time. An extension of this notion of rhythmic influence is social entrainment. Social entrainment posits that the temporal and rhythmic nature of individual behavior can also occur collectively in groups (Kelly).

In an examination of social entrainment in four-person groups, Kelly and McGrath (1985) found that time limits initially imposed during a first trial influenced group performance on subsequent trials. Basically, the pattern of behavior developed by each group (taking their initial time allocation into consideration) persisted throughout the following two trials even though the time allocation for completing the tasks differed in subsequent trials.

Ancona and Chong (1996) extended the notion of entrainment to organizations. They posit that worker behavior is greatly impacted by the temporal pacing and cyclical nature of work activities. Due to the structured nature of work, employees adjust their rhythms to synchronize with the external forces imposed by work. Often times the rhythmic patterns individuals develop remain even when the external pacer subsides. When a pattern of behavior persists despite changes in influencing conditions, entrainment is said to have taken place. Once behaviors are entrained, they can become somewhat difficult to change. In the case of groups or teams, patterns of behavior are established early on and eventually become the norm of the group (Tuckman, 1965). These norms dictate the manner in which teams interact and may become entrained in individual team members. As part of the transition or norming process, teams establish goals, strategies, and performance standards (Marks, Mathieu & Zaccaro, 2001). Furthermore, teams are influenced by their reward structures. In turn, the nature of how a team is rewarded may become entrained, which may affect team members' ability to adapt to reward structures.

Social Interdependence Theory

There has been widespread interest in how organizations should structure teams, what rewards/incentives should be offered, and how performance should be measured (Alper et al., 1998; Beersma, Hollenbeck, Humphrey, Moon, Conlon, & Ilgen, 2003; Tauer & Harackiewicz, 2004). Social interdependence theory states that "the way goals are structured determines how individuals interact, and the interaction pattern determines the outcomes of the situation" (Stanne, Johnson, & Johnson, 1999, p. 134). The type of goals established can dictate whether or not individuals will seek to work collaboratively towards collective accomplishment or individually towards gaining personal benefit.

The two major elements of social interdependence theory are cooperation and competition. Within a cooperative team design, team members' goals are positively linked, which means that as one person moves toward goal attainment, other members come closer to their goals as well (Alper et al., 1998; Stanne et al., 1999). A cooperative team's success is based upon the success of all members. Within cooperative teams, members can have individual goals as well as team goals. As one member reaches their individual goal, each and every other member of the team approaches individual success as well, which means that one member's effectiveness helps all other team members reach their goals. Cooperative systems emphasize group accomplishments, and are created through mutual assistance and the exchange of needed resources (Alper et al., 1998; Beersma et al., 2003).

Within a competitive environment, individuals' goals are separate. As one person attains his/her goals others are precluded or at least hindered from attaining theirs (Alper et al., 1998). Stanne et al. (1999) noted individuals engaged in a competitive system perceive their own goal success to be tied to the failure of their colleagues' goal attainment. As a result, individuals place their own goals above those of the team or the larger organization. Stanne et al. posit that competitive systems reinforce coercive action, manipulation of power, and conflict.

Cooperative and competitive teams, by their very nature, each emphasize different characteristics and goals. Competitive systems accentuate individual success, whereas cooperative teams strive for collective success. The cooperative drive for collective success can be characterized by team members sharing information, developing strategies, and exchanging ideas in order to maximize the effectiveness of all members. The discussion and transfer of knowledge from one team member to another ensures that all team members possess the information relevant and necessary to complete a task. However, this active interchange between members can be incredibly time-consuming (Beersma et al., 2003). In a competitive system, the knowledge and information possessed by one individual is not readily shared with other members. Withholding this information increases the likelihood of the individual's success while decreasing the potential for their teammates' success. Due to the reduced level of communication and exchange, competitive teams may encounter more difficulty in accomplishing tasks. However, for these same reasons competitive teams may actually operate faster (Beersma et al.). Researchers have found that cooperative systems tend to promote accuracy while having a negative effect on speed. On the other hand, competitive systems promote speed and have a negative effect on accuracy (Beersma et al.; Stanne et al., 1999). Historically, research has been supportive of cooperative group designs citing such benefits as increased group productivity, stronger positive relationships, and better psychological health (Stanne et al.).

In further examining social interdependence theory, Johnson et al. (2004) found supporting evidence indicating that cooperative teams tend to achieve a higher level of accuracy in goal attainment than competitive teams, yet they take much longer. Thus, cooperative teams are slower and more accurate, whereas competitive teams are faster and less accurate. The Johnson et al. finding highlights the influence of reward structure in devising organizational work teams.

Most notably, Johnson et al.'s (2004) findings indicate that team members become entrained to reward structures, and do not readily change their behavior in response to a new reward structure. A key open question then concerns the malleability of team reward structures. In Johnson et al.'s study, the reward structures of intact teams were changed. One intervention that may alleviate this entrainment and promote adaptation to the new reward structure is changing composition. To an organization wanting to change a team that is operating too competitively, Johnson et al.'s research suggests it is not enough to simply change the reward structure.

In the current study, we examine the effects of combining a change in reward structure with a change in composition. To do this, we examine teams at two points in time. First, we impose either a cooperative or competitive reward structure on the team and ask them to perform a task under the imposed reward structure in order to entrain members to either a cooperative or competitive reward structure. Next we reassigned teams so that they were comprised of either all competitive members, all cooperative members, or half cooperative and half competitive members. Teams were then asked to perform the same task with their new teammates under a cooperative reward structure, and we examined the ability of each type of team to adapt to the cooperative structure. Consistent with Johnson et al.'s (2004) findings, we expect teams that are initially rewarded competitively to continue to operate with greater speed but less accuracy than their cooperative counterparts.

Hypothesis 1: Competitively entrained teams will perform faster and less accurately than both cooperatively and mixed entrained teams.

Johnson et al. (2004) found information sharing was a key mediator of this relationship. Another potential mediator of this relationship is collaboration. Collaboration describes the extent to which team members work collectively towards a common goal. We expect cooperatively rewarded teams to engage in more collaboration than competitively rewarded teams, and we expect differences in collaboration to explain why team reward structure affects task performance (speed and accuracy).

Hypothesis 2a: Reward structure entrainment will affect the level of cooperation such that cooperatively entrained teams will engage in more collaboration than both competitively entrained teams and teams comprised of both cooperatively and competitively entrained members ("mixed teams").

Hypothesis 2b: Collaboration will mediate the relationship between reward structure entrainment and task performance (speed and accuracy).

The fast paced nature of modern business dictates that individuals will be exposed to a variety of organizational reward structures. Whether changing careers or being merged with new colleagues in an acquisition, workers will continually face the challenges of adapting to new environments. As part of this adaptation, reward structures will change requiring workers to adjust quickly to be successful. The current study was designed to offer a first look at how changing team composition affects adaptation to a new reward structure.

METHOD

Participants

Participants included 240 undergraduate psychology students at a large Southeastern University. Participants ranged from 16 to 60 years old, and 70% were female. Participants were randomly assigned to four-person teams. Students received course credit for participation.

Design and Procedure

The experiment consisted of three conditions (cooperative, competitive, and mixed-cooperative/competitive). These conditions were created by first having teams complete a task and become entrained to either a cooperative or competitive reward structure. Teams were then mixed so that a new set of teams comprising all cooperative, all competitive, or a mixture of cooperative and competitive team members was created. During the experimental task (time 2) all teams operated under a cooperative reward structure. Therefore our conditions refer to the composition of team members based on their reward structure at time 1. In the cooperative condition all four team members had worked under a cooperative time 1 reward structure. In the competitive condition all four team members had worked under a competitive time 1 reward structure. The mixed condition teams were comprised of two cooperatively and two competitively rewarded team members. At time 2 all teams had experienced a membership change from time 1, and operated under a cooperative reward structure.

Each condition consisted of participants randomly assigned to teams that were run two at a time. All teams engaged in the same type of task throughout the experiment. At time 1, teams in the first condition operated under a cooperative reward system, the teams in the second condition operated under a competitive system, and in the third condition half of the teams were cooperatively and half were competitively rewarded. At time 2, two members from each team within the specified conditions were switched to form two new teams within that condition. In the third condition, each team was comprised of an equal number of members from both cooperatively and competitively entrained teams. As an overall result, at time 2 there was a competitively entrained team, a cooperatively entrained team and a mixed entrainment team, all operating under a cooperative reward structure. At time 2, all teams were read instructions detailing a cooperative reward structure.

Task

The primary researchers were responsible for providing instructions, administering the task, keeping time, and tallying completion results. The raters charged with observing and rating information sharing and collaboration behaviors were trained by the primary experimenters and remained blind to both the hypotheses and conditions. Participants engaged in a puzzle building exercise designed to facilitate high interdependence. The task apparatus consisted of four individual, 25 piece, inset jigsaw puzzles. Each individual was charged with the completion of their respective puzzle.

Team members were each assigned to a corner of a room where one inset puzzle board and 25 pieces had been placed. Of the 25 pieces in each corner, 13 pieces were correct for that corner puzzle, while the remaining 12 pieces were comprised of four pieces from each of the three other puzzles. Participants were allotted a 2-minute period to examine their puzzles. After determining which pieces were incorrect for their puzzles, members were allowed to trade puzzle pieces with teammates during one of three exchange meetings. If teams negotiated pieces successfully, all members were able to complete their respective puzzles.

The task was chosen for the experiment based on a number of important considerations. Of paramount concern was the ability to measure individual and team performance in terms of speed and accuracy, which was easily done. In addition, the task required the team members to work together to succeed.

Manipulation

The participants in the cooperative condition (time 1) were told that their group scores would be determined by a combination of their team speed and the percentage of correct puzzle pieces for all four puzzles. Each teams' combined score was compared across the cooperative condition to determine an overall winning team, which was awarded a $40.00 cash prize to be split evenly between the four teammates. These same instructions were also provided to all time 2 conditions.

The participants in the competitive condition (time 1) were told that their individual scores would be determined by a combination of their team's speed and the percentage of correct puzzle pieces that each participant had upon completion of the task. The individual with the highest completion percentage and the fastest group time was the overall winner for the competitive condition, and was given a $20.00 cash prize. Thus, depending on condition, the goal was to either complete all four puzzles accurately in the shortest amount of time (cooperative reward structure), or for each individual to attempt to complete their individual puzzle regardless of the other team members (competitive reward structure).

Manipulation Check

Participants completed a manipulation check at time 1 to verify comprehension of the target reward structure for the purposes of entrainment. The manipulation check consisted of two items: (1) "Rewards for this task will be based solely on my own individual performance" and (2) "Rewards for this task will be based on how my group performs." Both items were rated on a 1- to 5-Likert scale anchored by 1 = "Strongly disagree" and 5 = "Strongly agree." An independent samples t test was conducted comparing the cooperative condition with the competitive condition for the first question (individual reward). The results for the cooperatively entrained teams indicated that the mean score for participants ($M = 2.17$, $SD = 1.15$) was significantly lower than the mean score for the competitively entrained teams ($M = 3.57$ $SD = 1.12$), $t(238) = -9.56$, $p < .001$. An independent samples t test was also conducted comparing the cooperative condition with the competitive condition for the second question (group reward). The results for the cooperatively entrained teams indicated that the mean score for participants ($M = 4.51$, $SD = .83$) was significantly higher than the mean score for the competitively entrained teams ($M = 3.74$ $SD = .97$), $t(238) = 6.60$, $p < .001$. The results of the manipulation check verified that overall participants correctly perceived the intended reward structure.

Measures

Team Performance

Team performance was operationalized as a combination of speed and accuracy. Speed was measured by the total time it took the team to complete all three of their exchange meetings. A team's accuracy was determined as the total number of correct pieces for all four team members combined. Individual accuracy scores were calculated as the number of correct pieces each team member had for their respective puzzles.

Information Sharing and Collaboration

Information sharing and collaboration were assessed through both experimenter observation and self-report. Three items were developed to assess the extent to which team members shared information: (a) "Individual team members shared the theme of their puzzle with the team"; (b) "Individual team members shared their four pieces with the team"; and (c) "Individual team members shared exact descriptions of puzzle pieces needed." Four items were developed to assess the amount of collaboration between members: (a) "Individual team members verbalized a strategy for coordinating the exchange of puzzle pieces"; (b) "The group agreed to work collaboratively in deciding how to exchange pieces"; (c) "The group collaboratively determined when to terminate each group exchange meeting"; and (d) "The group collaboratively determined when to convene each group exchange meeting." The items for information sharing were completed by both individual team members and independent raters. The independent raters also completed ratings for the four collaboration items. All responses were made on a 5-point Likert scale in which 1 = "Not at all" and 5 = "To a great extent." Coefficient alpha was .86 for the self-report measures. Within group agreement (r_{wg}) was calculated for information sharing at time 1 (r_{wg} = .75) and time 2 (r_{wg} = .93).

Data Aggregation

Since information sharing was measured at the individual level through participant self-report, the data was first analyzed for within group agreement and reliability before aggregating to the group level. Measures were aggregated in order to assess each construct at the team level. High agreement and reliability were found for all measures of both experimenter observation and participant self-report.

RESULTS

A one-way ANOVA was conducted comparing the differences in speed and accuracy between cooperative, competitive, and mixed teams at time 2. The omnibus F for speed was 1.02 (df = 2, 59, p > .05) indicat-

Table 7.1. Analysis of Variance for Performance

Source	SS	df	F	η^2	p
DV = Speed					
Reward structure	67,902.43	2	1.02	.03	.37
Error	1,896,036.90	57			
DV = Accuracy					
Reward structure	142.43	2	4.47	.14	.02*
Error	907.75	57			

Note: * $p < .05$.

ing no significant mean differences between conditions. The omnibus F for accuracy was 4.47 ($df = 2, 59$, $p < .05$) indicating the presence of significant mean differences (see Table 7.1). Upon further analysis cooperatively entrained teams ($M = 93.10$, $SD = 4.68$) were found to be significantly more accurate than competitively entrained teams ($M = 90.05$, $SD = 3.09$) with a mean difference of 3% ($p < .05$). Mixed teams ($M = 93.50$, $SD = 4.05$) were also found to be significantly more accurate than competitively entrained teams ($M = 90.05$, $SD = 3.09$) with a mean difference of roughly 3.5% ($p < .05$). There was no significant difference in accuracy between mixed and cooperatively entrained teams. These results provide partial support for Hypothesis 1.

To examine Hypothesis 2a, the differences in observed collaboration across the three time 2 conditions were analyzed through the use of a one-way ANOVA. The omnibus F for collaboration was 4.68 ($df = 2, 59$, $p < .05$) indicating the presence of significant differences in collaboration (see Table 7.2). Results of post hoc analyses revealed that cooperatively entrained teams ($M = 4.25$, $SD = 0.69$) were found to be significantly more collaborative than competitively entrained teams ($M = 3.53$, $SD = 0.75$). However, mixed teams ($M = 4.01$, $SD = 0.82$) were not significantly different than either competitively or cooperatively entrained teams. The results provide partial support for Hypothesis 2a.

Table 7.2. Analysis of Variance for Collaboration

Source	SS	df	F	η^2	p
Reward structure	5.34	2	4.68	.14	.01*
Error	32.54	57			

Note: * $p < .05$.

To further examine the impact of collaboration, a mediated regression analysis was conducted to investigate the potential for collaboration as a mediating variable in the relationship between reward structure and accuracy. Speed was not examined due to lack of a significant difference between conditions. In order to test the accuracy model, the two entrained reward structures (cooperation and competition) were dummy coded as vectors. To test the mediation hypothesis the steps proposed by Baron and Kenny (1986) were followed. First, the proposed mediator, collaboration, was regressed on reward structure. This yielded a significant beta weight, $t(59) = 3.23, p < .01$. Next, the dependant variable, accuracy, was regressed on reward structure, which yielded a significant beta weight for the first of the two vectors (cooperative), $t(59) = -2.14, p < .05$, but not for the second vector (competitive), $t(59) = -0.65, p > .05$. Third, accuracy was regressed on both collaboration and reward structure, which revealed that collaboration accounted for 15% of the variance in accuracy and reward structure added less than 7% beyond collaboration, which was not significant (see Table 7.3). When collaboration was controlled for, reward structure did not explain significant incremental variance in accuracy across the two vectors (cooperative entrainment and competitive entrainment) beyond that already explained by collaboration. The results provide partial support for Hypothesis 2b.

The differences in observed information sharing across the three time 2 conditions were analyzed through the use of a one-way ANOVA. The omnibus F for observer rated information sharing was 0.90 ($df = 2, 59, p > .05$) indicating no significant differences. The differences in self-reported information sharing across the three time 2 conditions were also analyzed by a one-way ANOVA. The omnibus F for information sharing

Table 7.3. Summary of Hierarchical Regression Analysis for Variables Predicting Accuracy ($N = 60$)

Independent Variable	B	ΔR^2	Total R^2
Step 1		—	.15**
Collaboration	.39**		
Step 2		.07	.22**
Collaboration	.31*		
Reward structure Vector 1	—		
Reward structure Vector 2	—		

Note: * $p < .05$, ** $p < .01$

was 0.02 ($df = 2, 59, p > .05$) indicating no significant differences in self-reported information sharing.

DISCUSSION

Overall, the current study provides support for the notion that reward structure impacts team performance. At time 2 both the cooperatively and competitively entrained teams appeared to carry their expected patterns of performance forward, suggesting that entrainment had taken place. Teams initially exposed to cooperative reward structures were more accurate than teams initially exposed to competitive reward structures. Mixed teams also faired better than their competitive counterparts achieving essentially the same level of performance as the cooperatively entrained teams. Thus, it appears that teams composed of members who initially operated under a competitive reward structure had a more difficult time adapting to the cooperative reward structure at time 2. This finding provides support for Johnson et al.'s (2004) notion of cutthroat cooperation. However, teams comprised of members with prior exposure to both cooperative and competitive reward structures (two from each condition) did not have any difficulty in adjusting, with respect to accuracy. The differences in performance between the two sets of teams illustrates the effects of entrainment and lends partial support for the findings reported by Beersma et al. (2003) and Johnson et al. (2004).

In addition, the researchers also set out to examine the influence of collaboration in the reward structure-performance relationship. More specifically, the researchers examined the mediating role of collaboration between prior reward structure entrainment and accuracy. Speed was not examined due to its nonsignificant relationship with reward structure. Collaboration was found to be a critical mechanism in defining the relationship between a team's entrained reward structure and their ability to produce accurate results. This would suggest that the institution of a cooperative reward structure engenders an environment of collaboration that promotes more accurate team performance.

An examination of information sharing revealed no differences between the time 2 conditions. Based on the literature, the researchers expected to see higher levels of information sharing in the cooperatively entrained teams as compared to the competitive and mixed teams. One explanation for this unexpected result may be the presence of a learning effect. Based on researcher observation, it appeared that the teams assigned to the time 1 competitive condition realized that their lack of communication and sharing of information hindered their performance. In order to effectively complete the puzzles, at least some level of information sharing was important. When faced with the second trial, where all conditions (teams) were cooperatively rewarded, the competitively entrained teams had the impetus to share more information. However, as illustrated in the results, the level of collaboration still differed, thus pointing out that even though competitively entrained teams were sharing more information, they were doing it somewhat begrudgingly.

Limitations

The generalizability of these results is somewhat limited. The participants in our study were all undergraduate students who participated for course credit as well as the opportunity for a cash prize. The age, level of experience, and maturation of the participants differs from that of a typical organization. Another issue regarding the participants is the fact that they were 70% female and 71% Hispanic, which is assuredly not representative of the typical populations within organizations across the country. Overall, the size and representativeness of the sample used could be improved to strengthen the findings.

Each session was conducted back-to-back, which meant that teams would go through their time 1 exposure (cooperative or competitive reward structure) and then move immediately to their time 2 exposure (cooperative reward structure). This rapid progression allowed for only limited initial exposure to a particular reward structure. This limited exposure may have inhibited the ability of team members to become fully entrained in their respective reward structures before progressing to the next set of conditions. As a result, the entrainment was likely too weak to have the type of impact one would expect from an employee who had been operating under the same reward structure day-in and day-out for a number of years. A final limitation could be the general lack of discrepancies concerning accuracy scores. Participants began each task with 13 out of 25 correct pieces for their respective puzzles, and thus each team had a floor for total accuracy scores around 50%. Therefore all accuracy scores were already confined to the range between 50-100, and ultimately the range shrunk to 78-100.

Future Research

The results of this study provided partial support for the research of both Beersma et al. (2003) and Johnson et al. (2004), as well as opened up some possible avenues of future research. The study could be modified by adding another session to the task, so as to ensure participants are fully immersed into their reward structure so that entrainment can take place. Having this additional session would allow for strategy development and learning to occur between time 1 and time 2. Then teams could be switched and mixed for a time 3 trial where changes could be measured. Another opportunity for researchers would be to examine various aspects of team composition, leadership, and shared mental models and how they impact a team working in either a cooperative, competitive, or mixed group. Having teammates with relatively high levels of cognitive ability, agreeableness, and extraversion may increase the communication and coordination between members, which in turn enhances performance. Training a team on various strategies may cause them to have a similar mental model, and thus improve the coordination between members and their overall performance. A final opportunity for future researchers could be to further examine the decision-making processes and abilities of cooperative, competitive, and mixed teams. It may be prudent to develop a more decision-oriented and intensive situation to effectively study how reward structures influence a team's decision-making processes and overall accuracy.

REFERENCES

Alper, S., Tjosvold, D., & Law, K. S. (1998). Interdependence and controversy in group decision making: Antecedents to effective self-managing teams. *Organizational Behavior and Human Decision Processes, 74*(1), 33-52.

Ancona, D., & Chong, C. (1996). Entrainment: Pace, cycle, and rhythm in organizational behavior. *Research in organizational behavior, 18*, 251-284.

Baron, R. M., & Kenny, D. A. (1986). The moderator-mediator variable distinction in social psychological research: Conceptual, strategic, and statistical considerations. *Journal of Personality and Social Psychology, 51*(6), 1173-1182.

Beersma, B., Hollenbeck, J. R., Humphrey, S. E., Moon, H., Conlon, D. E., & Ilgen, D. R. (2003). Cooperation, competition, and team performance: Toward a contingency approach. *Academy of Management Journal, 46*(5), 572-590.

Jenkins, D. G., Mitra, A., Gupta, N., & Shaw, J. D. (1998). Are financial incentives related to performance? A meta-analytic review of empirical research. *Journal of Applied Psychology, 83*(5), 777-787.

Johnson, M. D., Hollenbeck, J. R., Humphrey, S. E., Ilgen, D. R., & Jundt, D. (2004, August). *Cutthroat cooperation: Asymmetrical adaptation of team reward structures*. Paper presented at the annual meeting of the Academy of Management, New Orleans, LA.

Kelly, J. R. (1988). Entrainment in individual and group behavior. In J. E. McGrath (Ed.), *The social psychology of time: New perspectives* (pp. 89-110). Newbury Park, CA: Sage.

Kelly, J. R., & McGrath, J. E. (1985). Effects of time limits and task types on task performance and interaction of four-person groups. *Journal of Personality and Social Psychology, 49*, 395-407.

Marks, M. A., Mathieu, J. E., & Zaccaro, S. J. (2001). A temporally based framework and taxonomy of team processes. *Academy of Management Review, 26*(3), 356-376.

Stanne, M., Johnson, D. W., & Johnson, R. T. (1999). Social interdependence and motor performance: A meta-analysis. *Psychological Bulletin, 125*, 133-154.

Tauer, J. M., & Harackiewicz, J. M. (2004). The effects of cooperation and competition on intrinsic motivation and performance. *Journal of Personality and Social Psychology, 86*(6), 849-861.

Tuckman, B. W. (1965). Developmental sequence in small groups. *Psychological Bulletin, 63*(6), 384-399.

Wageman, R., & Baker, G. (1997). Incentives and cooperation: The joint effects of task and reward interdependence on group performance. *Journal of Organizational Behavior, 18*, 139-158.

CHAPTER 8

THE RELATIONSHIP BETWEEN SHARED LEADERSHIP AND TEAM PERFORMANCE AND SATISFACTION

Task Type Matters

Paul Pluta, Gregory Hyman, Ingrid Campbell, and Diana Keith

We investigated the relationships between the *planning and organizing, problem solving, support and consideration,* and *development and mentoring* dimensions of shared leadership and team performance and satisfaction. Fifty-six teams of undergraduate students (229 individuals) comprising three to eight members each performed either an action, creativity, or decision-making task. The relationship-oriented dimensions of shared leadership (*support and consideration, development and mentoring*) were positively related to satisfaction across all three tasks. Only *support and consideration* was related to performance across the three tasks. Task-oriented shared leadership (*planning and organizing, problem solving*) was positively related to satisfaction for the decision-making task. For the action task, both task-oriented and relationship-oriented shared leadership were related to satisfaction.

Refining Familiar Constructs: Alternative Views in OB, HR, and I/O, pp. 105–120
Copyright © 2007 by Information Age Publishing
All rights of reproduction in any form reserved.

Teams are commonplace in organizations, and are considered an important part of organizational development initiatives (e.g., Barrick, Stewart, Neubert, & Mount, 1998; Campion, Papper, & Medsker, 1996; De Dreu & Wiengart, 2003; Ilgen, 1999). The amount of autonomy afforded teams varies considerably both within and between organizations (Wellins, Byham, & Wilson, 1991). Thompson (2004) refers to the "team paradox," such that leaders are often necessary for effective team performance, but their very existence can undermine teamwork. Morgeson (2005) found that teams whose external leaders engaged in active coaching and sensemaking activities were less satisfied with leadership than teams with leaders who did not employ active intervention strategies. Supportive coaching and preparation were positively related to team members' judgments of leader effectiveness in Morgeson's study. The purpose of the present investigation is to determine whether leadership processes that are shared among group members are positively related to team performance and satisfaction. Furthermore, we seek to determine whether the pattern of relationships between shared leadership dimensions and performance and satisfaction varies by task type.

LEADERSHIP PROCESSES

The functional leadership paradigm posits the leader's role is to ensure that team members perform behaviors critical to both task accomplishment and group maintenance (Hackman & Walton, 1986). Teams often vary in the amount of autonomy they are afforded (Wellins, Bayham, & Wilson, 1991). These authors suggested that empowerment can follow a continuum, ranging from teams having basic housekeeping responsibilities to making decisions regarding team member discipline and compensation. Stewart and Barrick (2000) defined team self-leadership as the amount of authority and freedom teams have. However, this definition merely implies self-leadership in terms of team autonomy, without defining the specific leadership processes involved. Although he stressed the need for vertical leadership, Pearce (2004) acknowledged the value of shared leadership. This author suggested that groups need to be encouraged to exert both lateral and upward influence. Pearce advised that designated group leaders should promote and encourage members to engage in collective leadership behaviors. Hiller, Day, and Vance (2006) indicated that leadership process behaviors might be shared among members of autonomous teams. Hiller et al. investigated the relationship of four shared leadership processes of (a) *planning and organizing*, (b) *problem solving*, (c) *support and consideration*, and (d) *development and mentoring* to supervisor ratings of team effectiveness. The four dimensions are subsumed under the two higher-order task-oriented (*planning and organizing, problem solving*) and relationship-oriented (*support and consideration, development and mentoring*) aspects of leadership. These investigators found the dimension of *support and consideration* to be significantly related to team effectiveness.

Relationship-Oriented Shared Leadership and Performance

Riggio, Riggio, Salinas, and Cole (2003) found that, in general, group leaders selected for their socioemotional communication skills were judged more effective than leaders who did not possess these skills. These supporting, encouraging, and developing behaviors appear consistent with Hiller et al's (2006) two relationship-oriented collective leadership dimensions. Thus, we expect the relationship-oriented components of shared leadership (*support and consideration, development and mentoring*) will be positively related to group performance, regardless of the type of task being performed.

Shared Leadership and Task Type

Stewart and Barrick (2000) investigated the extent to which the relationships between self-leadership, intrateam processes, and performance are moderated by task type. These investigators defined team self-leadership in terms of the extent to which members conduct meetings, change work processes, or determine strategies, and so forth. We interpret these elements as being somewhat analogous to Hiller et al.'s (2006) task-oriented dimension. Stewart and Barrick (2000) found that greater self-leadership was related to better team performance for groups working on conceptual tasks versus behavioral tasks. Stewart and Barrick (2000) also investigated moderating effects of task type on the relationship between intrateam processes (i.e., communication, flexibility, shirking, and conflict) and performance. Intrateam processes in this context appear to capture behaviors loosely related to Hiller et al's (2006) relationship-oriented shared leadership dimension. Stewart and Barrick (2000) found a stronger negative relationship with performance for shirking and conflict when groups were performing a conceptual task versus when they were working on a behavioral task. In addition to discovering that the importance of intrateam processes varies by task type, Stewart and Barrick also found that intrateam processes mediate the relationship between group member interdependence and performance. Thus, although dimensions and definitions of key constructs appear to differ in important ways across studies, there is some indication that the various shared leadership processes might be more important for some types of tasks than for others.

Decision-Making Tasks

Riggio et al. (2003) suggested that socioemotional skills may be more closely related to group performance for group discussion tasks than for more clearly defined tasks. Additionally, groups whose leaders are highly concerned with group processes produce better decisions than groups whose leaders are more concerned with outcomes (Peterson, 1997). According to the model proposed by Zaccaro, Rittman, and Marks (2001), leader *planning* processes are directly related to the cognitive and motivational process that foster team effectiveness, and *development* processes influence the cognitive, motivational, and affective processes associated with effectiveness. However, these authors further posit that *problem solving* is related to all four processes (cognitive, motivational, affective, and coordination) that further influence team effectiveness.

Groups that think convergently focus on a narrow set of solutions to a problem (Goncalo, 2004). Decision-making tasks often involve asking a group of individuals with different goals and interests to arrive at the most optimal decision. Abad, Castella, Cuenca, and Navarro (2002) proposed that teams working on intellective tasks require a medium level of information richness, whereas teams working on a negotiation task perform best in conditions of high information richness. Thus, collective leadership processes that facilitate open and prolific information exchanges between team members should enhance performance and satisfaction for tasks that require both problemsolving and negotiation. Therefore, we expect both task- and relationship-oriented collective leadership will be positively related to satisfaction for a decision-making task. Furthermore, we expect *planning and organizing* collective leadership behaviors will be positively related to team performance for a decision-making task.

Creativity Tasks

Tasks involving the generation of ideas may be facilitated by thought divergence (Goncalo, 2004). Brainstorming is a prime example of such a task. Consistent with Goncalo, brainstorming tasks can be scored based on both the number of ideas generated (fluency) and the number of ideational shifts (flexibility).

The support and consideration component of collective leadership may promote group cohesiveness. Craig and Kelly (1999) referred to both task and interpersonal cohesiveness, which were found to have differential effects on team creativity. Interpersonal cohesiveness had no effect on performance, whereas task cohesiveness had a marginal but nonsignificant effect.

A brainstorming task can be considered an example of an additive task (Craig & Kelly, 1999). These investigators suggested that brainstorming tasks do not require the same level of group synergy and coordination commonly required by groups engaged in the generation of creative solutions to real-world problems. Thus, although relationship-oriented shared leadership may enhance interpersonal group cohesion, task-oriented collective leadership is expected to influence task performance on an additive task (i.e., brainstorming). Consequently, we expect that task-oriented collective leadership will be positively related to performance for the brainstorming task. However, relationship-oriented collective leadership will be positively related to satisfaction for the brainstorming task.

Action Tasks

Zaccaro et al. (2001) proposed a recurring phase model of team processes. Within a traditional input-process-outcome (IPO) framework, these authors proposed that teams engaged in ongoing tasks experience multiple performance episodes. Zaccaro et al. proposed that different team processes are important at different stages along the team performance continuum. During what these authors termed *action* phases, coordinating and monitoring behaviors are considered most effective, whereas planning and evaluation are thought to be most critical during *transition* phases. Additionally, interpersonal processes are posited to be important during both action and transition phases of the team performance cycle.

In the context of Hiller et al.'s (2006) model of collective leadership, one would expect that task-oriented collective leadership behaviors would be most critical during action phases of the team performance cycle. Additionally, one would expect that problemsolving and strategizing would be influenced by planning and organizing, and problemsolving collective leadership behaviors. Finally, social lubricant might facilitate consensus building and coordinated action. Therefore, we believe that both task- and relationship-oriented collective leadership process behaviors will be positively related to satisfaction and performance for the action task.

METHOD

Participants

Fifty-six teams of undergraduate students (229 individuals) comprising three to eight members each participated in this study. The decision making and creativity tasks utilized groups of students enrolled in a course in small group behavior, where they routinely participated in team-based tasks as part of the course curriculum. The groups for the action task were recruited from the psychology participant pool as part of an unrelated study. The mean age of the participants in this study was 20 years ($SD =$ 2.3 years).

Procedure

Teams performed either the decision-making, creative, or action task, each of which took approximately 45 minutes to complete. Groups were either performing their task as part of their coursework or as part of another unrelated research project. Thus, there was no random assignment to groups. After completing their respective tasks, each participant completed a questionnaire that contained measures of collective leadership and team satisfaction.

Decision-Making Task
Fifteen groups of 4 to 5 participants each took part in a decision-making task. The decision-making exercise was a group negotiation set up to avoid coalition building. It consisted of a multi-issue, multiparty, decision-making task that simulated a joint retail project with common areas and expenses. The goal was for the groups to arrive at the most optimal solution.

Creative Task
Ten groups ranging from 5 to 8 students each took part in a creative brainstorming task. This task required participants to generate as many ways as possible to classify fruits and vegetables. Participants were given an information sheet with different tips, such as (a) do not evaluate ideas, (b) express ideas as they come to mind, (c) build on the ideas of others, (d) and strive for quantity. This exercise was scored on two dimensions: total ideas produced and number of ideational shifts.

Action Task
Thirty-one groups ranging from 3 to 4 individuals each took part in a scavenger hunt. Participants were required to follow a list of clues to search for answers to questionnaire items. Each group was given the same questions with different wording to prevent the participants from forming one large cooperative group. The scoring of this exercise tracked number of correct answers in relation to total time to completion.

Measures

Collective Leadership

Hiller et al's (2006) collective leadership scale was adapted for use in the present study. These investigators conducted a factor analysis on the scale items, which resulted in the emergence of the following collective leadership dimensions: (a) *Planning and Organizing* (task), (b) *Problem Solving* (task), (c) *Support and Consideration* (relationship), and (d) *Development and Mentoring* (relationship). Internal consistency reliability estimates for the combined scale items on each of the four dimensions were generally high, ranging from .93 to .96. Sample items include, "Throughout your team exercise, how often did your team members share in setting the team's goals" and "Throughout your team exercise, how often did your team members share in providing support to team members who needed help?" Responses were made on a 5-point Likert-type scale where 1 = *Not at all* and 5 = *Very often*.

Team Satisfaction

A modification of the Job Diagnostic Survey (JDS; Hackman & Oldham, 1975) was used to measure team satisfaction. Responses were recorded on a Likert-type scale where 1 = *Strongly Disagree* and 5 = *Strongly Agree*. Items consisted of statements such as "I am satisfied with how my teammates and I work together" and "I am satisfied with the decisions that my teammates and I have made." Bishop, Dow, and Scott (2000) reported an internal consistency reliability estimate of .88 for the modified scale used in the present study.

RESULTS

Data Aggregation

Scale Reliability

The internal consistency reliability of the shared leadership questionnaire, at both the full-scale and subscale levels, was evaluated prior to data aggregation to the team level. The internal consistency reliability of the full-shared leadership scale for this sample was relatively high ($\alpha = .91$). Additionally, the internal consistency estimates for the *Planning and Organizing*, *Problem Solving*, *Support and Consideration*, and *Development and Mentoring* subscales were .84, .88, .74, and .79, respectively. For the *Task-Oriented* and *Relationship-Oriented* subscales, internal consistency estimates were .91 and .85, respectively. Given that the observed reliability estimates for all scales were reasonably high, we proceeded with data aggregation.

Group-Level Agreement

Prior to aggregating individual level data into a group composite, within-group agreement was assessed for each of the shared leadership subscales. The $r_{wg(j)}$ (James, Demaree, & Wolf, 1984) for all teams in the three task conditions were sufficiently high to justify aggregation to the team level. Thus, all subsequent analyses were conducted on data aggregated to the team level for the decision-making, creativity, and action tasks, with $n = 15$, $n = 10$, and $n = 31$, respectively.

Data Analyses

Results of the data analyses are presented in the Tables 8.1 through 8.4. Table 8.1 provides correlations between variables across all three task types. Tables 8.2, 8.3, and 8.4 report correlations for the decision-making, creativity, and action tasks, respectively.

Relationship-Oriented Shared Leadership and Performance

Across all three tasks, only *support and consideration* was significantly related to team performance ($r = .35, p < .01$). Thus, our first hypothesis received only partial support. The *development and mentoring* component of the relationship-oriented shared leadership dimension was not significantly correlated with performance for any of the team task conditions.

Shared Leadership and Satisfaction

Although not originally anticipated, all dimensions of shared leadership, with the exception of *planning and organizing*, were significantly related to team satisfaction across all three tasks. Thus, shared leadership appears to be related to team members' satisfaction with their teams across all types of tasks.

Decision-Making Tasks and Shared Leadership

Our hypothesis that both task- and relationship-oriented shared leadership would be related to satisfaction for the decision-making task was partially supported. The relationship between task-oriented shared leadership and team member satisfaction was significant ($r = .80, p < .01$). However, relationship-oriented shared leadership was not significantly correlated with satisfaction.

Our hypothesis with regard to the relationship between the *planning and organizing* dimension of shared leadership and performance for the decision-making task was also not supported. No significant linear relationship was found between these two variables.

Table 8.1. Team-Level Correlations Among Collective Leadership, Task Orientation, Performance and Satisfaction

Variables	N	M	SD	1	2	3	4	5	6	7	8
1. Planning and Organizing	56	4.03	0.52								
2. Problem Solving	56	3.93	0.51	.77**							
3. Support and Consideration	56	4.22	0.37	.44**	.49**						
3. Development & Mentoring	56	4.06	0.38	.47**	.55**	.61**					
4. Task Oriented	56	3.98	0.48	.93**	.95**	.50**	−.54**				
5. Relationship Oriented	56	4.15	0.34	.51**	.58**	.90**	−.89**	.58**			
6. Satisfaction	56	4.40	0.37	.23	.31*	.42**	−.35**	.29*	.42**		
7. Performance 1	56	175.11	242.53	.08	.21	.35**	−.03**	.16	.20	.17	
8. Performance 2	10	51.10	7.46	.16	.16	.17	.45	.16	.34	.31	.30

$*p < .05. **p < .01$

Table 8.2. Team-Level Correlations Among Collective Leadership, Task Orientation, Performance, and Satisfaction: Decision Task

Variables	N	M	SD	1	2	3	4	5	6	7
1. Planning and organizing	15	4.136	0.338							
2. Problem solving	15	4.131	0.257	.52*						
3. Support and consideration	15	4.407	0.217	.04	.07					
3. Development and mentoring	15	4.021	0.27	.14	.36	.54*				
4. Task oriented	15	4.133	0.257	.89**	.86**	.06	.28			
5. Relationship oriented	15	4.235	0.211	.09	.22	.86**	.89**	.17		
6. Satisfaction	15	4.444	0.239	.72**	.68**	.23	.23	.80**	−.23	
7. Performance 1	15	558.7	69.37	.27	−.13	−.23	−.15	.10	−.24	.16

$*p < .05. **p < .01$

Creativity Tasks and Shared Leadership

Contrary to our original hypothesis, task-oriented shared leadership was not significantly correlated with performance for the creativity task. Furthermore, no significant linear relationship was found between relationship-oriented shared leadership and team member satisfaction for the creativity task. Thus, shared leadership does not appear to be significantly related to team outcomes for a brainstorming task.

Action Tasks and Shared Leadership

Our hypothesis that both task- and relationship-oriented shared leadership would be significantly related to satisfaction and performance also received only partial support. Task-oriented shared leadership was positively correlated with team member satisfaction ($r = .47$, $p < .01$). Additionally, a significant and positive linear relationship was observed between relationship-oriented shared leadership and satisfaction ($r = .36$, $p < .05$).

DISCUSSION

Collective Leadership and Performance

Our first hypothesis received partial support. Only the *support and consideration* subscale of relationship-oriented collective leadership was positively related to performance across tasks. Consistent with Hiller et al.'s (2006) results, relationship-oriented collective leadership appears to be positively related to performance across task types. However, unlike Hiller et al., who found a significant relationship between the *development and mentoring* facet and measures of team performance, we were unable to replicate this finding. One possible explanation for these disparate results could be that Hiller et al. measured performance via supervisor ratings, whereas our performance measures were based on objective outcomes. Nevertheless, our results provide support for the idea that teams whose members are supportive and considerate of one another are likely to perform better than teams whose members do not exhibit these types of behaviors. However, no significant relationship was found between shared leadership and performance when examined at the task level of analysis. Thus, our third and fourth hypotheses were not supported. Although there was a positive linear relationship between *planning and organizing* and performance for the decision-making task, it did not attain significance. The positive correlations between collective leadership and performance for the creativity task were also nonsignificant.

Table 8.3. Team-Level Correlations Among Collective Leadership, Task Orientation, Performance and Satisfaction: Creative Task

Variables	N	M	SD	1	2	3	4	5	6	7	8
1. Planning and organizing	10	3.696	0.742								
2. Problem solving	10	3.736	0.709	.86**							
3. Support and consideration	10	4.357	0.313	.68*	.80**						
3. Development and mentoring	10	4.196	0.426	.73*	.88**	.84**					
4. Task oriented	10	3.718	0.698	.96**	.97**	.77**	.84**				
5. Relationship oriented	10	4.277	0.355	.74*	.88**	.95**	.97**	.85**			
6. Satisfaction	10	4.686	0.298	.06	.18	.42	.47	.13	.46		
7. Performance 1	10	140.2	27.6	.46	.18	.25	.12	.33	.18	.12	
8. Performance 2	10	51.1	7.46	.16	.16	.17	.45	.16	.34	.31	.30

$* p < .05. ** p < .01$

Table 8.4. Team-Level Correlations Among Collective Leadership, Task Orientation, and Performance: Action Task

Variables	N	M	SD	1	2	3	4	5	6	7	8
1. Planning and organizing	31	4.093	0.471								
2. Problem solving	31	3.896	0.504	.76**							
3. Support and consideration	31	4.087	0.397	.64**	.49**						
3. Development and mentoring	31	4.037	0.417	.57**	.55**	.63**					
4. Task oriented	31	3.987	0.459	.92**	.95**	.59**	.60**				
5. Relationship oriented	31	4.062	0.367	.67**	.58**	.90**	.91**	.66**			
6. Satisfaction	31	4.281	0.392	.47**	.42*	.34	.31	.47**	.36*		
7. Performance 1	31	0.779	0.314	.03	.01	−.16*	.06	.02	−.05	.08	

$* p < .05. ** p < .01$

Team Satisfaction

Relationship-oriented shared leadership behaviors were found to be positively related to team satisfaction across all three tasks, providing additional support for our first hypothesis. Thus, across tasks, groups whose members show support and consideration toward each other, and groups whose members attempt to develop and mentor their teammates are more satisfied than teams whose members perform fewer such behaviors.

For the decision-making task, task-oriented shared leadership behaviors were significantly positively related to team satisfaction. Thus, in partial support of our second hypothesis, the more team members shared in *planning and organizing* and *problem solving* activities, the higher their level of satisfaction. However, although the correlation coefficients were positive, relationship-oriented collective leadership was not significantly linearly related to satisfaction for the decision-making task.

In support of the idea of differential effects of shared leadership by task type, neither the performance scores nor the team satisfaction ratings for the teams working on the creativity task were significantly linearly related to shared leadership. Thus, our fourth and fifth hypotheses were not supported by the data. Because the brainstorming task represents a more pooled workflow arrangement, there was potentially less interaction among individual group members required for effective performance. Thus, collective-leadership might have little influence when teams perform additive tasks.

The action task also appeared to involve a high level of interaction among team members for effective performance. The task involved members using clues to plan and organize throughout the task performance process. Thus, both task- and relationship-oriented shared leadership behaviors were related to team members' satisfaction for the action task, providing partial support for our fourth hypothesis.

When taken as a whole, the results of our investigation provide some evidence that the pattern of relationships between shared leadership dimensions and team satisfaction varies by task type. The satisfaction of team members working on tasks requiring high levels of interaction is positively related to the relationship-oriented shared leadership behaviors exhibited within their respective groups. Additionally, teams that must interact and plan "on the fly" are more satisfied when members exhibit both task- and relationship-oriented shared leadership behaviors.

Limitations

Perhaps the most important limitation of the present investigation relates to the number of teams available for each task type. Our relatively small sample size at the group level may not have allowed us to detect significant differences between groups by task type.

The present study was also correlational in nature. Because there was no random assignment to groups, it is difficult to make causal inferences based on our results. There is also potential for common method bias associated with using self-report measures to assess both collective leadership and team satisfaction.

Additionally, the teams in our study were assembled for the relatively short duration of the tasks. The short life-cycles of the teams may not have allowed shared leadership to become salient to group members. The effects of shared leadership on task performance might emerge over time. Therefore, our failure to detect significant effects of shared leadership on performance might also be related to the lifetimes of the teams in our study.

One final limitation has to do with the fact that our study was conducted over different levels of analysis. Although our investigation was somewhat preliminary, and our goal was to simply examine where certain relationships exist, structural equation modeling would be the most appropriate analysis for a follow-up study. Now that we have more evidence for what relationships to expect, constructing and testing the fit of a conceptual model of the relationships explored in the present study is clearly a logical next step.

Future Research

Shared leadership is an interesting construct that deserves further investigation. As organizations continue to utilize semi-autonomous and self-managed groups, important leadership functions may have to be shared among team members. Future investigations should attempt to assess the role shared leadership behaviors play in influencing satisfaction and performance for more seasoned groups. Additionally, the effectiveness of different dimensions of shared leadership across task types, at the team level of analysis, will require a large number of teams for each task type in order for investigators to adequately assess significant differences in the effectiveness of shared leadership dimensions between tasks. Finally, field research would be helpful for investigating the potential real-world influence of shared leadership on group satisfaction and performance by task type. This knowledge could have implications for both selection and training.

CONCLUSION

The burgeoning use of autonomous work groups in organizations has presented investigators with a number of challenges. In order to adequately deal with the "team paradox" (Thompson, 2004) and take advantage of positive group reactions to external leaders' supportive and coaching behaviors (Morgeson, 2005), it is important to determine which facets of leadership processes should be supported and encouraged, so as to maximize both team performance and team member satisfaction. The present investigation revealed that the *support and consideration* facet of relationship-oriented shared leadership is related to satisfaction across the three task types studied. Thus, organizational efforts to train teams in relational skills appear to be on target. The relative importance of task- and relationship-oriented shared leadership also varies according to a group's task. Whereas group members are more satisfied when task-oriented shared leadership is emphasized for decision-making tasks, both task- and relationship-oriented shared leadership is related to satisfaction when the group is performing an action task. Leaders who wish to support and coach their teams would benefit from an awareness of what to support, based on what the team is working on at the time. Thus, the more we learn about the processes that contribute to team performance and satisfaction, the more we can assist organizations and leaders with advice on what to look for and when support and coaching are needed to improve satisfaction and maximize team performance.

AUTHOR'S NOTE

Correspondence concerning this article should be addressed to Paul Pluta, Department of Psychology, Florida International University, University Park, Miami, FL 33199. E-mail pplut001@fiu.edu

REFERENCES

Abad, A. Z., Castella, V. O., Cuenca, I. G., & Navarro, P. G. (2002). Teamwork in different communication contexts: A longitudinal study. *Psychology in Spain, 6,* 41-55.

Barrick, M. R., Stewart, G. L., Neubert, M. J., & Mount, M. K. (1998). Relating member ability and personality to work-team processes and team effectiveness. *Journal of Applied Psychology, 83,* 377-391.

Bishop, J. W., & Dow Scott, K. (2000). An examination of organizational and team commitment in a self-directed team environment. *Journal of Applied Psychology, 85,* 439-450.

Campion, M. A., Papper, E. M., & Medsker, G. J. (1996). Relations between work team characteristics and effectiveness: A replication and extension. *Personnel Psychology, 49,* 429-452.

Craig, T. Y., & Kelly, J. R. (1999). Group cohesiveness and creative performance. *Group Dynamics: Theory Research and Practice, 3,* 243-256.

De Dreu, C. K. W., & Weingart, L. R. (2003). Task versus relationship conflict, team performance, and team member satisfaction: A meta-analysis. *Journal of Applied Psychology, 88,* 741-749.

Goncalo, J. A. (2004). Past successes and convergent thinking in groups: The role of group-focused attributions. *European Journal of Social Psychology, 34,* 385-395.

Hackman, J. R., & Oldham, G. R. (1975). Development of the Job Diagnostic Survey. *Journal of Applied Psychology, 60,* 159-170.

Hackman, J. R., & Walton, R. E. (1986). Leading groups in organizations. In P. S. Goodman, et al. (Eds.) *Designing effective work groups* (pp. 72-119). San Francisco: Jossey-Bass.

Hiller, N., Day, D., & Vance, R. (2006). Collective enactment of leadership roles and team effectiveness: A field study. *Leadership Quarterly, 17,* 387-397.

Ilgen, D. R. (1999). Teams embedded in organizations: Some implications. *American Psychologist, 54,* 129-139.

James, L. R., Demaree, R. G., & Wolf, G. (1984). Estimating within-group interrater reliability with and without response bias. *Journal of Applied Psychology, 69,* 85-98.

Morgeson, F. P. (2005). The external leadership of self-managing teams: Intervening in the context of novel and disruptive events. *Journal of Applied Psycholog, 90,* 497-508.

Pearce, C. L. (2004). The future of leadership: Combining vertical and shared leadership to transform knowledge work. *Academy of Management Executive, 18,* 47-57.

Peterson, R. S. (1997). A directive leadership style in group decision making can be both virtue and vice: Evidence from elite and experimental groups. *Journal of Personality and Social Psychology, 72,* 1107-1121.

Riggio, R., Riggio, H., Salinas, C., & Cole, E. (2003). The role of social and emotional communication skills in leader emergence and effectiveness. *Group Dynamics: Theory, Research, and Practice, 7,* 83-103.

Stewart, G. L., & Barrick, M. R. (2000). Team structure and performance: Assessing the mediating role of intrateam process and the moderating role of task type. *Academy of Management Journal, 43,* 135-148.

Thompson, L. L. (2004). *Making the team: A guide for Managers* (2nd ed.). Upper Saddle River, NJ: Pearson Prentice Hall.

Wellins, R. S., Bayham, W. C., & Wilson, J. M. (1991). *Empowered teams*. San Francisco: Jossey-Bass.
Zaccaro, S. J., Rittman, A. L., & Marks, M. A. (2001). Team leadership. *The Leadership Quarterly, 12,* 451-483.

PART II

NEW PERSPECTIVES ON FAMILIAR CONSTRUCTS

CHAPTER 9

NEW PERSPECTIVES AND RESEARCH ON FAMILIAR CONSTRUCTS

Brian Perdomo, Kristin L. Cullen, and Daniel J. Svyantek

This section of the book has seven chapters and two critical analyses which provide new perspectives on important organizational concepts. These chapters share a common theme of striving. This striving is related to presenting new ways of understanding organizational constructs to provide both researchers and practitioners with new approaches to solve problems associated with these organizational constructs. Each chapter is based on the premise that, when presented with problems that seem impossible to solve, often the best results are achieved by finding new perspectives on the basic constructs being studied. New perspectives provide insights which illuminate the problems and improve the ability of organizational members to solve these problems. Therefore, each of the authors in this section of the book have explored new perspectives on common research areas in the IO literature. The following chapters seek to expand our knowledge of both macrolevel constructs (e.g., organizational change, workplace politics, and technological determinism) and microlevel con-

Refining Familiar Constructs: Alternative Views in OB, HR, and I/O, pp. 123–127
Copyright © 2007 by Information Age Publishing
All rights of reproduction in any form reserved.

structs (e.g., organizational citizenship behaviors, fit, and leadership) by offering new ways of understanding and studying these constructs.

This section begins with an organization development case-study. Using the action research model, Coghlan and Jacobs offer an interesting perspective of organizational change by investigating how conversations shape organizational change processes in practice. This chapter describes core processes of an organization development project in a residential healthcare provider organization. One goal of this project was to create a structure for the stakeholder groups in the organization. This structure would allow stakeholders to listen to each other and work together toward creating their own vision of how the organization can move into the future, according to its values and ethos. A second goal of the project was to study how such a third sector organization can respond to the demands for change from both its external and internal environments in a participative manner which stakeholders can engage in conversation and articulate what can be learned from the process. Through action research of an OD project complemented by semistructured interviews with participants, the authors gained a set of data and experiences that allows them to inquire into the relationship between conversations and change in more depth.

Benson and Adler approach organizational change by attempting to tie existing schools of strategy implementation (e.g., Rational Incrementalism, Egocentric Enactment, and Cognitive Renegotiation) with pertinent reward issues. While strategy implementation has been acknowledged as a fundamental and legitimate strategy making process, little has been discussed regarding how incentives affect the ability to 'just do it." Benson and Adler address this problem. They then seek to discuss these reward issues within the broader framework of human resources management (HRM) and organizational development. Their chapter suggests that strategy implementation is more than just implementing a strategic plan. They propose that certain kinds of reward systems are consistent with certain kinds of strategy implementation approaches. Without considering how strategy implementation differs within organizations and tying incentives to these variations, underlying assumptions about adequate employee compensation, and the effects of compensation may be unfounded. This chapter begins the discussion on how organizations actually reward employees to implement strategy in fulfilling organizational objectives.

Benson and Adler establish that an organization's strategy and reward system lay the foundation for equity perceptions. However, equity perceptions relate not only to an organization's reward system, but also to its political environment. The third chapter in this section is by Conner, Treadway, James, Stoner, and Hochwarter. This chapter examines the role of task interdependence in the relationship between workplace politics and work outcomes, such as satisfaction and turnover. This chapter presents the results of an empirical study using police officers as participants. It was found that police officers reporting high levels of task interdependence experienced lower levels of job and life satisfaction, and higher levels of turnover intent when politics were high. Conversely, those police officers reporting low levels of task interdependence did not report adverse effects of workplace politics perceptions. Based on their interpretation of the results, Conner et al. propose that managers may find it useful to incorporate workplace politics interventions with traditional organizational development activities to help develop programs aimed at increasing the efficacy of social interactions at work may enhance organizational effectiveness.

Another common outcome of interest in today's research literature is organizational citizenship behaviors (OCBs). The fourth chapter, by Harkins, Halbesleben, Beu, and Buckley, expand on the organizational citizenship construct by exploring the relationship between workplace deviance behaviors and inequity. The authors propose that there is a need to include workplace deviance behaviors (WDBs) within the fold of behaviors that individuals perform within organizations based on their perceptions of, and reactions to, treatment by the organization. Specifically, Harkins et al. state that WDBs are another type of behavior that employees embrace to align their perceptions of inequity within the firm, in the same manner as the more positively oriented (toward the organization) OCBs are. Through application of equity theory, the authors hypothesize that individuals are motivated to undertake OCBs/WDBs for other than their currently extended motivations. They discuss the manner in which this reconceptualization creates a new focus for OCB research, and suggest ways in which further work within the nomological network will lead to greater incremental contributions of the OCB literature in our understanding of organizational behavior broadly.

Two papers also deal with a proposed antecedent of important organizational constructs as equity perceptions and OCBs. These papers deal with the general issue of person-organization fit as an antecedent of organizational behavior.

A common antecedent of equity perceptions and citizenship behaviors is the degree of congruence between characteristics of the employee and the organization (person-organization fit). Scroggins and Benson extend this concept of person-job fit by introducing the idea of self-concept-job fit. Person-job fit is conceptualized as a multidimensional construct consisting of different types of fit (e.g., demand-abilities fit, supply-value fit, self-concept-job fit). Self-concept-job fit is defined and conceptually distinguished from other types of person-job fit by the authors. It is proposed that different types of person-job fit are differentially related to attitudinal and performance variables. The authors present a model that relates self-concept-job fit to experienced meaningful work. Meaningful work is hypothesized to relate to various outcome variables related to employee retention. The authors propose that organizations should focus on self-concept-job fit in order to increase applicant attraction and employee retention.

Svyantek, Cullen, Perdomo, and Goodman present an empirical study of the relationship of person-organization (PO) fit to job satisfaction. The authors propose that an interactionist approach to person-organization fit is critical for understanding organizational behavior in context. PO fit is assessed (1) using recognized statistical measures of PO fit (cf. the Edwards method) and (2) using measures of both employee and organizational characteristics and assessing the effects of their interactions on job satisfaction. This chapter describes an empirical study of the relationship between PO fit and job satisfaction. The organizational implications of the relationship between PO fit and job satisfaction are discussed using Schneider's (1987) Attraction-Selection-Attrition (ASA) framework to integrate the results of the study. The implications of this study support the importance of PO fit for predicting job satisfaction. The relationship of PO fit to job satisfaction, however, varies depending on the facet of job satisfaction used as the dependent variable of interest. This research study is also used to assess whether either of the two analytic approaches have more utility for organizations seeking to use PO fit to improve on important organizational criteria.

The final chapter is by Svyantek, Mahoney, and Cullen. The authors present a case study of warfare in the ancient Mediterranean world to explore the role of technological change and social systems in organizational productivity and change. This paper investigated the degree to which sociotechnical systems theory and technological determinism explain organizational effectiveness and efficiency. First, a brief review of technological determinism and sociotechnical systems is provided. Second, a description of warfare in the Mediterranean world over a 1,400 year period (1000 B.C to 400 A.D.) is given. Next, the degree to which technological change and social innovation affected organizational effectiveness during this period is analyzed. Finally, conclusions are offered about how to better understand the role of technology and social systems in organizational theory. They establish that technological and social changes occur in phases. The initial development of technology leads to social adjustment in the workplace. After this period of unrest, social change initiates new uses of technology leading to technological change and continuing the cyclical change process. The implications of these results for the relationship between technological and administrative innovations and organizational effectiveness are discussed.

Finally, the last section presents two critical analyses of new leadership perspectives using a book review format. Luchauer and Locander review *Finding Our Way: Leadership For and Uncertain Time* by Margaret Wheatley and show how all new ideas are not necessarily new. Dyck evaluates the book, *Resonant Leadership: Renewing Yourself and Connecting with Others Through Mindfulness* by Boyatzis and McKee. *Resonant leadership* is intended as a guide for leadership development. The book authors advocate a leader who is inspirational, creates a positive sentiment, and is connected with others.

The following chapters provide new perspectives on macro and microorganizational constructs. Each of these seven chapters and two critical analyses provides important points and should further the discussion of the constructs of their interest. These chapters have strived to present new ways of understanding organizational constructs that has both academic and practical utility. These chapters provide insights which illuminate the problems and improve the ability of organizational members to solve these problems. It is our hope that these chapters will both bring new ideas to these research areas and encourage further research and help the practitioner develop better organizational practices for improving organizational effectiveness and the quality of work life of employees.

CHAPTER 10

"LEARNING THROUGH LISTENING"

Conversation for Change in a Health-Care Provider

David Coghlan and Claus Jacobs

The aim of this paper is investigate the role of conversation in organizational change so as to enhance both theory and practice in this respect. As an investigation on how conversations shape organizational change processes in practice, we reflect on an interpretive case study in a health care organization. Through action research of an organization development (OD) project complemented by semi-structured interviews with participants, we gained a set of data and experiences that allows us to inquire into the relationship between conversations and change in more depth.

INTRODUCTION

"Learning Through Listening" was an action research project in Omega, a health-care provider organization in which service users, staff, members of management committees, trustees, managers, and central office staff were enabled to develop a capacity to change according to its values and ethos. The dual aim of the project was to create conditions in which the stakeholders could engage in conversation and listen to each other on what was important in the life of the organization and how actions could be derived as to move purposefully into the future Furthermore, the project provided an opportunity to study how an organization such as Omega can respond to demands for change from both its external and internal environments in a participative manner. The stated aims, therefore, were practical in that organizational actions by Omega were taken and theoretical in that knowledge and learning from Omega's experience can be used for like organizations.

This article introduces the role of conversation in organizational change; outlines OD, action research in the reported case study methodology; a detailed case report that systematically describes the intervention and a case analysis to present our findings. We complete the paper with conclusions and implications on the role of conversation for change in organizations.

THE ROLE OF CONVERSATION IN ORGANIZATIONAL CHANGE

To engage in conversation means to engage in change. The role of verbal communication for management in general (e.g., Mintzberg, 1975; Pondy, 1978) and for processes of change in particular (e.g., Barrett, Thomas, & Hocevar, 1995; Deetz, 1995; Heracleous & Barrett, 2001; Quinn, 1996; Weick & Quinn, 1999) has been widely acknowledged. While an instrumental approach considers language as a transfer of (unambiguous) information in achieving managerially relevant outcomes, an interpretive, constructionist perspective views conversation as a symbolic action contributing to developing shared meanings and identities (Evered, 1983; Smircich & Morgan, 1982). Such shared meanings are socially constructed through discursive and social interaction (Heracleous, 2004; Jacobs & Heracleous, 2005).

Embracing a interpretivist, constructionist view on language, Ford and Ford (1995) have emphasized the relevance of conversations for organizational change processes. Rather than assuming conversation as simply a tool for change, it is due to the performative character of speech acts that change is facilitated: "Change is a phenomenon that occurs within communication" (p. 542). Engaging in intentional change efforts means to deliberately change the discursively constructed reality of an organization and its participants. Based on Searle (1969), they suggest a typology of conversations that differ in content and orientation (initiative, understanding, performance and closure). While all play a specific role in change processes, dialogue, or to use their term, conversations for understanding provides a conversational mode to render privately held assumptions visible, to acknowledge and explore differences and, ultimately, to alter mental models (Ford & Ford, 1995, p. 563). In a similar line of argument, Crossan, Lane, and White (1999) emphasize equally the role of dialogue as central to processes of critical thinking, shared understanding and subsequent group coherence. Or, as Schein (1999, p. 209) suggests, "We have to listen to ourselves before we can really understand others."

Integrating these various aspects of conversations for understanding—or dialogue—for processes of organizational change, Scharmer (2001) offers a process archetype for organizational conversation that describes four generic stages of listening and conversing. He suggests two generic axes to distinguish conversational modes. First, conversation oriented toward the whole (primacy of the whole) or the parts (primacy of the parts). Second, the conversation can be follow a reflective or nonreflective mode. When combined these two frames form four modes of conversation in four fields, which suggest that conversations follow a path from "talking nice" through "talking tough" into a reflective mode of conversation to "generative dialogue."

Since language contributes to processes of meaning generation and sensemaking, conversations can be conceived of not only as a vehicle but as the very locus of organizational change (Ford & Ford, 1995). Thus, understanding change means to understand (and methodologically to participate in) conversations for change in organizational settings.

Interlevel Dynamics

To investigate how change moves through a system, different levels of aggregation are crucial. Coghlan and Rashford (2006; Coghlan, 1994; Rashford & Coghlan, 1994) distinguish four levels of behavior in organizations—the individual, the face-to-face team, the interdepartmental group and the organizational. The first level is the *bonding* relationship that the individual has with the organization and the organization with the individual. For the individual, this involves a utilization of membership and participation in the organization in order to meet personal life goals, while for management the core issue is to get a person committed to the goals, values and culture of the organization. The more complex approach to participation exists in establishing *effective working relationships in a face-to-face team*. An even more complex involvement exists in terms of the interdepartmental group type of interface where teams must be *coordinated* in order to achieve complex tasks and maintain a balance of power among competing political interest groups. Finally, the most complex, from the point of view of the individual, is the relationship of the total organization to its external environment in which other organizations are individual competitors, competing for scarce resources to produce similar products or services. The key task for any organization is its ability to *adapt* to environmental forces driving for change.

These levels of aggregation are systemically interlinked (Coghlan, 2002). There is a dynamic systemic relationship between individual bonding, team functioning, intergroup coordination and organizational adaptation (Rashford & Coghlan, 1994). Dysfunctions at any of the four levels can contribute to dysfunctions at any of the other three levels. An individual's level of stress can be expressed in dysfunctional behavior in the team and affect a team's ability to function effectively, which in turn affects the individual's ability to cope and ultimately the bonding relationship with the organization. If a team is not functioning effectively, it can limit the interdepartmental group's effectiveness that may depend on the quality and timeliness of information, resources and partially completed work from that team. If the interdepartmental group's multiple activities are not coordinated, the organization's ability to compete effectively may be affected. In the same vein, a change in an organization's socioeconomic environment can lead to a realignment of resources across the interdepartmental group, affecting the work of teams and individuals' bonding relationship with the changed or changing organization. In systemic terms, each of the four levels affects each of the other three.

Understanding how interlevel dynamics between individuals, within teams and across the interdepartmental group impact the process of, describing the need for change, defining the future state, assessing the present, and managing the transition state is critical to organization development and action research (Coghlan, 1994, 2002; Coghlan & Mc Auliffe, 2003). It is also critical to organizational learning as individual learning gets translated into team learning, team learning is generalized across the interdepartmental group in order that the organization may learn (Coghlan, 1997). Accordingly, the conversations that take place are not restricted to interpersonal settings, that is, individual to individual. They also takes place within teams/groups and between groups.

METHODOLOGY: ACTION RESEARCH AS CASE STUDY

Conversations in processes of change are highly local, contextual phenomena. Which methodology allows us to study these in a suitable research approach? In presenting an investigative case study, we are following in the line of Merriam's (1998) notion of the heuristic quality of case studies, that is, the potential of a case study to enhance our understanding of a phenomenon by exploring and exemplifying new or different meaning. In their study of conditioned emergence, MacIntosh and MacLean (1999) usefully introduce a case study to demonstrate some of their key theoretical arguments. Stake (2000) holds that it is due to the subjective character of case studies that propositional and experiential knowledge can be enhanced. Case material parallel actual experience of readers and feed into processes of creating awareness and understanding. As knowledge is socially constructed, "case study researchers assist readers in the construction of knowledge" (Stake, 2000, p. 442).

In the view of Gummesson (2000), the most demanding and far reaching method of doing case study is action research. Action research as an approach to research which aims at both taking action and creating knowledge or theory about that action (Argyris, 1993; Coghlan & Brannick, 2005; Reason & Bradbury, 2001). The outcomes are both an action and a research outcome, unlike traditional research approaches which aim at creating knowledge only. Action research works through a cyclical process of consciously and deliberately, (a) planning, (b) taking action and (c) evaluating the action, leading to further planning and so on. The second dimension of action research is that it is participative, in that the members of the system which is being studied participate actively in the cycles of planning, taking action and evaluation. This contrasts with traditional research where members are objects of the study. In action research the members identify issues, plan, implement and review action with the help of an action researcher who acts as a "friendly outsider" (Greenwood & Levin, 1998) and facilitates exploratory, diagnostic and action-oriented inquiry in the organization (Schein, 1995, 1999).

Organization development (OD) is an approach to planned change which is based on action research (Coghlan & Mc Auliffe, 2003). In organization development members of an organization are helped to perceive, understand and take action on issues facing them. Therefore it is an approach to organizational change that aims at enabling the organization to learn about itself as it engages in the process of change. The learning process is grounded in attention to process and reflecting on experience as the process is enacted. Central to the processes of organization development is the engagement of the members of the organization in visioning, taking action and reviewing (Beckhard & Harris, 1987; Marsick & Watkins, 1999).

A further characteristic of organization development is its distinctive model of helping (French & Bell, 1999). This model of helping is best characterized by process consultation which is a facilitative approach as contrasted with the more expert models adopted by most organizational consultants. In process consultation the consultant aims to be helpful to the client and so helps the clients explore issues, do their own diagnosis of what these issues mean and plan and take their own action (Schein, 1999). Much of this exploration is done through conversation and this research investigates how conversation was utilized in an OD project.

Our investigation therefore explores the case of an OD project in a health-care provider, Omega. We distinguish conceptually and analytically between the OD project called "Learning Through Listening" as the empirical phenomenon of study from the action research project on the OD project. The two differ in focus and key concepts. We also highlight the different roles both authors held in these two respective projects; the first named author acted as senior researcher while the second named author acted as facilitator with the members of Omega.

Action research is integrally linked to conversation. In the words of Greenwood and Levin (1998, p. 86), action research focuses on "keeping the conversation going ... through its methods aims to open horizons of discussion, to create spaces for collective reflection in which new descriptions and analyses of important situations may be developed as the basis for new action."

THE OD CASE STUDY: THE "LEARNING THROUGH LISTENING" PROJECT

The "Learning Through Listening" project was a 12-month organization development project within the Omega Foundation, a European-based health care provider. The project's objective was defined as building the capacity for change through creating a shared learning experience for participants which would be grounded in Omega values and mission enabling it to develop capabilities and processes for continued organizational learning and change.

Omega Foundation

The Omega Foundation provides residential care in 14 centers for people with physical and sensory disabilities. It has currently about 300 places in its centers with a total number of staff of around 400. The nine larger centers have between 20 to 35 permanent places, whereas the five smaller centers provide independent housing in a quasi-apartment setting for about 10 tenants each. In total, Omega has 287 permanent place as well as 32 respite places. The service users are assisted by 353 permanent staff as well as 104 community employment scheme workers. Local managers of the centres report directly to the CEO who is supported by a head office team that covers central function such as strategy and organization development, service user development, human resource management and training, financials and administration among others. The board of trustees in which voluntary members from the wider community as well as service users and staff are represented has the accountability for ensuring a quality service delivery as well as the strategic development of the Foundation.

At the core of Omega's service provision lies long-term supported accommodation service, which until the 1990s took the form of a traditional residential care model. Over the course of the last decade and in response to requests by service users, Omega's model of service has changed from an implicit benevolent paternalistic care model to an explicit professional service provision. The Omega Foundation provides three distinct services in its centres. Besides (1) long-term supported accommodation services, recent developments include (2) respite services and (3) outreach services.

The "Learning Through Listening" Process

In 1997 Omega was going through a period of serious change. Internally, this resulted in a change in governance structure, in policies and procedures, employment and funding operations. A major internal force for change was identified in the service users' changing needs and expectations with regard to the service provided by Omega. In response to these forces, an organization development project was initiated, with agreed objectives to build the capacity for change through creating a shared learning experience for participants, which would be grounded in Omega values and mission with a view to enabling it to develop capabilities and processes for continued organizational earning and change. To this end, work was done to create a friendly, catchy title for the project which would reflect Omega values. The outcome was "Learning Through Listening" and a special logo of the founder listening to a wheelchair user was used to head special notepaper to mark communications on the project.

The dual aim of the project was to (a) create conditions in which the stakeholders could engage in conversation together and listen to each other on what is important in the life of Omega and how it could create actions from the conversations in order to move purposefully into the future, and (b) study how an organization such as the Omega can respond to the demands for change from both its external and internal environments in a participative manner which stakeholders can engage in conversation and articulate what can be learned from the process. The stated aims, therefore, were both organizational actions by Omega and knowledge and learning from Omega's experience which would be useful to like organizations.

Design of the Intervention

The intervention was structured within the OD framework described earlier and was adapted to meet the contingencies as thrown up by the progress of the intervention. The project was designed to facilitate both the local and national agendas. At the local level, each of the local centres would engage in three individual days of an organization development process. On the first day, members (comprising management, staff and residents) of the local center would work together on (i) identifying contextual areas of change, (ii) articulating a desired future for the centre, and (iii) agreeing on plans for action. Implementation would then begin. On the second day, some months later, the data from the first day would be fed back and analyzed and the plans for action would be reviewed and adjustments to the implementation made, where required. On the third day, progress would be reviewed and the process evaluated. On this third day, neighboring centers would hold joint review and learning sessions. This was designed to support the development of the regional structure, as well as to manage the cost of the project. On this third day, centers would have an opportunity to reflect on their own learning and to share that learning with neighboring centers. The design was built around the cyclical nature of action and reflection, aimed to place a value on the independence of each center in order to build a sense of psychological safety and to maintain confidentiality so each centre could work through its own change issues.

The project constituted an OD intervention in this organization.[1] It aimed to create a structure to facilitate conversation about the present and desired future states of the organization, to enable stakeholders to take ownership of the change issues and to begin to empower themselves to map courses of action. Central to the design of the "Learning Through Listening" processes was the engagement of the members of the organization in visioning, taking action and reviewing. Drawing on Open Space Technology (Owen, 1997), what was seen as critical in the project was the ability to engage in dialogue through (a) the creation of an open space where participants would feel a sense of psychological safety and (b) where the participants would listen to one another and give voice to their own views. For the duration of the project, the second named author would work with each local center in the role of facilitator. His work would comprise several elements. First, he would approach each center in advance of the planned days and work with a local group to plan the meetings. Second, he would structure the space in which conversations would take place and would invite participants to explore the future of the organization together and he would facilitate the meetings (Coghlan & McIlduff, 1990). Third, he would facilitate reflection on experience and work with participants at exploring what they were learning.

Based on the idea that conversations for understanding or dialogue, (Schein, 1993; Watkins & Mohr, 2001), the workshop sessions would structured around three questions that were phrased in an integrative way in order to be mindful of differences in educational backgrounds and communicative skills of participants.

1. What do you really like about (your life, your work) in this centre/home? As most people in the organization had not been familiar with any type of group work, it would allow them to participate in a conversation that would start of in a positive, friendly mode.
2. What could be done even better? Based on the confidence built in the conversation around question 1, it was expected that participants would then speak up more freely with regard to opportunities for change.
3. How do we get there? Finally, concrete suggestions in terms of goals and action steps to be taken would follow from the discussion of question 3.

Records of conversations were kept. Points that were made were posted on flip charts, written up and brought back to the next meeting and checked for accuracy. The contributions would be shared and discussed and common themes extrapolated.

The process was structured around creating a conversational mode in a safe atmosphere so that reflective conversation could take place. Many groups began in a suspicious mode—why should this project be any different from other ones? The initial meetings were characterized by politeness, though often anger and frustration about elements in the life of a centre were be expressed early on and subsequent talking was tough. Some groups moved to engaging in reflective conversation around specific issues.

First and foremost, the goal was to provide a psychologically safe environment for conversation. Throughout the three separate days in each centre, as one would expect the conversation developed into at least an open talking-tough mode. Some sessions were driven by a reflective mode of conversation. Each of the different conversational modes can be useful depending on what is to be achieved. Most centres opted for separate session on days I and II, which would then lead into a joint session on day III. In most of the centers, the first session started off in a talking-nice mode: This was mainly due to the appreciative character of the first question. But more importantly, the initial question allowed most participants to get involved and to voice their views in a large group. To listen to many positive aspects of the participants' daily life and business created surprises for many participants. Especially the expression of mutual appreciation of service users and staff, led to a very healthy conversational mode. Based on this experience, it was either later that day or at least on day II of the process that groups switched into a debate or discussion mode.

The second question, focusing on opportunities, encouraged people to engage in a debate or discussion. Most of the debates and discussions were not necessarily in a talking tough mode as to threaten or hurt other stakeholders, but it was crucial to give space for concerns and problems that would not have been voiced elsewhere. Mainly service users had difficulties with the debate mode as they would not want to be considered as complacent about the service. The comment cited earlier, "You don't rock the boat with the people that you rely on!" points to one of the core issues of the entire project, how to encourage and enable people that consider themselves vulnerable to give feedback on their service? It is based on this feedback that the organization can develop a strategic vision of the service.

Reflection occurred in several small episodes within the debate mode: It was when people realized the bias of their views, the appreciation and acknowledgement of different views. Surprises about different perspectives and their validity were crucial in that regard. These episodes were considered most helpful when asked about the benefit of the project: First, they appreciated the space that was provided for conversation, and secondly, the quality of the conversation which they referred to that was achievable in an appropriate conversational setting.

As most centers opted for separate sessions on days I and II, day III was designed as a joint session. Groups had discussed and decided on which items to share with the other stakeholders on day III. The conversational mode was mainly "talking nice" as the mutual observation did not allow for an adequate openness due to the feeling of dependency, both from service users or staff point of view. At best, day III provided a platform to develop a nonthreatening mode for debate when people experienced that a facilitated meeting would help not to switch into mutual blaming and nagging.

FINDINGS

First Order Findings

Traditional research approaches typically focus on "findings," that is, issues named in the research which then form the basis for recommendations. In action research the focus is on outcomes which are explored in the next section. At the same time, there are some themes which emerged from the workshop sessions which can be noted. In action research, the focus is on outcomes of both a practical and theoretical nature. As an organization development project built on action research, the "Learning Through Listening" project has both important practical outcomes for Omega and theoretical outcomes for contributing to the theory and practice of dialogue in organizations. These outcomes emerged from the project as a whole that is from the three workshops with the three groups of stakeholder, both separately and together.

Practical Outcomes: Content

In their group workshops, *residents* first and foremost expressed appreciation the safety of the centres. In addition to that the service provided by staff was highly appreciated. Across all centers, residents faced a structural dilemma: There was a fear of giving even constructive feedback due to their high level of dependency or even vulnerability. As one service user put it, "you don't rock the boat with the people that you rely on!" Residents in most centres were concerned with staff training and induction as well as their own involvement in decision making processes in the centres. They focused on specific issues relating to staff rostering, range of services, meal facilities and menu.

The service quality was at the heart of the conversations. However, residents did not refer to "the service" they rather referred to specific forms in which they experienced the service, that is, the times to get up and be brought to bed, the quality of food, the general mood of the house, the communicative qualities of staff, and so forth. For example, the quality and variety of food for people with physical disabilities is a very prominent feature as this is one of the most important episodes during their day. It also gives a structure to their lives in the centers.

Another important issue was the possibility for residents to voice their concerns, critique or dissatisfaction. It is not only limited because of speech impairments that some residents might have, but because of a fundamental dilemma. Because of their perceived dependency and vulnerability, residents fear to give honest feedback as doing so could and does trigger subtle sanctions and responses by individual members of staff.

The benefit of the project was in their view to eventually have a space where they were able to address these issues. Both issues, service quality as well as the dilemma not being able to criticize the service quality, were voiced in a discursive arena where participants were able in a psychologically safe environment to discuss the validity and relevance of both points. Especially long-term residents who felt a certain agony toward the service were delighted to share their experiences with other residents initially and with staff in the third workshop. In one session, when one of the residents talked about her experience of the dilemma, other participants started laughing knowingly—and supported her view. It was clear that even though residents claimed their individuality and independence, they also realized that they share experiences, language and the way service quality is experienced.

Staff also expressed appreciation of the friendly and caring atmosphere. The top issue for staff in most centres were the staffing levels, that is, staff shortage. Fairness of pay was an issue as well, there did not seem to be a uniform pay scheme. Empowering the residents on the one hand and giving them freedom of choice without empowering the people that deliver that very service created certain tensions and frustrations in the centres ("Do staff have rights too?") There seemed to be a tension between the independence philosophy of the organization on the one hand and the medical model and/or ethos of care workers and nurses on the other. Staff also expressed concerns about role and responsibilities, rostering, relationship with management and training.

Staff members were mainly concerned with issues around their task of delivering the service. They referred to their job explicitly as serving and caring, whereby the meaning of "care" was explored in different centers differently: For one particular center staff, care was mainly the physical, medical, and hygiene aspect whereas in some other centres, staff emphasized the communicative aspects of caring. The notion of independence which is very prominent in the care provider's mission statement was also critically discussed. Does independence mean that residents can do everything they want—regardless of staff or organizational needs? Again, two opposing views could be identified: on the one hand, a rather paternalistic view that "I know what's good for you," on the other, a very consequent "Do what you want but pay for the consequences." For most staff, the opportunity to discuss and reflect on their daily business outside the daily requirements was new, and also showed them where differences in worldviews lie.

The *local managers* proved to be crucial throughout the project: Without their support, the impact and sustainability of the project would be very limited. They also are very influential in shaping organizational culture in the centres. There seems to be some irritancies with regard to roles and responsibilities between central office and center manager. If the local managers are considered classical middle managers, it should be made explicit. But that might jeopardize some managers' commitment. In addition to that some managers feel their possibility to give input in terms of strategic decision making has been very limited.

The local managers can be considered to be the interface between the local centres and central office. For example, in the house they refer to people as 'residents' whereas in discussions with central office, the official language requires to address them as "service users." Their commitment to the individual centre related very strongly to the perceived possibility to influence the overall strategy as well as the support they get from central office.

Practical Outcomes: Process

Vulnerability and a fundamental dilemma of residents were rendered visible. Even when asked to give feedback on the service quality to individuals or the organizations, residents refrained to do so for fear of repercussion. The fact that the project provided a space to voice and discuss this issue as a systematic blind spot of daily practice can be considered a proof of concept in itself. Communication between residents, staff and management was acknowledged to be central and in some centers a regular forum to continue conversation and dialogue was established and has continued. In some centers menus and meals times were reviewed and changed.

Listening became explicitly integral part of the core values of the organization as well as a key results area in its operative goals as outlined in its 2003 strategy statement. The "Learning Through Listening" project initiative can certainly claim some credit for this. From the very beginning, "Learning Through Listening" was considered a crucial module or step in larger participatory strategy development process. Even though formally the strategy process took place outside of the process, it was conducted in the spirit of the project. The generic design of the workshops as well as the overall design to integrate collective communications within and between stakeholder groups at the local, regional and national level provides a referent for future organization development interventions.

Second Order Findings

In our view, the project has broken new ground in exploring how reflective conversation can be conducted in different settings, the forms it takes and its role in organization development. It illustrates how the multiple perspectives of stakeholders can contribute to both problem definition and handling and the shaping of strategic direction.

Omega was going through the transition phase of change having changed its governance structures, employment and funding operations and policies and procedures. It was moving toward developing a strategic plan. The 'learning through listening' opened up a new change. Unfreezing took place in the initial contracting and early workshops where participants articulated their vulnerability. Changing took place as they engaged in dialogue and began to effect changes in the operations of the centres and in establishing structures for continuing conversation. The conversations in the workshops were always concrete and were relevant to the lives of the stakeholders (Weick, 1995). At time of writing, initial structural refreezing has been initiated in the formal identification of "listening" as a key result area in the strategic plan. This institutionalization of listening as a key result area, while it needs time to see how it works, is an important forum for continuing change, as discussed by Ford and Ford (1995)

"Learning Through Listening" as Action Research

As presented earlier, the research was conducted through action research which involves iterative cycles of action and reflection to generate both action and knowledge outcomes. Accordingly, a central element of research design was the reflection-in-action on the part of the facilitator as an action researcher with the members of Omega.

The issues which emerged at the workshop meetings were recorded on newsprint and were discussed in the groups. At subsequent meetings the details from previous meetings were presented so that participants were reminded of what had been said and could verify their accuracy. The facilitator captured his own experiences and reflections through field notes and journals. The two authors met regularly and explored these reflections both in terms of the advancement of the OD project and of the research. Distinguishing between the two proved to be useful as it helped attention to both action and research agendas. The themes were clustered and formed the basis for the semistructured interviews.

Of the seven centers that were included in the final analysis, all were included in the interview process. At each center one semistructured group interview with the local steering committee of the project, that usually comprised of local service manager, two staff members, and two residents was conducted. The questions were derived from the previous workshop sessions and included general questions that applied to all centers as well as specific questions for the local context. The open-ended questions included quality of service, degree of involvement, nature of conversational arenas and so forth. Subsequently a member validation was conducted by presenting the identified themes to the local steering committees for their consideration. These themes were then further explored in a set of 21 semistructured interviews with key informants from each centre and constituency. The transcribed interview data were analyzed through an iterative process of thematic coding and peer reviewing.

In keeping with the participative values of action research the practice of informed consent at all times during the project and the interview process respectively was ensured.

DISCUSSION

Conversation for Change

Central to processes of organization development and learning is the engagement of members of the organization in visioning, planning, taking action and reviewing. Weisbord (2004) notes that over the twentieth century there was an evolution of practice in the development of organizational meaning making and community formation. In the 1950s everybody solved problems. In the 1960s experts improved whole systems, and now in the twenty first century everybody improves whole systems. This engagement in systems improvement is enacted through conversation (Dixon, 1998). What is critical for such conversation to take place is (a) there be an open space where participants feel a sense of psychological safety and (b) the participants listen to one another, respect one another, suspend their own opinions to understand one other and give voice to their own views (Isaacs, 1999).

Rationality in discursive arenas then is not something external. Rationality, or the rules of the game are defined by participants, thereby not neglecting their relative power within that conversation. It is through the exchange and encounter of other views that we might get access to our own blind spots. Individual, abstract rationality in this view is replaced by a communal rationality that is created and enacted within a conversation: "to argue rationally is to 'play by the rules' favored within a particular cultural tradition" (Gergen & Thatchenkerry, 1996, p. 362).

The project has shown that a reflective conversation with primary stakeholders of the organization, that is, service users, staff members, managers and so forth, has rendered visible issues, themes and problems that had never been communicated before within the organization (Jacobs, 2003). Hence, the workshop sessions themselves but moreover the self-organized conversational arenas show how responsiveness impacts on people, when they felt and experienced seriously being listened to. In terms of the sufficient condition of responsiveness, Deetz (1995) argues for a dialogic communication that might be incomplete and partial, but "the reason I talk with others is to better understand what I and they mean, hoping to find new and more satisfying ways of being together" (p. 97). While acknowledging the difficulty of putting dialogic communication in practice, he concludes that involvement leads to participation. Involvement refers to the search for the better argument based on expert's knowledge, whereas participation is based "on giving voice to difference, negotiation of values and decisional premises, and the production of new integrative positions.... New positions are generated out of the 'subject matter' or 'otherness.' " The creation and provision of conversational arenas does not necessarily lead to an ad hoc participation of stakeholders. But involvement, as the project has shown, is likely to lead to authentic participation by stakeholders.

Overall, three aspects regarding conversational modes can be concluded. First, how was the space for conversation created? The decision whether to have joint or separate sessions proved to be crucial: The tradeoff between inclusion on the one hand, and a psychologically safe environment on the other was acknowledged. Most centers opted for getting "to the real stuff" by having separate sessions first. Centers that decided otherwise emphasized the benefits of a joint discussion. Second, how were people encouraged to participate in an open and honest discussion? The toughest part was getting started. Day I could be considered a confidence building measure. Complemented by an appreciative question, it is not surprising that the resulting conversation was mainly in a talking-nice mode. However, one function of question one was to get people involved into the conversation and make them feel safe in the group. A nonthreatening question for a start proved to be adequate. The switch into a debate was mainly driven by question of the facilitator as to their assumptions or theories-in-use as why and how certain things happen. In addition to that, each group had its prime movers, which where participants that saw the micro-political potential of the project. In order to not letting them highjack the process but benefiting from their contribution, it was through explicitly asking for assessment of their views by other participants. Thirdly, how is a reflective conversation facilitated? The reflective episodes did not occur because they were deliberately planned to happen. The overall framework and design of the project and its session did certainly have an orientation toward reflective conversation. This reflexive character of the project has to be acknowledged. However, reflective episodes, i.e. people acknowledging different views while questioning their own, people aiming at understanding ("verstehen") other viewpoints, did only occur after an appropriate amount of time and energy was spent in a debate. The next step then was to reflect on what people had said and heard as to learn the multiple rationalities behind certain statements. It is mainly the acknowledgement and understanding of different rationalities that makes reflective conversation a key aspect of an organizational and strategic development process.

Interlevel Dynamics

Interlevel dynamics and their impact on levels of aggregation were central to the project. Each individual, whether resident, staff member, trustee, volunteer, member of a management committee, has a bonding relationship to the organization. This relationship is experienced very differently by members of the different groups and varies from individual to individual. The project aimed at strengthening the relationships in ways that are appropriate to the different constituencies by the process of creating the open space in which conversation and listening could take place. The project also aimed at addressing the functional and residential groups and teams in which individuals work and live. Therefore, there was attention to the strategic and operational issues of how each center functions, how committees work and how people work together to deliver the service to the residents. It also attended to how the different groups coordinate their efforts, whether it be the resident, staff and management committee within a center or the many centers within the national organization, or between the foundation office and the local centers. Finally, the ultimate aim of the project was to help the strategic and operational adaptation of the whole organization in a changing world. The project attempted to create an open space for conversation across and between all levels: individual to individual within the same group (residents and staff), group to group (residents to staff, center to local centers) and organization to its external stakeholders.

Learning Responsiveness

Individual and organizational learning are considered two distinct levels of learning. In terms of responsive aspects, learning levels outline the potential myopia and maladaptive learning through persistent routines and mental models. Responsiveness refers to sensitivity and acknowledgment of the existence and potential relevance of data that are in conflict with current mental models that might be outdated cognitive interpretation frameworks (Jacobs, 2003; Jacobs & Coghlan, 2005). Responsiveness in terms of learning level would contribute to the development of shared understanding through a participative culture. Conversational arenas in which different privately held cause-effect- assumptions are made explicit and visible, become intelligible. The conversational mode for such an assessment of mental models should not be competitive in nature. A reflective, dialogical interaction holds promise to render the differences visible and to agree on a shared view on a certain state of affairs, which in turn serves as an interpretation and relevance filter at a collective or even organizational level. Given that mental models, shared cognitive maps, and interpretation or sensemaking frameworks are the link between the individual and the organizational level of learning, the prerequisites or discursive conditions are of interest. It is with adequate conversational settings or discursive arenas that shared experience can be reflected upon, equivocality can be rendered visible and shared understanding might occur. An active responsiveness could enable the process of linking individual with collective learning.

The guiding question at the level of a stakeholder group is: how can a stakeholder group or individuals in such a group contribute to an active responsiveness? As for the necessary condition, that is, the creation of conversational arenas, self-organized, autonomous public spheres might be an appropriate way in that regard. As the example of one center showed, two stakeholder groups were willing and able to organize conversational arenas for themselves. On the one hand, the residents' advocacy group in which themes and issues of relevance and importance to them can be voiced in a psychologically safe setting. And, the staff's "Learning Through Listening" group that aimed at reflecting on operational issues outside the context of formal staff meetings. Both arenas obviously could have been prevented by management, but only for the sake of losing the perception of these stakeholder groups that management was nonresponsive per se. Insofar, both groups had more relative power in this particular case. Exploring the boundaries for self-organized conversational arenas can be a challenging but very fruitful endeavour on the way to active responsiveness. The project showed that talking and listening to stakeholders in a specific way allowed rendering visible issues and themes that had never been explored in public in this organization. Hence, while acknowledging the limits of generalizing from this single case, the project experience and reflection suggests that such specific conversational arrangements in terms of setting and mode are useful for exploring and understanding stakeholder needs.

As for the sufficient condition, how can stakeholders themselves learn the skills of reflective conversation? As Deetz (1995) has suggested, involvement leads to participation. Insofar, learning participation is a reflexive process. Participation and reflective conversation can be learned by participating in conversational arenas. Tracing surprises and paradoxes, discussing them in a curious rather than restricting manner allows for exploring own privately held assumptions about one self and others.

As for the sufficient condition, despite the broad knowledge that organization development consultants seem to hold regarding exercises and trainings for groups and individuals within a certain conversational setting. The key implication seems to be that in contrast to most organization development concepts, which assume sensitivity, openness, willingness, and ability of participants as an existing prerequisite for participants to engage in reflective conversations, this project would suggest that active responsiveness in such processes is concurrently developed as the process evolves. Hence, organization development consultants and managers should be attentive to responsive qualities in their interventions and their processes rather than assuming that responsiveness already exists prior to any intervention.

CONCLUSIONS

This article has outlined some of the core processes of an organization development project in a residential health-care provider organization in which a structure was created for the stakeholder groups in the organization, listen to each other and work together toward creating their own vision of how the organization can move into the future, according to its values and ethos. The aim of this organization development-action research project was to create conditions in which the stakeholders could engage in reflective conversation together and listen to each other on what is important in the life of the organization and how it could create actions from the conversations in order to move purposefully into the future. A second aim was to study how such a third sector organization can respond to the demands for change from both its external and internal environments in a participative manner which stakeholders can engage in conversation and articulate what can be learned from the process.

NOTE

1. A total of seven centers were included in the case study. All centers were invited to participate in the project. However, five did not participate for different reasons. One center did not participate in order to avoid confusion with a parallel total quality management project that was in progress. Two centers did not participate as they were in were in the process of changing management at the time of the process. Another two centers chose not to participate having discussed the usefulness in a preliminary meeting with the facilitator. Eight centers opted to participate in the

project. The central office and the Board of Trustees opted for one session each respectively.

REFERENCES

Argyris, C. (1993). *Knowledge for action*. San Francisco: Jossey-Bass.
Barrett, F. J., Thomas, G. F., & Hocevar, S. P. (1995). The central role of discourse in large-scale change: A social construction perspective, *Journal of Applied Behavioral Science, 31*(3) 352-372.
Beckhard, R., & Harris, R. (1987). *Organizational transitions*. Reading, MA: Addison-Wesley.
Coghlan, D. (1994). Organization development through inter-level dynamics, *International Journal of Organizational Analysis, 2*(3), 264-279.
Coghlan, D. (1997). Organizational learning as a dynamic interlevel process. In M. A. Rahim, R. T. Golembiewski, & L. E. Pate (Eds.), *Current topics in management* (Vol. 2, pp. 17-44). Greenwich, CT: JAI Press.
Coghlan, D. (2002) Interlevel dynamics in systemic action research, *Systemic Practice and Action Research, 15*(4), 273-283.
Coghlan, D., & Brannick, T. (2005). *Doing action research in your own organization* (2nd ed.). London: Sage.
Coghlan, D., & Mc Auliffe, E. (2003). *Changing healthcare organizations*. Dublin, England: Blackhall.
Coghlan, D., & McIlduff, E. (1990) Structuring and nondirectiveness in group faciltitation. *Person Centered Review, 5*(1), 13-29.
Coghlan, D., & Rashford, N. S. (2006). *Organizational change and strategy: An interlevel dynamics approach*. London: Routledge.
Crossan, M. M., Lane, H. W., & White, R. E. (1999). An organizational learning framework: From intuition to institution. *The Academy of Management Review, 24*(3), 522.
Deetz, S. (1995). *Transforming communication: Transforming business*. Creskill, NJ: Hampton.
Dixon, N. M. (1998). *Dialogue at work*. London: Lemos and Crane.
Evered, R. (1983). The language of organizations. The case of the navy. In R. Evered (Ed.), *Organizational symbolism* (pp. 109-121). Greenwich CT: JAI Press.
Ford, J. D., & Ford, L. W. (1995). The role of conversation in producing intentional change in organizations, *Academy of Management Review, 20*(3), 541-570.
French, W., & Bell, C. (1999). *Organization development* (6th ed.). Upper Saddle, River, NJ: Prentice-Hall.
Gergen, K. J., & Thatchenkery, J. T. (1996). Organization science as social construction: Postmodern potentials, *Journal of Applied Behavioral Science, 32*(4), 356-377.
Greenwood, D., & Levin, M. (1998). *Introduction to action research*. Thousand Oaks, CA: Sage.
Gummesson, E. (2000). *Qualitative methods in management research* (2nd ed.). Thousand Oaks, CA: Sage.

Heracleous, L., & Barrett, M. (2001). Organizationa change as discource: Communicative actions and deep structures in the context of information technology implementation. *Academy of Management Journal, 44*(4), 755-778.
Heracleous, L. (2004). Interpretive approaches to organizational discourse. In D. Grant, N. Phillips, C. Hardy, L. Putnam, & C. Oswick. (Eds.), *Handbook of organizational discourse* (pp. 175-192). Thousand Oaks CA: Sage.
Isaacs, W. (1999). *Dialogue and the art of thinking together.* New York: Doubleday.
Jacobs, C. (2003). *Managing organizational responsiveness.* Wiesbaden, Germany: Deutscher Universitats-Verlag.
Jacobs, C., & Coghlan, D. (2005). Sound from silence: On listening in organizational learning, *Human Relations, 58*(1), 115-118.
Jacobs, C., & Heracleous, L. (2005). Answers for questions to come—Reflective dialogue as an enabler of strategic innovation. *Journal of Organizational Change Management.*
MacIntosh, R., & MacLean, D. (1999). Conditioned emergence: A dissipative structures approach to transformation. *Strategic Management Journal, 20*(4), 297-316.
Marsick, V. J., & Watkins, K. E. (1999). *Facilitating learning organizations: Making learning count.* London: Gower.
Merriam, S. B. (1998). *Qualitative research and case study applications in education.* San Francisco: Jossey-Bass.
Mintzberg, H. (1975), The manager's job: Folklore and fact. *Harvard Business Review, 53,* 100-110.
Owen, H. (1997). *Open space technology.* San Francisco: Berrett-Kohler.
Pondy, L. (1978). Leadership is a language game. In L. Pondy (Ed.), *Leadership. Where else can we go?* (pp. 87-101). Durham, NC: Duke University Press.
Quinn, J. (1996). The role of "good conversation" in strategic control. *Journal of Management Studies, 33,* 381-394.
Rashford, N. S., & Coghlan, D. (1994). *The dynamics of organizational levels.* Reading, MA: Addison-Wesley.
Reason, P., & Bradbury, H. (2001). *Handbook of action research.* London: Sage.
Sackmann, S. (1989). The role of metaphors in organization transformation. *Human Relations, 42,* 463-485.
Scharmer, O. (2001). Self-transcending knowledge: Sensing and organising around emerging opportunities, *Journal of Knowledge Management, 5*(2), 137-150.
Schein, E. H. (1993). On dialogue, culture and organizational learning, *Organizational Dynamics, 22*(2), 40-51.
Schein, E. H. (1995). Process consultation, action research and clinical inquiry: Are they the same? *Journal of Managerial Psychology, 10*(5), 14-19.
Schein, E. H. (1999). *Process consultation revisited: Building the helping relationship.* Reading, MA: Addison-Wesley.
Searle, J. R. (1969). *Speech acts: An essay in the philosophy of language,* London: Cambridge University Press.
Smircich, L., & Morgan, G. (1982). Leadership: The management of meaning. *Journal of Applied Behavioral Science, 18,* 257-273.

Stake, R. E. (2000). Case studies. In N. Denzin & Y. Lincoln (Eds.), *Handbook of qualitative research* (pp. 435-454). Thousand Oaks, CA: Sage.

Watkins, J. M., & Mohr, B. J. (2001). *Appreciative inquiry: Change at the speed of imagination.* San Francisco: Jossey-Bass.

Weick, K. E. (1995). *Sensemaking in organizations.* Thousand Oaks, CA: Sage.

Weisbord, M. E. (2004). *Productive workplaces revisited.* San Francisco: Jossey-Bass.

CHAPTER 11

THE IMPLEMENTATION OF STRATEGY AND ORGANIZATIONAL REWARD SYSTEMS

AN OVERLOOKED AREA IN THE STRATEGIC MANAGEMENT OF HUMAN RESOURCES

Philip G. Benson and Terry R. Adler

We explore strategy implementation relative to organizational pay and propose that strategy implementation is related to reward systems. Our primary contributions are: one, tying existing schools of strategy implementation thought that include Rational Incrementalism, Egocentric Enactment, and Cognitive Renegotiation with pertinent reward issues; and second, discuss these reward issues within the broader framework of human resource management (HRM) and organizational development. Our investigation suggests that strategy implementation is more than just implementing a strategic plan. We propose that certain kinds of reward systems are consistent with certain kinds of strategy implementation approaches.

Organizations face the difficult task of implementing organizational strategy, or "just doing it," without an adequate grasp of how these changes affect employee reward systems (Martell, Gupta, & Carroll, 1996). Consequently, many leading business researchers have suggested that the study of strategy implementation is the most underdeveloped topic of the strategy making process (Dobni & Luffman, 2003; Gibbons, 2001; Gupta & Govindarajan, 1984; Mintzberg, 1994). Mintzberg (p. 226) strongly states that the primary weakness of research regarding strategy implementation, in general, is how the strategy making process really does work in organizations.

From a practitioner view, strategy implementation appears also to be among the most difficult tasks facing managers at all organizational levels (Rapert, Velliquette, & Garretson, 2002). For instance, how organizations reward employees for doing a good job has been an important question in the human resource management (HRM) literature (Davis-Blake & Pfeffer, 1989; Ferris, Hochwarter, Buckley, Harrell-Cook, & Frink, 1999; Gerhart & Rynes, 2003; Michlitsch, 2000). The implementation of organizational pay and reward systems is much more than an administrative task, as Schendel and Hofer (1979) suggest, and their role in the further implementation of strategy can be crucial. Compensation systems may be inadequately conceived and managed, with significant and potentially negative outcomes for the organization. Consider that Corboy and O'Corrbui (1999) found nearly 70% of strategic plans and strategies are never successfully implemented. Could this be related to employee perceptions that organizational reward systems are not adequate, or not consistent with the behavior required for successful implementation of strategy? We suggest that the lack of attention to organizational reward systems is one of the critical issues in proper strategy implementation success.

Our paper provides a classification scheme of current strategy implementation theory relative to organizational pay, an examination of reward systems relative to strategy making processes, and a discussion of reward issues relative to broader issues of HRM and organizational development. We suggest that certain kinds of reward systems are consistent with certain kinds of strategy implementation approaches, and first it is necessary to describe a model of how strategies are implemented in organizations.

A NEW CLASSIFICATION SCHEME OF STRATEGY IMPLEMENTATION

In 1981, Lawler published a now classic text on the role of pay systems in organizations, wherein he took the view that approaches to employee compensation, and changes in those systems, represent a form of organizational development. Since that book was published, much has been written on the growing role of "strategic" models of human resource management, and much of this literature goes far beyond the mere technical and design aspects of pay systems (see Galbraith & Nathanson, 1978, or Kogut, 1991, as examples).

If Lawler (1981) is correct, then pay systems can be a profound source of impact on organizational functioning, even to the point of impacting the nature of other organizational processes. What is critical, and has been increasingly recognized, is that HR practitioners should use such powerful tools to aid the implementation of the strategies deemed important for the organization, and without this tie-in, HR practices become stand-alone policies that fail to truly impact broader organizational functioning. Indeed, when the policies implemented by the HR practitioner are inconsistent with the broader organizational goals and vision, HR can actually end up working against the rest of the organization, making implementation of broad organizational strategies less likely to succeed than if HR did nothing.

Thus, one can consider the role that HR plays in the implementation of broad organizational strategies. HR practitioners can engage in various programs to improve strategy implementation, but in this paper we focus primarily on the role of reward systems. What reward practices are consistent with various approaches to strategy implementation?

Additionally, pay and reward plans may not be of a "one-size-fits-all" nature. The critical issue in strategic HRM is to fit HR practices to other administrative and organizational functions. Baron and Kreps (1999), for example, argue that HR practices must be consistent with each other, and consistent with other organizational practices, if effective results are to be expected. While many firms have adopted innovative HRM practices, relatively few have looked at the systematic relationships among HR practices, and the need for broader approaches to implementation (Ichniowski, Kochan, Levine, Olson, & Strauss, 2000).

In addition, even those scholars who have considered the relationships among HR practices and organizational functioning have often taken a limited view of the phenomena. Generally, the alignment of various HR practices (see Baron & Kreps, 1999) has been considered, as has the relationship of bundles of HR practices to overall organizational success (Ichniowski et al., 2000). We specifically consider the impact that reward practices have in the implementation of other strategic plans in organizations. To sort and classify past work on strategy implementation, we propose three main schools of thought, following closely the model of Adler, Boje, and Black (2004): (1) Rational Incrementalism; (2) Egocentric Enactment; and (3) Cognitive Renegotiation. The theory we develop will suggest that approaches or "schools of thought" vary on dimensions of definition of strategy implementation, theme, and integrating mechanisms. Each school addresses different fundamental issues of strategy implementation but these schools of thought do overlap in some areas. Each school of thought has a unique working definition of strategy implementation. In addition, each has implications for the HR systems consistent with its implementation, and the "best practices" in employee reward systems that are critical for strategy implementation.

Rational Incrementalism

In the Rational Incrementalism framework, strategy implementation can best be thought of as organizational strategy that is not only planned but managed. Therefore, managers are capable of not only looking into future organizational issues, but also deciding what issues to pursue at all levels of the organization. The emphasis is on partitioning work linearly through analysis with the focus of implementation on corporate leadership. Rational Incrementalism creates personal and organizational awareness, understanding, and commitment necessary to implement strategies effectively. Resources can be appropriately and increasingly committed and rewarded, and employees are rewarded for achieving results.

Rational Incrementalism is desirable so that resources can be appropriately and increasingly committed to projects that implement the strategic plan. Thus, rewards are tied to smaller but more clearly developed pieces of work in the strategic plan. Not surprisingly, strategy implementation is narrowly viewed as "achieving results" in strategy making (Andrews, 1980, p. 28) and these results are dictated by top management in the strategic plan (Beer & Eisenstat, 2000; Heracleous, 2000).

Porter (1980, p. xiv), for example, provides a framework for what we are calling Rational Incrementalism. Many strategic analysis tools for formulation of strategic plans are clearly defined and are used to comprehensively analyze a firm's industry, "its future evolution, to understand its competitors and its own position, and to translate this analysis into a competitive strategy for a particular business." Methods like strengths, weaknesses, opportunities, and threats (SWOT), Porter's five-forces model, value-chain analysis, strategic mapping, and strategy profiling are traditionally taught in the formulation of strategy from a narrow, prescriptive viewpoint (Andrews, 1980; Littler, Aisthorpe, Hudson, & Keasey, 2000; Porter, 1980).

The balanced scorecard (Kaplan & Norton, 1992, 1993), as determined by top management, is also one of the few methods designed for the implementation of strategy from a strategic plan. The balanced scorecard is a method (Brewer, 2002; Gumbus & Lyons, 2002; Kaplan & Norton, 1996a, 1996b) to facilitate the translation of critical stakeholders' goals down the hierarchy of an organization. This process helps to make explicit the links between strategy and strategic goals and the daily work of individuals (Brewer, 2002; Gumbus & Lyons, 2002). Indeed this method has been adopted by over 50% of the Fortune 100 firms (Gumbus & Lyons, 2002) and includes such organizations as AMD (Advanced Micro Devices), Apple Computer, (Kaplan & Norton, 1993) and even very diversified conglomerates such as Philips Electronics (Gumbus & Lyons, 2002). While individuals may be involved to some degree in setting their organizational goals and measurements, they are constrained to do so in ways that meet the goals set by those higher in the organization. Typically the actual processes to achieve these end states are not specified; however, there are other implementation orientations such as stage-gate models that do specify a process.

Many theorists and consultants in this school use stage-gate models to manage strategic implementation decisions to achieve results aspired to in the strategic plan. The management of strategic portfolios is a prime example where stage-gate modeling is typically applied (Lorange, 1998). A typical stage-gate model has several names today such as "phase-review," "gating," "road-mapping," or "new product development" processes. Cooper, Edgett, and Kleinschmidt (1998, p. 21) (see Figure 11.1 for a generic stage-gate model) describe how stage-gate processes allow for more "effective," or rational, implementation of portfolio management because "gates are where Go/Kill decisions are made on individual projects, and hence where many of the resources are allocated." Thus, current strategy implementation models like scenario analysis fit the Rational Incrementalism philosophy in the allocation of resources to adapt to future change.

Resource allocations are typically reviewed and allocated at each gate between stages by corporate leadership. Wheelwright and Clark (1992) describe four organizations that vary in the extent of executive review at each gate. In general, though, each stage of strategy implementation is designed to gather information needed to move a project forward and to modify resource allocations. Thus, Cooper et al. (1998) suggest that the stage-gate process is best characterized by "fuzzy gates" where tailoring of stages and gates is allowed to facilitate executive decision-making in resolving conflict situations. The nature of incremental resource allocation at subsequent gates means that the potential for organizational conflict increases as stages are progressively realized.

Conflict within organizations is thus best resolved when top management resolves disputes between individuals and teams implementing strategy. Thus, we propose the following hypotheses:

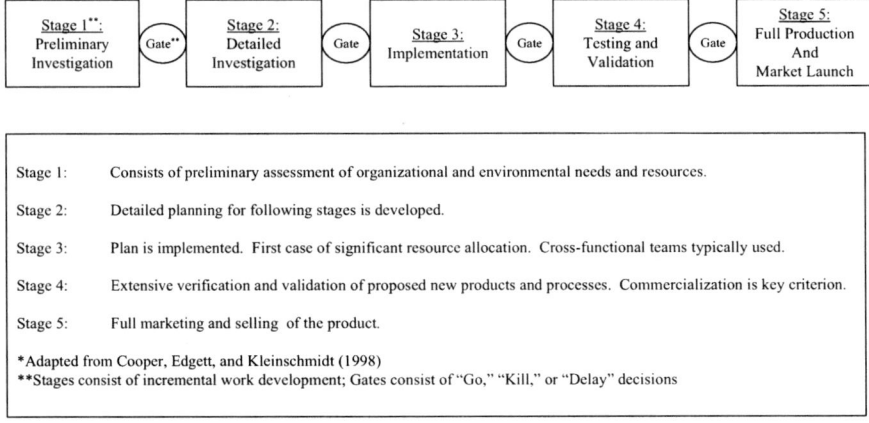

Figure 11.1. Generic stage-gate model.

Hypothesis 1: The use of rational incremental schemes for strategy implementation will be characterized by an internal organizational leadership.

Hypothesis 2: The use of rational incremental schemes for strategy implementation will lead to compensation based on work identified in the strategic plan.

The next classification of strategy implementation thought integrates terms like strategic spontaneity and social context.

Egocentric Enactment School

We define Egocentric Enactment as a market focused view in acquiring and disposing of organizational resources. One could argue that the "competitive advantage," "image management," and "push-pull marketing" practices of strategy management are grounded in this school. Consider Ansoff's (1979) argument that "resource scarcity makes it necessary to plan not only the 'front' interface with the market but also the 'rear' interface with the sources of supply" (p. 43). Thus, this school is firmly established in the institutional and resource dependence approach to strategy implementation. While the Rational Incrementalism school views personal leadership as the tie that binds strategy formation with strategy implementation, what we are calling the Egocentric Enactment school suggests that the interdependence between these two concepts is best characterized by "living off" that interface. Martell et al. (1996) describe how firms that differentiate tend to use market leadership compensation practices. Thus, the true barometer of an organization's reward system is dictated by environmental concerns.

Strategy implementation is, therefore, defined by Parsons (1960), an institutional theorist, as the disposal of firm outputs and the mobilization of resources necessary to get firm outputs out the door. The first priority of firms is to set goals that effectively allow for the compensation of resources that put firms in a position to remain competitive (Parsons, 1960, p. 29). Zucker (1988), representative of theorists in this school of thought, would add that organizations can construct their own environments based on the firm's relationship within its institutional environment (Meyer & Rowan, 1977; Weick, 1979). The Egocentric Enactment school view of strategy implementation is from a prescriptive lens since firms are to "enact" and "co-opt" their environments to acquire and reward their employees. The importance of the environment in strategy implementation is a defining characteristic of this school of thought and one that clearly dominates the open-systems perspective found in organizational theory (Scott, 1992).

While other strategy implementation schools would consider environmental issues in their analysis (see Schendel & Hofer, 1979), the Egocentric Enactment school views the environment with elevated status in the decision-making process, especially with regard to how an organization's resources are affected by its boundaries. The Egocentric Enactment school thus expands strategy implementation to enact an organization's culture on the firm's environment. Strategy is culture, according to Weick (1979), and the intent of this school of thought is to impose, or enact, your culture on the environment as needed (e.g., spontaneity). This would make strategy implementation very difficult to achieve given the changing and dynamic nature of market environments (Schendel & Hofer, 1979). However, staying true to resource dependence and institutional theory, environments also affect organizational strategy. The tension, or conflict, organizations experience in rewarding employees effectively is primarily due to the tension in enacting culture and reacting to environmental pressures.

While some would argue that the dynamism of organizational environments is overrated (Mintzberg, 1994), theorists in this school would maintain that the environment is both a cause and benefactor of conflict in organizations. For instance, as organizations integrate environmental concerns into firm-level decisions, organizations adapt and become more similar through mimicry (DiMaggio & Powell, 1983). Thus, institutional power is elevated, according to Zucker (1988), by adapting to structures and processes that meet environmental needs.

Therefore, market and industry characteristics are key considerations in achieving the best fit between a firm's strategic implementation and environmental conditions and demands regarding compensation systems (Dobni & Luffman, 2003). Other studies by Selznick (1949) described how firms co-opt their environments by absorbing new elements into the leadership of a firm, or policy determining structure, as a means of averting threats to its stability or existence. The same could be said of organizations like Enron today where firms co-opt resources from the environment at the cost of taking away resources from other firms in their industry (Witt & Behr, 2002).

The study of the implementation of corporate strategy in the Egocentric Enactment school is thus focused on how strategy implementation assists firms in compensating employees to adapt to environmental pressures. Objective data with regard to HRM/performance linkages thus are examined in the spontaneous compensation of employees. With regard to the Egocentric Enactment school, Weick (1979) states that "plans become excuses for interaction ... plans are a pretext under which several valuable activities take place in organizations" (p. 11). The use of strategic planning, or analysis, is not a useful activity as plans "bother about the best method of accomplishing an accidental result" (Bierce, 1946, p. 327). The onus of strategy making falls clearly in the dynamics of strategy implementation as strategy formulation represents an internal activity and strategy implementation represents an external focus in enacting a firm's environment. Thus, an organization's boundary determines the extent of integration between strategy formation and strategy implementation.

The accuracy of strategy formation significantly lags practical and realistic concerns and as Cohen and March (1976) suggest, plans become symbols, games, and excuses for these interactions. The enactment of a firm's environment across an organization's boundary is where strategy implementation becomes a valuable activity in the Egocentric Enactment school of thought. Egocentric Enactment, therefore, implies the prescriptive determination of organizational resources. We thus propose the following hypotheses with regard to this school of thought:

Hypothesis 3: An Egocentric Enactment perspective of strategy implementation will be associated with less successful implementation of strategic plans.

Hypothesis 4: The use of an Egocentric Enactment perspective of strategy implementation will be associated with more objective market data in the compensation of employees.

The next category focuses upon collective learning processes as key definition, theme, and integrating mechanism are discussed.

Cognitive Renegotiation School

The onus for determining how strategy is implemented differs from the previous schools of thought we have discussed so far in that unlike the Rational Incrementalism school where the personal leadership of top management integrates, or the Egocentric Enactment school where the boundary conditions between the organization and the environment dictate what and how resources are acquired and disposed of, this school of thought places its emphasis on the degree of centralization between thinking and doing in an organization. Key concepts in the Cognitive Renegotiation school are that implementation may precede formation sometimes and likewise formation may precede implementation. Strategy implementation becomes a notional idea based on the strategy making process being recursive where strategy planning sometimes precedes strategy implementation and vice versa. Therefore, strategic planners sometimes become the implementers and sometimes strategic implementers become the planners. It is the process of renegotiation between planning and implementation that adds value to organizations and what makes strategy implementation so complex. Thus, employees are rewarded based on how well they renegotiate strategy plans with top management based on implementation shortfalls and constraints. Organizations use terms like "360 reviews" to emphasize the value of integration between planning and doing.

The Cognitive Renegotiation school attempts to improve our understanding of why this renegotiation is so difficult. Investigators in this framework would point to the fallacy of separating strategy formation from strategy implementation. As Majone and Wildavsky (1978) put it, "literal implementation is literally impossible" (p. 116) due to the separation of analysis from synthesis. According to Mintzberg (1994), analysis (e.g., planning) and synthesis cannot and should not be separated in the strategy making process. Strategy implementation is best characterized as a process of collective learning where strategies emerge and intervention is done organizationally (Mintzberg, 1994, pp. 286-87). Many authors have investigated HRM/performance linkages here with regard to the effects of consensus and commitment in achieving strategic decisions (Dooley, Fryxell, & Judge, 2000; Kim & Mauborgne, 1993; Michlitsch, 2000; Rapert et al., 2002)

Mintzberg (1994) would add that emphasis on consensus and commitment is dependent on a firm's degree of centralization. The formation-implementation dichotomy "collapses" and consensus and commitment occur based on how decisions are made in an organization. If a centralized structure is used, then the formulator implements as in an entrepreneurial organization. If a decentralized structure is evident then implementers formulate, such as in a research and development laboratory (Mintzberg, 1994). The implementation of strategy is thus best accomplished when top management and employees share the process.

Researchers, however, do not necessarily separate strategy formation from strategy implementation. For instance, Andrews (1980), representative of the Rational Incrementalism school, states that "the formulation of strategy is not finished when implementation begins" (p. 106). This is a clear recognition that the two "phases" of strategy making overlap and this overlap is best managed, according to the Rational Incrementalism school, by senior leadership.

The didactic of the Cognitive Renegotiation school of thought is the continual renegotiation between formulators and implementers in the strategy making process. Thinking and acting are combined and characteristically recursive, dependent on how organizational strategies emerge, are recognized, and managed by senior management and strategic planners. The balance between analysis and synthesis hangs on the degree senior management and strategic planning is centralized within an organization. Thus, social context is somewhat considered in the strategy making process.

While the Cognitive Renegotiation school of thought is descriptive, unlike the previous prescriptive models, this school of thought provides little assistance in offering a cohesive explanation for why organizations plan at all and possibly less understanding of how rewards match performance. If analysis and synthesis occur recursively, then how does strategy offer unique value that organizational theorists, decision-making, organizational behaviorists, and industrial-organization economists do not already provide? If strategy implementation is "crafting" rather than "planning" as Mintzberg (1987) suggests, then the ultimate conclusion is that this school of thought remains exactly that—a school of thought dependent on the crafters, or artisans, at the time with less emphasis on rewarding adequately or fairly. Thus, while intuition and "gut-feel" have a part to play in strategy implementation, we argue that this perspective on rewarding employees may lead to perceptions of procedural and distributive injustice (Kim & Mauborgne, 1993). The following hypotheses are proposed with regard to this school of thought:

Hypothesis 5: A Cognitive Renegotiation perspective of strategy implementation will be associated with shared implementation of strategic plans between top management and employees.

Hypothesis 6: The use of a Cognitive Renegotiation perspective of strategy implementation will be associated with less procedural justice in the compensation of employees.

Hypothesis 7: The use of a Cognitive Renegotiation perspective of strategy implementation will be associated with less distributive justice in the compensation of employees.

Hypothesis 8: The use of a Cognitive Renegotiation perspective of strategy implementation will be associated with no clear strategic plan until after strategy is fully implemented.

DISCUSSION

Becoming reflective, some may argue that the implementation of strategy is not even a bona fide and worthy avenue of study in the strategy making process. Some theorists even claim that strategy implementation is akin to organizational change. Yet, we would argue that not only is strategic implementation a separate set of activities, practitioners recognize the uniqueness of strategy implementation to further current work or possibly change future direction (Pettigrew, 1985; Porter, 1980; Rapert et al., 2002).

The question thus changes to how firms and researchers understand how strategy is implemented in an organization. We have presented three alternative explanations of strategy implementation found in organizations: Rational Incrementalism, Egocentric Enactment, and Cognitive Recognition. Each has its own unique characteristics and effects on the reward and compensation of organizational employees.

In the Rational Incremental school, employees are rewarded for sticking to the plan and getting work accomplished. Rewards are clearly identified and partitioned when parts of the plan are successfully completed. Unfortunately, the plan can quickly become obsolete due to many influences so rewards may be given to individuals for completing work in the strategic plan that is neither effective nor adequate. We are reminded of Kerr's (1975) article of how organizations can reward behavior that is contrary to the goals of the organization. The Rational Incremental school of thought seems to be ripe for furthering Kerr's notion of ineffectiveness.

The Egocentric Enactment school rewards individuals and teams based on what the market says is appropriate. Thus, an organization faces the unfavorable task of integrating their rewards based on many competing, complex, and unstable influences in the marketplace. Many universities face these challenges as faculty are rewarded for scholarly work that is externally determined, yet have to promote and tenure faculty internally based on what the market dictates. Integrating faculty promotions between departments and colleges within a university is therefore both time-consuming and complex as each college and department faces unique market forces that influence a faculty's ability to conduct research and publish manuscripts. Many firms face similar issues as they recruit and retain human resources from a constrained resource pool.

The last school of thought is the Cognitive Renegotiation framework. Rewards are based on how individuals and teams communicate with top management in the collaborative implementation of strategy. There is clearly recognition that strategic plans and the market will not only change, but that the strategic plan may be entirely perfunctory in responding to the market. In other words, trust and communication between top management and individuals is absolutely necessary to simultaneously implement strategy and then find a plan that allows them to implement in a particular market. Thus, Mintzberg (1994) suggests that strategy planning should better be thought of as "crafting" incorporating both planning and implementation together as an organization discovers what they should be doing while they are doing it.

The Cognitive Renegotiation school recognizes how difficult strategy implementation is because of integrating internal factors like getting teams to cooperate effectively with external factors like how market forces change unpredictably. Rewarding individuals becomes a spontaneous moment because top management makes quick value judgments about what is good behavior and what is not. Top management thus 'knows it when they see it' but not before. Creativity is much this way as found in research and development, new product development, and entrepreneurial firms (Wheelwright & Clark, 1992). Individuals are typically allowed time to innovate and then are rewarded when their innovations become successful. Unfortunately, it is difficult to surgically recreate what and who determined success so rewards often fail to adequately compensate.

CONCLUSION

As we have discussed, the range of thought on strategy implementation that has been examined over the years is quite broad (Mintzberg, 1987; 1994). While strategy implementation has been acknowledged as a fundamental and legitimate strategy making process, little has been discussed regarding how incentives affect the ability to "just do it." Prior investigations, in general, have contributed much to the debate about the resources and processes necessary to adequately compensate employees. Certainly, many of the proposed relationships in this paper could be subjected to further, empirical analysis. We propose that without considering how strategy implementation differs within organizations and tying incentives to these variations, underlying assumptions about adequate employee compensation may be unfounded. Our intent is to begin discussion on how organizations actually reward employees to implement strategy in fulfilling organizational objectives.

AUTHOR'S NOTE

An earlier form of this paper was presented at the annual meeting of the Irish Academy of Management, Trinity College Dublin, on September 2, 2004. Address all correspondence to the first author.

REFERENCES

Adler, T. R., Boje, D., & Black, J. (2004, August). *Strategic social theatre: More than "just doing it" in the emergent implementation process.* Paper presented at the Annual Academy of Management Conference, Business Policy and Strategy Division, New Orleans, LA.

Andrews, K. (1980). *The concept of corporate strategy.* Homewood, IL: Irwin.

Ansoff, H. (1979). *Strategic management.* London: Macmillan.

Baron, J. N., & Kreps, D. M. (1999). *Strategic human resources: Frameworks for general managers.* Hoboken, NJ: Wiley.

Beer, M., & Eisenstat, R. (2000). The silent killers of strategy implementation and learning. *Sloan Management Review, 41,* 29-41.

Bierce, A. (1946). *The collected writings of Ambrose Bierce.* New York: The Citadel Press.

Brewer, P. (2002). Putting strategy into the balanced scorecard, *Strategic Finance, 84*(7), 44-52.

Cohen, M., & March, J. (1976). Decisions, presidents, and status. In J. March & J. Olsen (Eds.), *Ambiguity and choice in organizations* (pp. 132-142). Bergen, Norway: Universitetsforlaget.

Cooper, R. G., Edgett, S. J., & Kleinschmidt, E. J. (1998). *Portfolio management for new products.* Reading, MA: Perseus.

Corboy, M., & O'Corrbui, D. (1999). The seven deadly sins of strategy. *Management Accounting, 77,* 29-31.

Davis-Blake, A., & Pfeffer, J. (1989). Just a mirage: The search for dispositional effects in organizational research. *Academy of Management Review, 14,* 385-400.

DiMaggio, P. J., & Powell, W. W. (1983). The iron cage revisited: Institutional isomorphism and collective rationality in organizational fields. *American Sociological Review, 48*, 147-160.

Dobni, C. B., & Luffman, G. (2003). Determining the scope and impact of market orientation profiles on strategy implementation and performance. *Strategic Management Journal, 24*, 577-585.

Dooley, R., Fryxell, G., & Judge, W. (2000). Belaboring the not-so-obvious: Consensus, commitment, and strategy implementation speed and success. *Journal of Management, 26*, 1237.

Ferris, G. R., Hochwater, W. A., Buckley, M. R., Harrell-Cook, G., & Frink. (1999). Human resource management: Some new directions. *Journal of Management, 25*, 385-415.

Galbraith, J. R. & Nathanson, D. A. (1978). *Strategy implementation: The role of structure and process*. St. Paul, MN: West.

Gerhart, B., & Rynes, S. L. (2003). *Compensation: Theory, evidence, and strategic implications*. Thousand Oaks, CA: Sage.

Gibbons, P. (2001). Managing strategy implementation. *Irish Journal of Management, 22*, 213-215.

Gumbus, A., & Lyons, B. (2002). The balanced scorecard at Philips Electronics, *Strategic Finance, 84*(5), 45-49.

Gupta, A., & Govindarajan, V. (1984). Business unit strategy, managerial characteristics, and business unit effectiveness at strategy implementation. *Academy of Management Journal, 27*, 25-41.

Heracleous, L. (2000). The role of strategy implementation in organizational development. *Organization Development Journal, 18*, 75-87.

Ichniowski, C., Kochan, T. A., Levine, D. I., Olson, C., & Strauss, G. (2000). What works at work: Overview and assessment. In C. Ichniowski, D. I. Levine, C. Olson, & G. Strauss (Eds.), *The American workplace: Skills, compensation and employee involvement* (pp. 1-37). Cambridge, England: The Cambridge University Press.

Kaplan, R. S., & Norton, D. P. (1992, January-February) The balanced scorecard—Measures that drive performance, *Harvard Business Review, 70*, 71-79.

Kaplan, R. S., & Norton, D. P. (1993, September-October). Putting the balanced scorecard to work. *Harvard Business Review, 71*, 134-147.

Kaplan, R. S., & Norton, D. P. (1996a, January-February). Using the balanced scorecard as a strategic management system, *Harvard Business Review, 74*, 75-85.

Kaplan, R. S. & Norton, D. P. (1996b). Linking the balanced scorecard to strategy, *California Management Review, 39*(1), 53-79.

Kerr, S. (1975). On the folly of rewarding A, while hoping for B. *Academy of Management Journal, 18*, 769-783.

Kim, W., & Mauborgne, R. (1993). Procedural justice, attitudes, and subsidiary top management compliance with multinationals' corporate strategy decisions. *Academy of Management Journal, 36*, 502-527.

Kogut, B. (1991). Joint ventures and the option to expand and acquire, *Management Science, 37*, 19-33.

Lawler, E. E., III. (1981). *Pay and organization development*. Reading, MA: Addison-Wesley.
Littler, K., Aisthorpe, P., Hudson, R., & Keasey, K. (2000). A new approach to linking strategy formulation and strategy implementation: An example from the UK banking sector. *International Journal of Information Management, 20*, 411.
Lorange, P. (1998). Strategy implementation: The new realities. *Long Range Planning, 31*, 18-30.
Majone, G., & Wildavsky, A. (1978). Implementation as evolution. *Policy Studies Review Annual, II*, 103-117.
Martell, K., Gupta, A., & Carroll, S. (1996). Human resource management practices, business strategies, and firm performance: A test of strategy implementation theory. *Irish Business and Administrative Research, 17*, 18-36.
Meyer, J., & Rowan, B. (1977). Institutionalized organizations: Formal structure as myth and ceremony. *American Journal of Sociology, 83*, 340-363.
Michlitsch, J. (2000). High-performing, loyal employees: The real way to implement strategy. *Strategy & Leadership, 28*, 28.
Mintzberg, H. (1987, July/August). Crafting strategy. *Harvard Business Review, 65*, 66-75.
Mintzberg, H. (1994). *The rise and fall of strategic planning*. New York: Free Press.
Parsons, T. (1960). *Structure and process in modern society*. New York: Free Press.
Pettigrew, A. M. (1985). *The awakening giant: Continuity and change in Imperial Chemical Industries*. Oxford, England: Blackwell.
Porter, M. 1980. *Competitive strategy: Techniques for analyzing industries and competitors*. New York: Free Press.
Rapert, M., Velliquette, A., & Garretson, J. (2002). The strategic implementation process: Evoking strategic consensus through communication. *Journal of Business Research, 55*, 301.
Schendel, D., & Hofer, C. (Eds.). (1979). *Strategic management: A new view of business policy and planning*. Boston: Little, Brown.
Scott, R. (1992). *Organizations: Rational, natural, and open systems*. Englewood Cliffs, NJ: Prentice-Hall.
Selznick, P. (1949). *TVA and the grass roots*. Berkeley: University of California Press.
Weick, K. (1979). *The social psychology of organizing*. Reading, MA: Addison-Wesley.
Wheelwright, S., & Clark, K. (1992). *Revolutionizing product development: Quantum leaps in speed, efficiency and quality*. New York: The Free Press.
Witt, A., & Behr, P. (2002, July 31). Losses, conflicts threaten survival: CFO Fastow ousted in probe of profits. *The Washington Post*, p. A01.
Zucker, L. (1988). *Institutional patterns and organizations: Culture and environment*. Cambridge, MA: Ballinger.

CHAPTER 12

TASK INTERDEPENDENCE AS A MODERATOR OF POLITICS-WORK OUTCOMES RELATIONSHIPS

Deondra Conner, Darren Treadway, Matrecia James, Jason Stoner, and Wayne Hochwarter

Past research has sought to identify factors that moderate the relationship between politics perceptions and work outcomes. The current study focused on a previously uninvestigated moderator, task interdependence, which is defined as the level of interaction between organizational members. We propose that politics perceptions and task interdependence would interaction such that those who reported close interactions with organizational members would be adversely affected by workplace politics. Data gathered from 221 police officer strongly supported our proposed relationships. Specifically, those reporting high levels of task interdependence experienced lower levels of job and life satisfaction, and higher levels of turnover intent when politics were high. Conversely, those reporting low levels of task interdependence did not report adverse effects of workplace politics perceptions. Implications of these findings, strengths and limitations, and avenues for future research are provided.

INTRODUCTION

Significant reviews of the literature have linked politics perceptions with a host of adverse outcomes such as lower levels of job satisfaction and commitment, and higher levels of tension and turnover intent (Ferris, Adams, Kolodinsky, Hochwarter, & Adams, 2002; Kacmar & Baron, 1999). Given the strength of research reported in these reviews, it may appear that politics perceptions habitually lead to negative consequences. However, there is evidence to suggest that the direct relationship between politics perceptions and negative work outcomes may not exist for all individuals. For example, Christiansen, Villanova, and Mikulay (1997) asked, "Are all workers impacted by politics equally, or do organizational politics affect the attitudes of some individuals but not others?" (p. 710). It is our contention that the level of interaction among workers will predict when politics perceptions lead to adverse reactions. More specifically, when individuals work closely with others, rely on the efforts of coworkers, and perceived their work activities to have an impact on employees in their proximal work setting, the adverse effects of politics should be more pronounced. Conversely, when individuals perceive low levels of task interdependence, we anticipate that perceived politics would have only a minimal impact on work outcomes.

In the current study, we assess the ability of perceived politics and task interdependence to interactively predict three job outcomes: job satisfaction, intent to leave, and life satisfaction. Job satisfaction and intent to turnover have served as often-observed outcomes in previous politics perceptions research (Hochwarter, Perrewé, Ferris, & Guerico, 1999; Kacmar & Baron, 1999). Although life satisfaction has yet to receive empirical attention in this particular domain, its significant relationship with job satisfaction in past research (Hart, 1999; Sumer & Knight, 2001) suggests that vocational factors may have an impact on constructs not directly related to the execution of work tasks.

ORGANIZATIONAL POLITICS

Organizational politics has been defined as "behavior not formally sanctioned by the organization, which produces conflict and disharmony in the work environment by pitting individuals and/or groups against one another, or against the organization" (Ferris, Frink, Galang, Zhou, Kacmar, & Howard, 1996, p. 234). Research addressing the phenomenon of organizational politics has proceeded along two central streams: political behaviors and political perceptions. Taken together, these streams represent an increasingly voluminous amount of research that seeks to define the context, actions, and consequences of self-directed behavior within organizations.

Recent attention has focused more closely on the second research stream—the determination of the antecedents and consequences of an individual's perceptions of organizational politics. Interest into the impact of perceptions of organizational politics on work experience spans over two decades beginning with the work of Gandz and Murray (1980). Grounded in the work of Lewin (1936), it is the contention of researchers in this field that individuals act not upon reality, but on their *perceptions* of reality. Therefore, of critical importance to the study of politics within organizations is the manner in which perceptions of political behavior are formed and consequently affect an individual's work-related experience.

The Search for Moderating Variables

As noted, previous work has examined the relationship between perceived politics and outcomes such as job anxiety, job satisfaction, and organizational withdrawal (Cropanzano, Howes, Grandey, & Toth, 1997; Ferris & Kacmar, 1992; Gilmore, Ferris, Dulebohn, & Harrell-Cook, 1996; Hochwarter et al., 1999). Additionally, theory and research has suggested that politics perceptions-work outcomes relations are likely moderated by a number of contextual and dispositional variables. In general, understanding of and control over the work environment have been constructs most often employed as moderators (Ferris, Russ, & Fandt, 1989; Ferris et al., 2002). Theoretically, politics can be considered a source of stress in the immediate work environment and we expect comparably debilitating consequences as other workplace stressors (Ferris et al., 1996). Empirical research supports the efficacy of these moderators in that the negative impact of politics perceptions is greatest for those with do not possess an adequate level of control or understanding (Ferris et al., 1993; Ferris, Frink, Gilmore, & Kacmar, 1994).

In addition to this line of research, academicians have sought to identify other factors capable of moderating the relationship between perceived politics and work outcomes. For example, previous work has employed supervisor-subordinate goal congruence (Witt, 1998), self-efficacy (Bozeman, Perrewé, Hochwarter, & Brymer, 2001), and affective commitment (Hochwarter et al., 1999) as moderators. In an attempt to build on these works, the current study conceptualizes task interdependence as a factor capable of either increasing or lessening the adverse effects of politics perceptions. Specifically, we posit that the level of work interaction perceived by sample respondents will predict whether politics affect work outcomes. Specifically, we contend that those perceiving high levels of task interdependence will be more adversely impacted than those who report lower levels of task interdependence.

TASK INTERDEPENDENCE

Task interdependence can be defined as the degree to which members of a group depend on each other for information and resources, and work together to complete tasks (Campion, Medsker, & Higgs, 1993; Johnson & Johnson, 1989; Shaw, Duffy, & Stark, 2000; Van der Vegt, Emans, & Van de Vliert, 2000). Some scholars extend this concept to also reflect individual group members' perceptions of job design relative to dependency on other workers for task accomplishment (Shaw et al., 2000; Van der Vegt et al., 2000; Wageman, 1995). This extension of task interdependence takes into account individual group members' discretion as to how much they actually feel they work together at task accomplishment. Hence, task interdependence is an element of group structure and job design that involves collective action (actual and perceived in the case of individual affective states).

At a macrolevel, this construct takes the forms of pooled and/or sequential interdependence. Both pooled (varied order) and sequential (fixed order) interdependence involve the coordination and combining of processes and inputs to complete a task (Thompson, 1967; Van de Ven & Ferry, 1980; Wageman, 1995). Task interdependence is also distinguished from its closely associated counterpart-outcome interdependence. Outcome interdependence involves collective consequences or group rewards (in contrast to individual rewards) and can be mutually exclusive from task interdependence (Van der Vegt et al., 2000; Wageman, 1995).

Previous Task Interdependence Research

Much of the previous research involving task interdependence has examined the interactive effects of combining task with outcome interdependence (DeMatteo, Eby, & Sundstrom, 1998; Mitchell & Silver, 1990). In general, the moderating effects of task interdependence have been empirically demonstrated in studies determining a proper mix (if any) between task and outcome interdependence. For example, Miller and Hamblin (1963) found that group-level performance was greatest at balanced levels of task and outcome interdependence. More recent work has revealed similar conclusions (Wageman & Baker, 1997). However, Rosenbaum et al. (1980) found that groups performed best when given group rewards (as opposed to hybrid or individual rewards) for performance on highly interdependent tasks. Johnson and Johnson (1989) examined mixed models of interdependence and concluded that pure interdependent models were better for group performance than hybrid models of interdependence.

Similarly, Wageman (1995) demonstrated that group performance was higher under conditions where task and outcome interdependence were either of an individual or of a group nature, exclusively (as opposed to mixed or hybrid combinations). Other studies have shown that low levels of task interdependence and high levels of outcome interdependence can reduce individual effort and performance (Kidwell & Bennett, 1993; Wageman & Baker, 1997). Correspondingly, Van der Vegt et al. (2000) found that high levels of job complexity offset the negative effects of mismatched task and outcome interdependence on job satisfaction and job commitment.

Individual-Level Analysis and Affective Outcomes

Group-level research has shown that task interdependence is related to collective performance and satisfaction (Campion et al., 1993; Campion, Papper, & Medsker, 1996). However, with so many studies focusing on group level analyses, recent work has begun to call for more exploration of "individual-level performance outcomes in the group context" (Shaw et al., 2000, p. 259). Van der Vegt et al. (2000) echoed this suggestion, arguing that, "Little is known about how group members affectively respond to intragroup interdependence" (p. 634). Furthermore, since an element of task interdependence involves the perceptions of individual group members, it is important to better understand their perceptions and affective states. This form of awareness is important because the degree of required task interdependence as perceived by the individual and the level of cooperation may vary among members of a group (Wageman, 1995).

For example, Pearce and Gregerson (1991) found a positive relationship between an individual's felt responsibility for work and task interdependence. Anderson and Williams (1996) demonstrated that task interdependence was positively related to the frequency with which employees sought help with task-related problems. In a study of group member satisfaction and performance, Shaw et al. (2000) found that task interdependence and preference for group work activities were positively associated with satisfaction and performance. Also at the individual level, Van der Vegt et al. (2000) reported a positive relationship between task interdependence and individual job satisfaction and commitment.

In general, research has linked task interdependence with a variety of positive affective outcomes (Kiggundu, 1983). Other investigations, however, have shown task interdependence to lead to adverse consequences (Brass, 1985). For example, research suggests that task interdependence may hamper performance by providing inaccurate information, increasing distrust of other members of the group, and interrupting the flow of resources (Van Der Vegt et al., 2000). Steiner (1972) refers to these impediments as "process losses." Further, task interdependence has the capacity to provide individuals the power that may be used to exploit or frustrate others (Earley & Northcraft, 1989). Research suggests that employees have the opportunity to withhold resources as work group members become more interdependent (Raven, 1992). In sum, it may be premature to assume that task interdependence is always coupled with positive outcomes.

The Interactive Effects of Task Interdependence and Politics Perceptions

Substantial research has sought to examine the conditions under which politics perceptions lead to negative reactions (Ferris et al., 1989, 2002). What is absent in the literature, however, is an assessment of whether task interdependence has a significant effect on this relationship. To address this gap in the current literature, we will test an interactive model of task interdependence-politics perceptions. In doing so, we are assuming that the level of task interdependence will influence reactions that individuals have to politics perceptions.

On the one hand, it may be plausible that task interdependence may be viewed as a factor able to ameliorate the negative consequences of politics. Indeed, Maslyn and Fedor (1998) suggested that individuals might be able to insulate themselves from the harmful effects of politics by actions initiated by their immediate work group (i.e., high task interdependence). Hence, it may on the surface appear that individuals may come together as a group to neutralize workplace politics.

Nonetheless, it is our contention that task interdependence will promote negative consequences. Task interdependence refers to the manner in which group members exchange resources for the purpose of completing an assigned task (Brass, 1985). It is posited that individuals occupying political environments will manipulate resources and relationships differently than those occupying nonpolitical settings. Past research has described political behaviors as the promotion of self-interests (Kacmar & Baron, 1999; Porter, Allen, & Angle, 1981), at the expense of organizational goals (Ferris et al., 1989). Further, research has shown political behavior to be directed toward important decision makers (Cropanzano et al., 1997) using tactics perceived by most as disreputable (Mintzberg, 1983).

In groups with high interdependence, the activities of one individual have a significant bearing on others. Hence, if an individual is acting with only self-interests in mind and at the expense of what is best for the larger organization (as well as his or her immediate group members), conflict is likely to increase. In this regard, individuals are likely to withhold resources from one other to ensure that they are viewed in a positive light. In addition, resentment is likely to surface if individuals are sacrificing the good of the work group for personal gain. Further, if is it perceived that individuals are directing self-interested work activities (i.e., ingratiation, sucking up, brownnosing, etc.) toward important decision makers instead of focusing on the activities of the immediate work group, negative reactions should develop. Finally, disreputable tactics are likely to be viewed more negatively in environments where there are close and frequent interactions among group members. In sum, task interdependence is expected to lead to positive outcomes when it stimulates the expansion of cooperative behaviors among group members. However, since political environments are described as conflict-laden in which competition for scare resources is intense, it is unlikely that positive attributes will materialize in settings requiring high levels of interdependence.

The Current Study

In the current study, we contend that politics perceptions and task interdependence will interact to predict three job outcomes: job satisfaction, intent to leave, and life satisfaction. Job satisfaction and intent to turnover represent two of the most frequently examined consequences of politics perceptions (Cropanzano et al., 1997; Hochwarter et al., 1999; Kacmar & Baron, 1999). Conversely, the link between politics perceptions and life satisfaction has yet to be delineated in previous work. By not doing so, researchers may have failed to capture to totality of the work experience. For example, previous research has shown life satisfaction to relate to work-related factors such as organizational commitment and job satisfaction (Tepper, 2000). In addition, life satisfaction has been affected by the characteristics inherent in the task and the overall work itself (Judge & Watanabe, 1993; King & Hautaluoma, 1987). As research continues to examine the boundary between one's work and nonwork life, included variables that occupy both of these domains appears to be warranted.

In addition, we see the potential for variables to affect the relationship between independent and dependent variables, and hence, were controlled for in the current research. Specifically, demographic variable such as age, gender, and tenure have been shown to predict the dependent variables used in the current study (Kacmar & Ferris, 1989). In addition, previous research has described negative affect (NA) and positive affect (PA) as the dispositional underpinnings of job satisfaction (Staw, Bell, & Clausen, 1986), as well as correlating with turnover intent (Cropanzano, James, & Konovsky, 1993), and life satisfaction (Iverson & Maguire, 2000). Moreover, previous research has found it useful to control for leader-member exchange (LMX) when predicting work outcomes (Maslyn & Fedor, 1998). Finally, to obtain the greatest appreciation of the relationship between our independent variables and life satisfaction, we controlled for the percentage of time individuals considered themselves happy (Fordyce, 1997).

METHOD

Participants

We administered surveys to 221 law enforcement officials who were participating in training activities at work. Individuals were given time at the end of the training session to complete the survey. Participation was voluntary and anonymity was guaranteed to all. All 211 participants elected to complete the survey. The sample consisted of primarily males ($n = 192$, 87%), while the average age of respondents was approximately 42 years ($SD = 8.31$). Respondents averaged roughly 4 years of position tenure ($SD = 5.07$). Individuals were asked to report the number of individuals that represented their immediate work group. On average, individuals reported working closely with five individuals ($M = 4.92$, $SD = 5.17$), indicating an sufficient level of task interdependence.

Measures

Task Interdependence

The reciprocal interdependence subscale of Pearce and Gregersen's (1991) scale was used to measure task interdependence. The 5-item scale had "I must frequently coordinate my work efforts with others" and "The way that I perform my job has a significant impact on others" as representative items. A 7-point format was used (1 = *strongly disagree* to 7 = *strongly agree*).

Politics Perceptions

Kacmar and Carlson's (1997) measure was used to tap politics perceptions. The 15-item scale had "It is safer to think what you are told than to make up your own mind" and "Agreeing with powerful others is the best alternative in this organization" as representative scale items. A 7-point format was used (1 = *strongly disagree* to 7 = *strongly agree*).

Positive and Negative Affect

Affective disposition was measured using the 20-item Positive and Negative Affect Scale (PANAS; Watson, Clark, & Tellegen, 1988). Participants responded to words such as *distressed, jittery,* and *nervous* for NA and *interested, enthusiastic,* and *attentive* for PA. Possible responses ranged from *very slightly or not at all* (1) to *extremely* (5).

Leader-Member Exchange (LMX)

Five items from Graen and Cashman's (1975) scale were used to measure LMX (Dunegan, Duchon, & Uhl-Bien, 1992). "My supervisor recognizes my potential," and "I can count on my supervisor for help when I need it" are two representative items. Responses were scored using a 5-point response format (1 = *strongly disagree* to 5 = *strongly agree*).

Life Happiness

Respondents were asked to indicate the amount of time they are happy using a 0 – 100% scale (Fordyce, 1977; Judge & Locke, 1993).

Job Satisfaction

Job satisfaction was measured using a 5-item subscale of Brayfield and Rothe's (1951) index (Judge, Locke, Durham, & Kluger, 1998). "Each day of work seems like it will never end" (reversed coded), and "Most days I am enthusiastic about my work" are characteristic items that were measured with a 7-point format (1 = *strongly disagree* to 7 = *strongly agree*).

Life Satisfaction

Life satisfaction was measured using a 5-item scale (Diener, Emmons, Larsen, & Griffith, 1985). "I am satisfied with my life in general" and "In most ways my life is close to ideal" are two scale items. A 7-point scoring format was used (1 = *strongly disagree* to 7 = *strongly agree*).

Turnover Intent

Intent to turnover was measured using three items from a scale developed by Camman, Fichman, Jenkins, and Klesh (1979). Items included "I often think about quitting," and "I will probably look for a different job in the next year." A 7-point scoring format was used (1 = *strongly disagree* to 7 = *strongly agree*).

Data Analysis

Moderated multiple regression (MMR) analysis was used to test for the three two-way interactions (Cohen & Cohen, 1983). In the first step, age, gender, and position tenure were entered. For job satisfaction and intent to turnover, NA, PA, LMX, politics perceptions, and task interdependence were entered in the second step. For life satisfaction, NA, PA, percentage of time happy, politics perceptions, and task interdependence were entered in step two. For all dependent variables, the politics perceptions-task interdependence interaction term was entered in the third step. MMR analysis tests for the significance of the increment in criterion variance explained by the interaction term beyond that explained by the main effect constructs.

RESULTS

Assessment of Construct Adequacy

Because the self-report survey contained measures of both independent and dependent variables, we conducted a Harmon single-factor test (Podsakoff & Organ, 1986) to determine construct uniqueness and to assess the effects of common method variance. All independent and dependent variables were included in the analysis. A single factor failed to emerge when using an eigenvalue of 1.0 as a minimum criterion. Also, the strongest factor explained a modest level of criterion variance (i.e., 17%) suggesting construct distinctiveness. Finally, reliability estimates for all variables were adequate (e.g., ≥ .70).

Correlations and Reliability Estimates

Table 12.1 reports descriptive statistics for study variables. Dependent variables were only modestly correlated (*r*'s ranging from .28 to -.44). In general, relationships reported in Table 12.1 are consistent with respect to both direction and magnitude with results provided in previous research (Kacmar & Baron, 1999; Cropanzano et al., 1997).

Table 12.1. Means, Standard Deviations, Reliability Estimates, and Intercorrelations Among Study Variables

Variable	M	SD	1	2	3	4	5	6	7	8	9	10	11	12
1. Age	41.91	8.31	NA											
2. Gender[1]	1.13	.30	-.17	NA										
3. Position tenure	4.10	5.07	.40	-.02	NA									
4. Negative affect	1.67	.48	-.19	.01	-.06	(.77)								
5. Positive affect	3.72	.59	-.09	.03	-.17	-.19	(.89)							
6. LMX	3.83	.80	.12	-.05	-.08	-.21	.23	(.82)						
7. % of time happy	77.22	16.17	-.05	.13	-.08	-.38	.33	.32	NA					
8. Politics perceptions	4.03	.99	.15	.01	.19	.11	-.28	-.41	-.22	(.82)				
9. Task interdependence	4.01	.46	.05	-.03	-.09	.17	.18	-.06	-.10	.12	(.70)			
10. Job satisfaction	5.60	.84	-.18	-.09	-.13	-.19	.54	.35	.35	-.33	.05	(.73)		
11. Turnover intent	1.91	1.17	.02	.11	.01	.27	-.31	-.28	-.11	.30	-.06	-.44	(.84)	
12. Life satisfaction	5.14	.96	-.04	.02	.09	-.29	.27	.23	.36	-.10	-.03	.28	-.22	(.86)

$N = 221$
$r > .12, p < .05$
[1] Gender was coded "1" for male and "2" for female
Coefficient alphas on the diagonal

Regression Analyses

Table 12.2 shows the results of our hierarchical regression analyses. As shown, age, PA, and LMX predicted satisfaction. The politics perceptions-task interdependence interaction explained incremental variance in job satisfaction scores ($b = -.23$, $\Delta R^2 = .02$, $p < .05$). Further, gender, NA, PA, politics perceptions, and task interdependence predicted intent to turnover. In the third step, the politics perceptions-task interdependence interaction term explained additional variance ($b = .31$, $\Delta R^2 = .02$, $p < .05$). Finally, position tenure, NA, PA, and percentage of time happy predicted life satisfaction. The interaction term entered in the third step was significant and explained incremental variance ($b = -.44$, $\Delta R^2 = .04$, $p < .01$). These results support our contention that task interdependence moderates the relationship between politics perceptions and work outcomes.

Following past research (Stone & Hollenbeck, 1989), three levels of task interdependence scores were plotted: At one standard deviation above the mean, at the mean, and at one standard deviation below the mean. Results for the dependent variables are shown in Figures 12.1, 12.2, and 12.3. Consistent with our proposed associations, politics had

Table 12.2. Results of Hierarchical Regression Analyses Predicting Job Satisfaction, Turnover Intent, and Life Satisfaction

Variable	Job Satisfaction		Turnover Intent		Life Satisfaction	
	b	ΔR^2	b	ΔR^2	b	ΔR^2
Step 1:						
Age	−.02*		.01		−.01	
Gender	−.31		.39*		.02	
Position tenure	.01	.05	−.01	.01	.02*	.02
Step 2:						
Negative affect	−.14		.61**		−.40*	
Positive affect	.67**		−.36*		.27*	
LMX	.24**		−.17			
Happy					.02**	
Politics perceptions (A)	−.09		−.27**		.01	
Task interdependence (B)	.03	.38**	−.30*	.24**	.08	.21**
Step 3:						
A x B	−.23*	.02*	.31*	.02*	−.44**	.04**

$N = 221$
* $p < .05$
** $p < .01$

the most deleterious impact on outcomes when task interdependence was perceived as high. Surprisingly, job satisfaction and life satisfaction increased as politics increased when task interdependence was perceived as low.

DISCUSSION

As team-based work structures have become commonplace in organizations, the need to better understand affective reactions to group processes has become more important (Guzzo & Shea, 1992). The current study was designed to increase our understanding of group processes by examining the interactive effects of task interdependence and politics perceptions on work outcomes. Results strongly supported our contention that politics perceptions lead to deleterious outcomes when individuals reported high levels of task interdependence. Critical to the successful completion of work-related activities is the sharing of materials, information, expertise, and other resources (Cummings, 1978). Since definitions of organizational politics often focus on the manipulation of resources for personal gain (Burns, 1961; Frost & Hayes, 1977; Pfeffer, 1981), it is apparent that close interactions with coworkers have the potential to increase self-serving behaviors that are designed to protect or secure the interests of the actor.

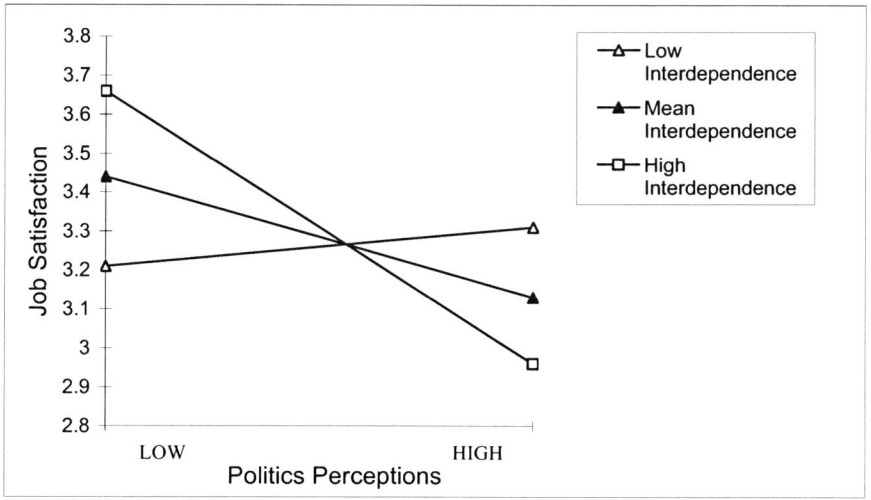

Figure 12.1. Interactive effects of politics perceptions and task interdependence on job satisfaction. Formula to plot (.84 + (−.23f) x P) + (.97f − .27).

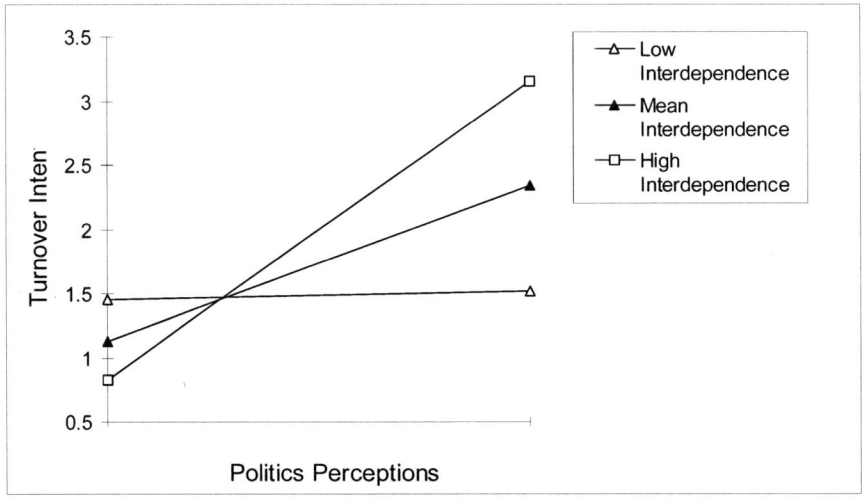

Figure 12.2. Interactive effects of politics perceptions and task interdependence on turnover intent. Formula to plot $(1.51 + (.23f) \times P) + (.95f - .3.31)$

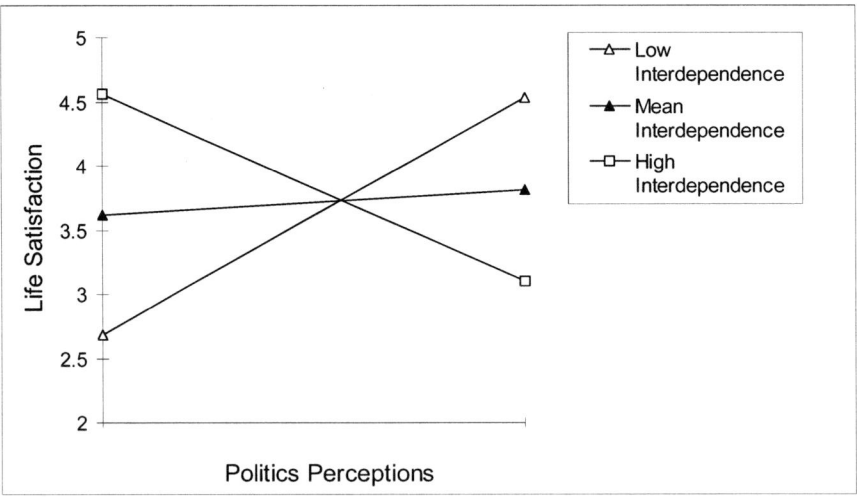

Figure 12.3. Interactive effects of politics perceptions and task interdependence on life satisfaction. Formula to Plot $(1.81 + (-.44f) \times P) + (1.89f - 4.04)$.

In addition to confirming the negative consequences of politics perceptions for high interdependence groups, results shown in Figures 12.1 and 12.3 indicate that job and life satisfaction *increased* concomitantly with politics for those reporting low levels of task interdependence. These findings call into question the conclusion that increases in politics perceptions are always coupled with a proliferation of negative consequences. What might explain these contradictory results? Previous work has suggested that some individuals may *prefer* working in a political environment (Hochwarter, 2003; Pfeffer, 1981) and that this environment can be used to obtain a strategic advantage. When there is low interdependence among employees, perhaps much of the competition for desired rewards is eliminated.

Study Strengths and Limitations

The current study has several strengths that need to be noted. First, the sample consisted of a homogeneous group (i.e., police officers), which allows for a greater depth of understanding. In addition, the sample was comprised of individuals that were a part of a naturally occurring work group with a nondefined level of task interdependence. Finally, we were able to control for factors previously substantiated to explain variance in job satisfaction, turnover intent, and life satisfaction scores.

The study contains limitations that require discussion. First and foremost, the data collection was cross-sectional and relied exclusively on information gather from a single source. This research strategy immediately suggests the potential influence of common method bias. We are confident that the effect of common method bias is nominal for two reasons. First, correlations of study variables reported in Table 12.1 are not of the magnitude to suggest construct redundancy. Second, we undertook additional tests (i.e., a Harmon one-factor test) to assess the potential influence of common method bias. Although it is impossible to completely eliminate the possibility of common method variance, it does not appear that it is unduly problematic in the current study. Further, a strength of the study may be also considered a weakness. Specifically, the dependence on practicing patrol officers as the single source of data calls into question the external generalizability of our findings.

Avenues for Future Research

Given the limitations noted above, research will need to examine the relationships reported here in a wider array of environments using a data collection strategy that relies on multiple sources. In addition, future studies should expand the operationalization to include other outcome variables. Although it was important to include affective responses in the current study (Duffy, Shaw, & Stark, 2000), incorporating performance-related outcomes represents a logical extension of the current research (Jehn, Northcraft, & Neale, 1999).

Although we suggested that politics and interdependence affect work and nonwork outcomes by increasing conflict, this intermediate linkage was not explicitly examined. Previous research indicates that conflict may possess an important association with task interdependence and work outcomes (Duffy et al., 2000; Jehn et al., 1999). Employing qualitative methods to assess the underlying relationship between politics, interdependence, conflict, and work outcomes appears warranted.

Finally, it may be fruit to examine group level predictors and outcomes. For example, the current study included factors examined at the organization-level (e.g., politics perceptions), at the group-level (e.g., task interdependence), and at the individual level (job satisfaction, intent to leave, and life satisfaction). Assessing the impact of group-level politics (Maslyn & Fedor, 1999) and task interdependence on group level performance and satisfaction (Van der Vegt, Emans, & Van de Vliert, 2001) may potentially be informative.

Conclusion

Saavedra, Earley, and Van Dyne (1993) suggested that "work groups can exercise some choice in how they plan, coordinate, and execute, goals and feedback may predispose group members to work collectively or independently on the group's tasks" (p. 61). Results from this investigation suggest that individual may be predisposed to act independently when they are situated in an environment fraught with politics. From a practical perspective, managers may find it useful to incorporate workplace politics interventions with traditional organizational development activities. Since both team-based structures and workplace politics are likely to be in existence for some time, developing programs aimed at increasing the efficacy of social interactions at work may enhance organizational effectiveness.

AUTHOR'S NOTE

Address correspondence to Dr. Wayne Hochwarter, College of Business, Tallahassee, FL 32306-1110, (850) 644-7849 (Office), (850) 644-7843 (Fax), whochwar@cob.fsu.edu

REFERENCES

Anderson, S. E., & Williams, L. J. (1996). Interpersonal, job, and individual factors related to helping processes at work. *Journal of Applied Psychology, 81,* 282-296.

Bozeman, D. P., Perrewé, P. L., Hochwarter, W. A., & Brymer, R. A. (2001). Organizational politics, perceived control, and work outcomes: Boundary conditions on the effects of politics. *Journal of Applied Social Psychology, 31,* 486-503.

Brass, D. (1985). Technology and the structuring of jobs: Employee satisfaction, performance and influence. *Organizational Behavior and Human Decision Processes, 35,* 216-240.

Brayfield, A., & Rothe, F. (1951). An index of job satisfaction. *Journal of Applied Psychology, 35,* 307-311.

Burns, T. (1961). Micropolitics: Mechanisms of institutional change. *Administrative Science Quarterly, 6,* 257-281.

Cammann, C., Fichman, M., Jenkins, D., & Klesh, J. (1979). *Michigan organizational assessment questionnaire.* Unpublished manuscript.

Campion, M. A., Medsker, G. A., & Higgs, C. A. (1993). Relations between work group characteristics and effectiveness: Implications for designing effective work groups. *Personnel Psychology, 46,* 823-850.

Campion, M. A., Papper, E. M., & Medsker, G. J. (1996). Relations between work team characteristics and effectiveness: A replication and extension. *Personnel Psychology, 49,* 429-452.

Christiansen, N., Villanova, P., & Mikulay, S. (1997). Political influence compatibility: Fitting the person to the climate. *Journal of Organizational Behavior, 18,* 709-730.

Cohen, J., & Cohen, P. (1983). *Applied multiple regression/correlation analysis for the behavioral sciences* (2nd ed.). Hillsdale, NJ: Erlbaum.

Cropanzano, R., Howes, J. C., Grandey, A. A., & Toth, P. (1997). The relationship of organizational politics and support to work behaviors, attitudes, and stress. *Journal of Organizational Behavior, 18,* 159-180.

Cropanzano, R., James, K., & Konovsky, M. (1993). Dispositional affectivity as a predictor of work attitudes and job performance. *Journal of Organizational Behavior, 14,* 595-606.

Cummings, T. (1978). Self-regulating work groups: A socio-technical analysis. *Academy of Management Review, 3,* 625-634.

DeMatteo, J. S., Eby, L. T., & Sundstrom, E. (1998). Team-based rewards: Current empirical evidence and directions for future research. *Research in Organizational Behavior, 20,* 141-183.

Diener, E., Emmons, R., Larsen, R., & Griffin, S. (1985). The satisfaction with life scale. *Journal of Personality Assessment, 49,* 71-75.

Duffy, M., Shaw, J., & Stark, E. (2000). Performance and satisfaction in conflicted interdependent groups: When and how does self-esteem make a difference. *Academy of Management Journal, 4,* 772-782.

Dunegan, K., Duchon, D., & Uhl-Bien, M. (1992). Examining the link between leader-member exchange and subordinate performance: The role of task analyzability and variety as moderators. *Journal of Management, 18,* 59-76.

Earley, P., & Northcraft, G. (1989). Goal setting, resource interdependence, and conflict. In M. Rahim (Ed.), *Managing conflict: An interdisciplinary approach* (pp. 161-170). New York: Praeger.

Ferris, G. R., & Kacmar, K. M. (1992). Perceptions of organizational politics. *Journal of Management, 18*, 93-116.

Ferris, G. R., Adams, G. L., Kolodinsky, R. W., Hochwarter, W. A., & Ammeter, A. P. (2002). Perceptions of organizational politics: Theory and research directions. In F. Dansereau & F. J. Yammarino (Eds.), *Research in multi-level issues: The many faces of multi-level issues* (Vol. 1, pp. 179-254). Oxford, England: JAI Press.

Ferris, G. R., Brand, J. F., Brand, S., Rowland, K. M., Gilmore, D. C., King, T. R., et al. (1993). Politics and control in organizations. In E. J. Lawler, B. Markovsky, J. O'Brien, & K. Heimer (Eds.), *Advances in group processes* (Vol. 10, pp. 83-111). Greenwich, CT: JAI Press.

Ferris, G. R., Frink, D. D., Galang, M. C., Zhou, J., Kacmar, K. M., & Howard, J. L. (1996). Perceptions of organizational politics: Predictors, stress-related implications, and outcomes. *Human Relations, 49*, 233-266.

Ferris, G. R., Frink, D. D., Gilmore, D. C., & Kacmar, K. M. (1994). Understanding as an antidote for the dysfunctional consequences of organizational politics as a stressor. *Journal of Applied Social Psychology, 24*, 1204-1220.

Ferris, G. R., Russ, G. S., & Fandt, P. M. (1989). Politics in organizations. In R. A. Giacalone & P. Rosenfeld (Eds.), *Impression management in the organization* (pp. 143-170). Hillsdale, NJ: Erlbaum.

Fordyce, M. (1997). Development of a program to increase personal happiness. *Journal of Counseling Psychology, 24*, 511-521.

Frost, P. J., & Hayes, D. C. (1977). *An exploration in two cultures of political behavior in organizations.* Paper presented at the conference on Cross-Cultural Studies of Organizational Functioning, University of Hawaii, Honolulu.

Gandz, J., & Murray, V. (1980). The experience of workplace politics. *Academy of Management Journal, 23*, 237-251.

Gilmore, D. C., Ferris, G. R., Dulebohn, J. H., & Harrell-Cook, G. (1996). Organizational politics and employee attendance. *Group and Organization Management, 21*, 481-494.

Graen, G., & Cashman, J. (1975). A role-making model of leadership in formal organizations: A developmental approach. In J. Hunt & L. Larson (Eds.), *Leadership frontiers* (pp. 143-165). Kent, OH: Kent State University Press.

Guzzo, R., & Shea, G. (1992). Group performance and intergroup relations in organizations. In M. Dunnette & L. Hough (Eds.), *Handbook of industrial and organizational psychology* (pp. 269-313). Palo Alto, CA: Consulting Psychologist Press.

Hart, P. (1999). Predicting employee life satisfaction: A coherent model of personality, work and nonwork experiences, and domain satisfactions. *Journal of Applied Psychology, 84*, 564-584.

Hochwarter, W. (2003). The interactive effects of pro-political behavior and politics perceptions on job satisfaction and affective commitment. *Journal of Applied Social Psychology, 33*, 1360-1378.

Hochwarter, W. A., Perrewé, P. L., Ferris, G. R., & Guercio, R. (1999). Commitment as an antidote to the tension and turnover consequences of organizational politics. *Journal of Vocational Behavior, 55,* 277-297.

Iverson, R., & Maguire, C. (2000). The relationship between job and life satisfaction: Evidence from a remote mining community. *Human Relations, 53,* 807-839.

Jehn, K., Northcraft, G., & Neale, M. (1999). Why differences make a difference: A field study of diversity, conflict, and performance in workgroups. *Administrative Science Quarterly, 44,* 741-763.

Johnson, D. W. & Johnson, R. T. (1989). *Cooperation and competition: Theory and research.* Edina, MN: Interaction Book Co.

Judge, T., & Locke, E. (1993). Effect of dysfunctional thought processes on subjective well-being and job satisfaction. *Journal of Applied Psychology, 78,* 475-490.

Judge, T., & Watanabe, S. (1993). Another look at the job satisfaction-life satisfaction relationship. *Journal of Applied Psychology, 78,* 939-948.

Judge, T., Locke, E., Durham, C., & Kluger, A. (1998). Dispositional effects on job and life satisfaction: The role of core evaluations. *Journal of Applied Psychology, 83,* 17-34.

Kacmar, K. M., & Baron, R. A. (1999). Organizational politics: The state of the field, links to related processes, and an agenda for future research. In G. R. Ferris (Ed.), *Research in personnel and human resources management* (Vol. 17, pp. 1-39). Stamford, CT: JAI Press.

Kacmar, K. M., & Carlson, D. S. (1997). Further validation of the Perceptions of Politics Scale (POPS): A multi-sample approach. *Journal of Management, 23,* 627-658.

Kacmar, K. M., & Ferris, G. R. (1989). Theoretical and methodological considerations in the age-job satisfaction relationship. *Journal of Applied Psychology, 74,* 201-207..

Kidwell, R. E., Jr., & Bennett, N. (1993). Employee propensity to withhold effort: A conceptual model to intersect three avenues of research. *Academy of Management Journal, 18,* 429-456.

Kiggundu, M. (1983). Task interdependence and task design: Test of a theory. *Organizational Behavior and Human Performance, 31,* 145-172.

King, W., & Hautaluoma, J. (1987). Comparison of job satisfaction, life satisfaction, and performance of overeducated and other workers. *Journal of Social Psychology, 127,* 421-433.

Lewin, K. (1936). *Principles of topological psychology.* New York: McGraw-Hill.

Maslyn, J., & Fedor, D. B. (1998). Perceptions of politics: Does measuring different foci matter? *Journal of Applied Psychology, 84,* 645-653.

Miller, L., & Hamblin, R. L. (1963). Interdependence, differential rewarding, and productivity. *American Sociological Review, 28,* 768-778.

Mintzberg, H. (1983). *Power in and around organizations.* Englewood Cliffs, NJ: Prentice-Hall.

Mitchell, T. R., & Silver, W. S. (1990). Individual and group goals when workers are interdependent: Effects on task strategies and performance. *Journal of Applied Psychology, 75,* 185-193.

Pearce, J. L., & Gregerson, H. B. (1991). Task interdependence and extra-role behavior: A test of the mediating effects of felt responsibility. *Journal of Applied Psychology, 76,* 838-844.
Pfeffer, J. (1981). Management as symbolic action: The creation and maintenance of organizational paradigms. In L. L. Cummings & B. M. Staw (Eds.), *Research in organizational behavior* (Vol. 3, pp. 1-52). Greenwich, CT: JAI Press.
Podsakoff, P., & Organ, D. (1986). Self-reports in organizational research: Problems and prospects. *Journal of Management, 12,* 531-544.
Porter, L. W., Allen, R. W., & Angle, H. L. (1981). The politics of upward influence in organizations. In L. L. Cummings & B. M. Staw (Eds.), *Research in organizational behavior* (Vol. 3, pp. 109-149). Greenwich, CT: JAI Press.
Raven, B. (1992). A power/interaction model of interpersonal influence: French and Raven thirty years later. *Journal of Social Behavior and Personality, 7,* 217-244.
Rosenbaum, M. E., Moore, D. I., Cotton, J. L., Cook, M. S., Hieser, R. S., Shovar, M. N., et al. (1980). Group productivity and process: Pure and mixed reward structures and task interdependence. *Journal of Personality & Social Psychology, 39,* 626-642.
Saavedra, R., Earley, P., & Van Dyne, L. (1993). Complex interdependence in task-performing groups. *Journal of Applied Psychology, 78,* 61-72.
Shaw, J. D., Duffy, M. K., & Stark, E. M. (2000). Interdependence and preference for group work: Main and congruence effects on the satisfaction and performance of group members. *Journal of Management, 26,* 259-279.
Staw, B., Bell, N., & Clausen, J. (1986). The dispositional approach to job attitudes: A lifetime longitudinal test. *Administrative Sciences Quarterly, 31,* 56-77.
Steiner, I. (1972). *Group processes and productivity.* New York: Academic Press.
Stone, E., & Hollenebck, J. (1989). Clarifying some controversial issues surrounding statistical procedures of detecting moderator variables: Empirical evidence and related matter. *Journal of Applied Psychology, 74,* 3-10.
Sumer, H., & Knight, P. (2001). How do people with different attachment styles balance work and family? A personality perspective on work-family linkage. *Journal of Applied Psychology, 86,* 653-663.
Tepper, B. (2000). Consequences of abusive supervision. *Academy of Management Journal, 43,* 178-190.
Thompson, J. D. (1967). *Organizations in Action.* New York: McGraw-Hill.
Van der Vegt, G., Emans, B., & Van de Vliert, E. (2001). Patterns of interdependence in work teams: A two-level investigation of the relations with job and team satisfaction. *Personnel Psychology, 54,* 51-69.
Van der Vegt, G., Emans, B., & Van de Vliert, E. (2000). Team members' affective responses to patterns of intragroup interdependence and job complexity. *Journal of Management, 26,* 633-655.
Van de Ven, A. H., & Ferry, D. L. (1980). *Measuring and assessing organizations.* New York: Wiley.
Wageman, R. (1995). Interdependence and group effectiveness. *Administrative Science Quarterly, 40,* 145-180.

Wageman, R., & Baker, G. (1997). Incentives and cooperation: The joint effects of task and reward interdependence on group performance. *Journal of Organizational Behavior, 18,* 139-158.

Watson, D., Clark, L., & Tellegen, A. (1998). Development and validation of brief measures of positive and negative affect: The PANAS scale. *Journal of Personality and Social Psychology, 54,* 1063-1070.

Witt, L. A. (1998). Enhancing organizational goal congruence: A solution to organizational politics. *Journal of Applied Psychology, 83,* 666-674.

CHAPTER 13

ORGANIZATIONAL CITIZENSHIP BEHAVIORS

Concept Redefinition, Inclusion, and Reconceptualization

Jason Harkins, Jonathon R. B. Halbesleben,
Danielle S. Beu, and M. Ronald Buckley

The literature concerning organizational citizenship behaviors (OCBs) has traditionally relied upon a broad definition which is the extant definition from the original conception of OCBs. In order to refocus the construct of OCBs, we explicate the need for inclusion of workplace deviance behaviors (WDBs) within the fold of behaviors that individuals perform within organizations toward some end. Specifically, we believe that WDBs are another type of behavior that employees embrace to align their perceptions of inequity within the firm, in the same manner as OCBs. Through application of equity theory, we argue that individuals are motivated to undertake OCBs/WDBs for other than their currently extended motivations. Moreover, we argue that the appropriate conceptualization of OCBs/WDBs falls in line with previous conceptualizations of political/support behavior in organizations. We discuss the manner in which this reconceptualization creates a new focus for OCB research, and suggest ways in which further work within the nomological network will lead to greater incremental contributions of the OCB literature in our understanding of organizational behavior broadly.

Across myriad research topics in the social sciences, conflicting empirical reports suggest that knowledge bases rest on shaky ground (Hubbard, Vetter, & Little, 1998). Many examples of the difficulty with building a body of research can be identified. One is the concept of "brand loyalty" in Marketing, which "as a construct has little to no functional utility in the context of model or theory" (Tarpey, 1974). Another is "leadership" in management that is "in ferment at the present time, probably because there are so few dominant positions" (Miner, 2003). This failure stems not from a lack of measurement or attempted measurement, but from insufficient construct development and construct measurement lacking parsimony. The definitional/construct development issues faced by these areas create difficulties for researchers trying to test propositions, and the imprecise construct measurement depreciates the value of studies done because of an inability to replicate studies and build a common body of knowledge. These areas and others like them require more efficient construct space definition and more precise measures in order to develop as a legitimate area of inquiry. The organizational citizenship behavior (OCB) construct is one that could benefit from further construct development. In fact, Bolino, Turnley, and Niehoff (2004) have made some cogent suggestions concerning the refinement of this construct.

OCBs have been an issue of increasing interest since Organ first defined the concept as "individual behavior that is discretionary, not directly or explicitly recognized by the formal reward system, and that in the aggregate promotes the effective functioning of the organization" (Organ, 1988, p. 4). This definition, still the most widely used in the OCB research, is very broad with a number of definitional drawbacks (Organ, 1997). The research on OCBs has considered citizenship behaviors from a variety of perspectives, therein creating a number of competing taxonomies which seek to explain what is known about individuals undertaking this form of organizational activity.

Deviance behaviors within organizations have become an area of active scholarly research of late. Workplace deviance behaviors (WDB) research really developed with Robinson and Bennett's (1995) definition "behavior [of organizational members] that violates significant organizational norms and in doing so threatens the well-being of an organization, its members, or both" (p. 556). The development of this construct has paralleled the development of OCBs in many ways (i.e., similar: survey questions, antecedents, motivations, etc.) which has created some doubt as to whether or not the separation of the constructs is because they are distinct in their theoretical underpinnings or because of the items used in measurement. We will argue that the separation is artificial and that WDBs and OCBs are two extremes of a continuum.

Equity theory (Homans, 1961) provides a theoretical base for explaining OCBs and WDBs within the workplace. Equity theory argues that people are concerned with both the inputs and outputs of themselves and referent others (both within and outside their organization) (Adams, 1963). We will argue that this balancing of inputs and outputs creates situations where individuals create balance in their minds through the initiation of OCBs or WDBs according to whether their inequity is positive or negative.

Two particularly interesting findings on OCBs have come out of the literature: (1) some researchers suggest that managers who wish to encourage OCBs at work should reward employees for undertaking OCBs (Schnake & Dumler, 1997) and (2) the available empirical evidence suggests that managers are influenced by OCBs when completing performance ratings and making other related decisions (Podsakoff, MacKenzie, Paine, & Bachrach, 2000). These findings create a situation whereby one may question the motivation underlying OCBs (Bolino, 1999). By reexamining the literature on OCBs and considering some political behavior literature, we argue that OCBs are not always "selfless" acts, but may actually fit in the scope of political behaviors.

We begin the article by reviewing the relevant literature on OCBs, looking at the definitions, taxonomies, and conceptualizations. We then indicate the definitional concerns faced within the OCB literature as it currently is used. At this time we also call for a more concise and encompassing taxonomy to reduce the differences between current taxonomies. The definitional issues raised also call for a new definition of OCBs and one is offered which is more in line with the original conception. Once a new definition of OCBs has been established, we indicate a need for consideration and acknowledgement of WDBs in OCB research. By pointing out the slight conceptual differences between OCBs and WDBs we argue for a combination of the WDB and OCB constructs into one construct, political behavior, containing both extremes. Negative OCBs (e.g., OCBs intended to manage impressions rather than from an altruistic motive; cf. Bolino, 1999) have not yet been well-integrated within OCB research. We then introduce equity theory as a means of exploring the motivation behind many behaviors currently classified as OCBs (WDBs). After offering a definition of political/support behaviors, the lack of a need for politics to be perceived as negative actions is explained and examples are given. Finally, we offer some suggestions for future research in the field of OCBs and WDBs.

REVIEW OF OCB DEFINITIONS, TAXONOMIES, AND CONCEPTUALIZATIONS

The OCB construct has grown considerably since its initial conceptualization, yet the vast majority of studies done in the area rely upon Organ's (1988) original definition. In addition to defining OCBs, Organ (1988) also created a taxonomy of different behaviors to specify behaviors which were included as OCBs. The taxonomy categorized OCBs into five dimensions: **altruism,** which is helping behavior aimed at another person (such as helping a sick coworker out), **sportsmanship,** which is a negative action that an individual refrains from performing (such as complaining about little things), **courtesy,** which is keeping others informed about what is going on (such as informing subordinates of upcoming changes), **civic virtue,** which is participation in the political life of the organization (such as attending meetings and keeping informed about organizational decisions), and **conscientiousness,** which is helping behavior aimed at the organization (such as doing more work than is required for the job).

Although most of the studies use Organ's (1988) definition of OCB, other definitions, taxonomies, and conceptualizations exist. These definitions all have their roots in Organ's original definition, but the changes create many subtle and not so subtle differences. Table 13.1 contains a listing of the varied definitions encountered in the literature. The definitions listed in Table 13.1 only refer to overall definitions of the overarching OCB and WDB constructs, not to any of the various subareas from which a great variety of taxonomies have been developed.

The definitions provided in Table 13.1 vary greatly in their specificity regarding what OCBs and WDBs are and how to distinguish behavior of employees at work that are OCBs and WDBs from those that are not. For OCBs, the argument could be made that all of these definitions serve to bound the construct; they are not used in conjunction with each other in academic papers. If each author creates his/her own boundaries, which vary from Organ's (1988) "A readiness to contribute beyond literal contractual obligations" to Moorman and Hartland's (2002) "behaviors that help units work more efficiently and effectively" to Zellars, Bennett, and Duffy (2002) "omission of OCBs is not punishable," then what exactly an OCB is becomes difficult to establish. Articles which attempt to conduct empirical work on the OCB construct encounter substantial difficulties in light of the fact that there is not agreement among current authors in the area regarding what OCBs are. As such, we argue that Table 13.1 indicates that, OCB is a concept in a state of "construct ambiguity."

Researchers present a number of OCB taxonomies, which are different from Organ's (1988) original taxonomy. However, the taxonomies tend to exhibit a large degree of overlap with the definitions of the original five-

Table 13.1. Definitions of Organizational Citizenship Behavior/Workplace Deviance Behavior

OCBs represents individual behavior that is discretionary, not directly or explicitly recognized by the formal reward system, and that in the aggregate promotes the effective functioning of the organization. (Organ, 1988, p. 4)	Voluntary behavior [of organizational members] that violates significant organizational norms and in doing so threatens the well-being of an organization, its members, or both (Robinson & Bennett, 1995, p. 556)
In an organizational context behaviors are deliberative and reflective rather than spontaneous and are, therefore, governed by fairness consideration (Organ, 1988; Organ & Konovosky, 1989)	Any intentional action by members of organizations that violates core organizational and/or societal norms (Vardi & Wiener, 1996)
A readiness to contribute beyond literal contractual obligations (Organ, 1988)	
Functional, extrarole, prosocial behavior, directed at individuals, groups, and/or an organization (Schnake, 1991)	Any behavior that brings harm, or is intended to bring harm to the organization, its employees, or its stakeholders (Gaiacalone & Greenberg, 1997)
Are inherently moral in that the actor chooses to perform a behavior that is beneficial to another person generally regarded as virtuous over one that is not (Graham, 1995; Ryan, 2001; Solomon, 1992)	Adverse reactions to perceived unfairness by disgruntled employees toward their employer (Skarlicki & Folger, 1997)
Behavior that contributes to the maintenance and enhancement of the social and psychological context that supports task performance (Organ, 1997, p. 91)	An act that betrays the trust of either individuals or the organizational community (Moberg, 1998)
Do not directly support the technical core ... but rather influence the social and psychological environment of organizations. OCBs are more discretionary and less constrained by work-process technology and other task features than in-role activities (Diefendorff, Brown, Kamin, & Lord, 2002)	Attempted injurious or destructive behavior initiated by either an organizational insider or outsider that is instigated by some factor in the organizational context (O'Leary-Kelly, Griffin, & Glew, 1996)
Help units work more efficiently and effectively (Moorman & Harland, 2002)	Any form of behavior by individuals that is intended to harm current or previous coworkers, or their organization (Baron & Neuman, 1996; Folger & Baron, 1996)
From the manager's perspective ... extra-role employee efforts that increase organizational effectiveness and efficiency (Ryan, 2002)	
Omission of OCBs is not punishable (Zellars et al., 2002)	
Employee efforts that go "above and beyond the call of duty" (Bolino & Turnley, 2003)	
Behaviors that are not directly enforceable ... and they are representative of the special or extra efforts that organizations need from their workforce in order to be successful (Bolino & Turnley, 2003)	Nontask behaviors that have negative organizational implications (Puffer, 1987)

part taxonomy in Organ (1988). The overlap shows that many different writers in the area consider the inclusiveness of behaviors in the original to be strong, yet some view the exact classification by Organ to be either too inclusive or too restrictive. For example, Van Dyne, Graham, and Dienesch (1994) present a taxonomy including social participation (overlap with altruism and courtesy), loyalty (overlap with sportsmanship and some civic virtue), obedience (overlaps with civic virtue and conscientiousness), and functional participation (which has no overlap in Organ) (LePine, Erez, & Johnson, 2002). Another conceptual framework for the dimensions of OCB is found in Morrison's (1994) work. Her taxonomy includes: altruism (overlap with altruism and courtesy), conscientiousness (slightly more restrictive than Organ's consciousness), sportsmanship (almost identical to Organ), involvement decisions (overlap with civic virtue and a piece of sportsmanship), and "keeping up with changes" (overlap with civic virtue and consciousness) (LePine et al., 2002).

Not only have others created taxonomies based upon reclassifying the behaviors people exhibit into different levels of category depth, but there has also been classification according to the beneficiary of the OCB. Williams and Anderson (1991) originally provided the taxonomy focused in this way and developed a two category classification: OCBI, or OCBs that benefit other organizational members (overlaps with altruism and courtesy), and OCBO, or OCBs that benefit the organization (overlaps with sportsmanship, civic virtue, and conscientiousness). Coleman and Borman (2000), empirically developed a similar taxonomy to Williams and Anderson (1991), finding categories of interpersonal citizenship performance (OCBI), organizational citizenship performance (OCBO), and job-task citizenship performance, which is behavior which reflects extra effort and persistence on the job, dedication to the job, and the desire to maximize one's own job performance (unrelated to Organ's taxonomy, but similar to Van Dyne et al.'s (1994) functional participation).

It would be incorrect to draw the conclusion that OCB is the only conceptualization of this type to be included in the literature. There are in fact, four similar conceptualizations: extra-role behavior (cf. Van Dyne, Cummings, & Park, 1995), prosocial organizational behaviors (cf. Brief & Motowildo, 1986; George, 1990, 1991; George & Bettenhausen, 1990; O'Reilly & Chatman, 1986), organizational spontaneity (cf. George & Brief, 1992; George & Jones, 1997), and contextual performance (cf., Borman & Motowildo, 1993, 1997; Borman, White, & Dorsey, 1995; Motowidlo & Van Scotter, 1994)—all of which occur in the literature and deal with the same idea of employees enacting behaviors that are "above and beyond the call of duty" (Bolino & Turnley, 2003). Certainly there are differences in what exactly each of these conceptualizations refers to; however, as study of the different conceptualizations has increased, the differences have diminished. The distance separating the most recent definition provided by Organ (1997) and the other conceptualizations has shrunk to the point where the terms, for better or worse, are now used interchangeably by many authors.

OCB Definitional Issues

The majority of researchers examining the OCB construct still use the definition proposed by Organ (1988), indicated above. This is due in no small part to the rapid operationalization of the typology by Podsakoff, MacKenzie, Moorman, and Fetter (1990). This operationalization created a valid measure to easily assess OCBs from a supervisor's perspective. However, Organ's original definition leaves some issues which need to be addressed by future researchers. Before research can truly look at antecedents and consequences of OCBs, two words/phrases from the original definition of OCBs need clarification and two additional issues need to be addressed.

Organ's (1988) definition includes only *individual* OCBs, yet this construct may be used at the group or organization level of measurement and analysis (Schnake & Dumler, 2003). Today, groups and teams, formed from the lowest level workers to top management, permeate the world of business. As individuals start working in an organization, they often join work groups, and these groups are a part of everyday processes. In self-managed teams, workers perform all tasks and when making certain decisions, they will put the team first because they strongly identify with the team. To this end, groups are able to, and do, engage in OCBs. One example is Southwest Airlines, where groups are used to interview employees and make hiring decisions for the organization. Individuals are brought in and interview with the groups with which they would work once in the organization, and if one person says they do not think the potential new hire is right, then the applicant is not hired. Since interviewing and making hiring decisions are not in the job descriptions of all the individuals in the group, and since the group undertakes the process and makes the decision, the group undertakes an OCB. OCBs in this area would likely not occur for many of the individuals but for the presence and identification with the group.

Effective functioning of the organization is another issue that researchers need to address when using the Organ (1988) definition. Due to the nature of groups, OCBs do not necessarily promote effective functioning of the organization. In some groups, having one person doing that extra little bit inspires everyone to do bigger and better things (synergy), but in other groups one member working extra hard is an invitation to others to do less (free ride). When one member of a group decides to go "above and beyond the call of duty," the other members do not necessarily hold their effort and work constant, but instead some of them may engage in social loafing (Kidwell & Bennett, 1993). This process can easily be noticed by taking a close look at groups of students in business schools working on projects. When it becomes apparent one member wants to do a particularly good job on a project, those prone to social loafing will decide to reduce their quality and quantity of work because they know the work will get done. For example, if one person in an assigned group in an MBA program is known to be a conscientious student who is driven to submit a project that is as good as the team can do, certain individuals, having this knowledge, will reduce their output (sometimes to 0) without fear that the project will be incomplete, or to their thinking, even inferior. This move toward social loafing, especially if there is no within team accountability (i.e. there are no peer evaluations), occurs within groups prior to any work being done. This forces the other group members into extra effort (OCBs) and the group produces the same or less of a product than would have been generated with equal effort from all members of the group (no OCBs).

We propose that the definition of OCBs must become more restrictive concerning the behaviors that fall within this categorization. Researchers need to be able to clearly indicate that the behaviors being studied are OCBs, and thus something of interest and not indicative of a relatively straightforward performance-reward relationship. OCBs' roots are in the area of psychology, which defines prosocial behavior as behavior "voluntarily and expressly directed toward the benefit of someone else with no apparent prospect of immediate extrinsic reward to the behavior" (Organ 1988). This definition clearly delineates OCB from non-OCB and signals clear situational markers (e.g., lack of extrinsic rewards). Despite what could be argued to be a temporal issue (see Mitchell & James, 2001 for an explanation of how we have failed to include time in many of our theories), this is the definition that we believe best articulates what Organ and scholars since then have been trying to capture in OCBs.

CONSTRUCT SPACE REFINEMENT: INCLUDING WDBS

OCBs have been conceptually thought to encompass a number of beneficial outcomes for organizations, including enhancing coworker and managerial productivity, freeing up resources so they can be used for more productive purposes, and reducing the need to devote scarce resources to purely maintenance functions (MacKenzie, Podsakoff, & Fetter, 1991, 1993; Organ, 1988, 1990; Podsakoff, Ahearne, & MacKenzie, 1997; Podsakoff & MacKenzie, 1994, 1997). Of course the greatest potential benefit of OCBs is the increase in overall organizational effectiveness (Podsakoff et al., 1997; Walz & Niehoff, 2000). However, organizational functioning is not necessarily enhanced by OCBs. There are times when members perform OCBs instead of in-role behaviors, thus day-to-day functioning suffers, likely detracting from organizational effectiveness (Bolino, 1999). For example, well intentioned behaviors, such as coworkers helping out with others' computing problems, have been linked with substantial costs to the organization (Bulkeley, 1992).

There are other behaviors that employees exhibit, however, which can create negative efficiency through intentioned acts. These acts are referred to as workplace deviance behaviors (WDBs). WDBs are defined as "voluntary behavior [of organization members] that violates significant organizational norms and in doing so threatens the well-being of an organization, its members, or both" (Robinson & Bennett, 1995, p. 556). The impact of these actions has been the focus of recent theoretical and empirical work (cf. Robinson & Greenberg, 1998). Much of the work in this area has focused on looking at the impact of deviance in terms of costs to organizations through heightened stress, increased absenteeism and turnover, and lowered morale (Braverman, 1993; Filipczak, 1993; Kedjijian, 1993; Kurland, 1993; Murphy, 1993; Slora, Joy, & Terris, 1991). Development of WDBs has not been restricted to individual implications, however. Dunlop and Lee (2004) have looked at the performance implications of WDBs in the workplace using both subjective and objective measures of performance

WDBs have a significant effect on overall effectiveness; Bourke (1994) found that workplace theft (a form of WDB) alone costs U.S. organizations between $10 and $120 billion annually. Dunlop and Lee (2004) also found that WDB also has a significant effect on reducing performance of the overall business unit. The negative effects within the organization of WDBs are easy to see, but it has not been considered in the majority of literature dealing with OCBs (Dunlop & Lee, 2004 is a notable exception).

Given the potential of significant negative influence on organizational effectiveness, there is a need for further study of WDBs. Researchers have delineated a wide variety of potential antecedents of WDBs, including personality (Giacalone & Knouse, 1990; Lee, Ashton, & Shin, 2005), perceived injustice or inequity (Greenberg, 1990, 1993), and social processes occurring amongst employees (Greenberg, 1997; Robinson & O'Leary-Kelly, 1998). These antecedents are very similar to the antecedents of OCBs when looked at in a negative context. It is not just the similarity between the antecedents and the consequences, but the similarity between types of behaviors (conscientiousness and production deviance), as well as similarity in measurement type and questions (Kelloway, Loughlin, Barling, & Nault, 2002) that are noteworthy.

With the definition of WDBs operating at the same level of employee action (i.e., voluntary action taken outside of job expectations), studies have looked at how WDBs and OCBs both act in the same work environment (see Table 13.1 for similarities between definitions offered for OCBs and WDBs) (Dunlop & Lee, 2004; Lee & Allen 2002). Despite the finding by Kelloway et al. (2002) that OCBs and WDBs are distinct constructs, there are still some questions if this is the case (Liden, Wayne, Jaworski, & Bennett, 2004). The Kelloway et al. (2002) findings argue that WDB operates as a unique construct, but one highly correlated to OCBs, which we believe is an artificial separation driven by measurement issues rather than the theoretical background behind the concepts.

The argument behind both OCBs and WDBs in the workplace is focused on explaining why individuals do what they do that is outside of normal work requirements and expectations. OCB research has only focused on how these positive extra-role behaviors can be explained in light of predictable extrinsic rewards. WDB research has instead focused on explaining the nature of these extra-role behaviors within organizations which clearly violates organizational norms. Measurement of the two constructs has trended toward artificially separating the underlying questions toward the extreme of either concept in order to get clearly differentiable results.

The links in the literature suggest a potential construct-space relationship between OCBs and WDBs. Not only are the antecedents and consequences similar in that they are presented as almost diametrically opposed, but the construct spaces appear to overlap. This suggests that a construct respecification that includes WDBs may be of value. WDB provides a negative anchor on a scale that until now had only positive and less positive as anchors. Without the adjustment of the construct space, further research in this area is not measuring the full variability of responses that are due to OCBs in organizations.

The previous discussion suggests a considerable overlap between the constructs of OCBs and WDBs. As such, we propose:

Proposition 1: WDB and OCB share the same construct space

EQUITY MOTIVATIONS OF OCBS/WDBS

With Adams' (1963) advancement of equity theory, it became clear that individuals compare their inputs and outputs at work with others. The comparison that individuals make between their inputs and outputs is not "rational," in the sense that they do not merely compare themselves with workers with similar responsibilities in the firm or the industry. Instead, individuals decipher their equity or inequity by comparing themselves to various referent others; be they family members, college friends, or neighbors. When this comparison has been done, and the existence, or lack thereof, of equity is decided, individuals work to restore their equity (if it does not currently exist).

Deutsch (1985) laid out three means for individuals to restore equity: demand for compensation, retaliation, or justification. The first means of restoring equity, demand for compensation, is action based, but is completely within the confines of a normal work behavior: asking for a raise for work well done. The third method, justification, is done in the mind of the individual and would not exhibit itself in an individual's behavior. Retaliation, the second method, however, we argue is what individuals do when exhibiting OCBs/WDBs in the workplace.

The focus on negative inequity by Deutsch (1985) is understandable as this is the inequity that Americans feel most clearly. In this situation, individuals perceive that they are not getting their due and whether or not the first method has been tried, individuals engaged in WDBs are trying to restore equity. By shirking on the job, stealing office supplies, or using company frequent flier miles for personal reasons, individuals are moving their input/output ratio closer to the ideal they perceive in their mind. "Retaliatory behavior" can occur with positive inequity, where individuals perceive their ratio is too much in their favor. In this instance, the individual chooses to engage in OCBs to right the ratio. This is classified as a retaliatory behavior because the individual is paying the organization back in kind to make the equity ratio equal, and in this case paying back in kind is a positive action.

OCB/WDB AS POLITICAL/SUPPORT BEHAVIOR

With the explosion of OCB research in the mid- and late 1990s, the concept became firmly entrenched as a more "selfless" or "altruistic" action undertaken by good people. However, researchers have begun to question the assumption that OCBs are done without concern for oneself (Bolino, 1999; Bolino & Turnley, 2003; Bolino et al., 2004; Rioux & Penner, 2001). While one cannot argue that there are not good people out there engaging in selfless acts for their organizations, we believe that many of the behaviors currently labeled OCBs and WDBs are instead political/support behaviors. We realize there are some behaviors which the OCBs construct captures that are very specific and ultimately promote organizational effectiveness without any desire for extrinsic value, however, the vast majority of OCBs behaviors which are exhibited could actually be undertaken with some intention toward achieving some extrinsic value, even if said value is never "cashed in" (idiosyncratic credit).

The above discussion suggests that both OCBs and WDBs have the potential to be considered a form of political/support behavior. A current debate in the politics literature questions if organizational support and political behavior are two ends of a continuum of behavior or not. While Andrews and Kacmar (2001) find support for the two as distinct constructs, Nye and Witt (1993) and Randall, Cropanzano, Bormann, and Birjulin (1999) argue that political behavior and organizational support are ends of a spectrum. We side with those researchers who argue that political and organizational support behaviors are ends of a spectrum because the absolute presence of one precludes the existence of the other and empirical findings have them very highly correlated (Andrews & Kacmar, 2001 find a –.72 correlation).

Politics has been defined in a number of ways, as such, we have chosen to look at politics as "actions by individuals which are directed toward the goal of furthering their own self-interests without regard for the well-being of others or their organization" (Kacmar & Baron, 1999, p. 4). We conceptualize support from an individual level. Although the literature has previously looked at support as a group or organization level construct, the way in which individuals conceive of an organization as supportive is based on the actions of individuals within the organizational context. As such, we argue that the definition of organizational support as "members view organizations as supportive when they are rewarded beyond what is dictated by formal policies" (Andrews & Kacmar, 2001, p. 349) can be equally well argued for individuals. Individuals within organizations can act to give and receive support to/from other individuals by accomplishing the same actions. By exploring both sides of this continuum, we have argued for a construct that speaks to both the good and the bad that can be generated when extra-role behavior is undertaken. Second, the definition fits particularly smoothly into the context of the organization.

Given the definition of political/support behavior we are led to the conclusion that the two probably overlap in terms of their construct space. This leads to the following:

Proposition 2: The current definition of OCB has considerable overlap with the construct space of "political/support behavior."

Critical to the overlap is the notion that political/support behavior in and of itself is not bad. Politics and political skill are a necessary part of organizational life (Ferris, Perrewé, Anthony, & Gilmore, 2000). Politics allow individuals to get things accomplished in a smooth, gracious manner (Ferris et al., 2000) that would otherwise require a power struggle. Nearly all of the examples of OCBs provided in the extant OCBs literature can be looked at from a political/support perspective for motive. Take for example, training a new recruit. An employee who takes on this responsibility not only gets the value of training the recruit "the right way," s/he also is noticed for a willingness to train the recruit, not only by top management with regard to a set of behaviors to be evaluated, but also by the recruit as a good individual willing to help out; this is individual support. While this does fall within Organ's (1988) definition of an OCB, the definitional issues still exist (See Bolino, 1999 for a discussion of how to determine if behaviors are OCBs or impression management).

To further support the political behavior argument of OCBs, we can look at the empirical ties between OCBs and rewards and OCBs and performance ratings. Dulebohn, Murray, and Ferris (2004) found that influence tactics' relationship to performance ratings were completely mediated by leader reward behavior, whereas OCBs had direct effects on performance ratings. While this finding casts doubt on the similarity between influence tactics and OCBs in relation to performance ratings, political/support behaviors can be seen based on empirical support for the relationship between the frequency of OCBs and rewards.

As Podsakoff et al. (2000) found, reward contingencies influence the frequency of organizational citizenship behavior. Furthermore, they found that employees are not indifferent to the rewards made available by the organization. Managers administer rewards contingent upon citizenship behavior (Allen & Rush 1998). The findings indicate that individuals do more OCBs when rewards for said behaviors are frequent, recognizable, and differential (i.e., make a difference to the person receiving the reward in some way). The interaction between OCBs and performance ratings in organizations is similar to the above relationship between OCBs and rewards. MacKenzie et al. (1991, 1993), MacKenzie, Podsakoff, & Rich (2001), and Werner (1994) found that managers take OCBs into account when evaluating the performance of their subordinates.

Generally, there has been relatively little study done on the downsides of OCBs, and the little that has been done has had sparse success in finding what causes one to engage in an organizational citizenship behavior that is positive versus OCBs that are negative. Schnake (1991) indicates that it is the motive which separates what we consider OCBs from impression-management behaviors. This need to understand the motive of individuals before being able to assess whether an OCB is positive or negative may creates some difficulties for managers in organizations Since it is the case that not every manager would interpret the same action from the same employee in the same way, the separation between positive and negative OCBs seems merely in the eye of the beholder. This leads to another problem with negative OCBs, how do researchers assess motivation? Bolino (1999) suggests a number of propositions to distinguish OCBs motives from impression management motives when the behaviors are similar. The downsides of OCBs all seem to stem from misplaced motivation, and yet that is surely what happens in organizations.

In the same way that OCBs reveal themselves as political behaviors, WDBs may also be politically motivated behaviors. Considering the earlier argument for the consideration of WDBs as sharing the same construct space as OCBs; if we argue that OCBs are political/support behaviors, it only makes sense that WDBs are as well. Again an example can be particularly illustrative. For instance, when an individual chooses to not pass on telephone messages, that individual is choosing to cause problems for the individual who is not receiving the messages. This will cause the person not receiving the messages grief, both from being unable to get the messages, as well as from whoever called and left a message, thereby reducing his/her power. Also, if this instance occurs frequently enough with important phone calls, the person not receiving the calls could run into performance difficulties that are noted by the supervisor for future reference.

Proposition 3: The current definition of WDB holds considerable overlap with the construct "political behavior."

RECOMMENDATIONS FOR FUTURE RESEARCH

First, we suggest that if OCBs and WDBs are found to be overlapping constructs, they need to be researched together to give a more parsimonious picture of the behaviors studied. We also propose that if researchers continue to use Organ's (1988) definition of OCBs, they need to recognize that it exists as part of the broader construct of political behavior. If we successfully made the argument that OCBs and WDBs share a construct space, researchers also need to recognize WDBs as part of the political behavior construct. Without this adjustment by future researchers, the continuation of research in this area will be of little value.

OCB research has been increasing in popularity for over a decade now, but the focus needs to change to evaluating these behaviors as political behaviors. OCB/WDB research has paid considerable attention to predicting specific behaviors. A number of antecedents and consequences have come to light, as well as the associations and interactions between constructs within the taxonomies. This research should continue, but a political framework may be more useful in explaining the behaviors. When researchers use the broad definition of OCBs, we are confident that the inclusion of this political framework will facilitate the study of the role of OCBs in organizations.

Future research in the area needs to take a closer look at the individuals being studied and evaluate if the majority of employees, as OCB literature to this point posits, really are motivated by helping the company, fellow employee, or supervisor out altruistically, or if they are politically motivated. Completing research where the motivation of the individual is considered and measured is surely very difficult, but nonetheless it needs to be done to provide a clear picture of what behaviors people are undertaking and why.

CONCLUSION

OCB research has been developing for more than a decade, and as such an impressive body of research has been developed. The nature of the research that has been done, however, is falling into a pattern whereby new authors are taking a taxonomy of behaviors and empirically testing antecedents or consequences without consideration for the many facets of the construct.

The OCB literature to date has more than 30 behaviors classified as OCBs that have been studied (Podsakoff et al., 2000). With such a great number and variety of behaviors and categories of behavior being studied, comparison between studies becomes problematic. Ultimately, researchers need to look closely at the nomological network that represents OCBs and decide what the construct is and any lawful relationships that exist between it and other constructs. Without this work, the relative merit of additional study may be diminished due to a lack of construct understanding and parsimony. There is a need to develop more comprehensive theory in order to determine what exactly constitutes an organizational citizenship behavior and some consensus needs to occur.

In this article we have posited the need to redefine OCBs from the Organ (1988) definition most commonly used in research. As such, we have presented a definition of OCBs, which we believe better represents the true nature of the construct. The definition presented is very narrow, but focuses on those tasks that employees undertake which are truly done for no extrinsic reward. This definition will significantly change future OCBs research when evaluating antecedents and consequences of OCBs.

Finally, we contend that OCBs, as currently conceptualized, are political behaviors. The implications of this are many. First of all, this alters what researchers will study and the relevant literature that is used for future study. The move into a political behavior area would reduce or eliminate many of the criticisms of OCBs as they are currently studied, including the in-role/extra-role argument. Also, political behavior provides a motivational basis which removes the distinction between impression management and OCBs. Finally, political behavior promotes, and provides an easy transition for the transfer of WDBs into the same construct space as OCBs.

AUTHOR'S NOTE

Address correspondence to: M. Ronald Buckley, University of Oklahoma, Division of Management Norman, OK 73109-0450. Submitted to: *Organizational Analysis*, September, 2004. Revised and resubmitted to *Organizational Analysis*, February, 2005.

REFERENCES

Adams, J. S. (1963). Towards an understanding of inequity. *Journal of Abnormal & Social Psychology, 67*(5), 422-436.

Allen, T. D., & Rush, M. C. (1998). The effects of organizational citizenship behavior on performance judgments: A field study and a laboratory experiment. *Journal of Applied Psychology, 83*, 247-260.

Andrews, M. C., & Kacmar, K. M. (2001). Discrimination among organizational politics, justice, and support. *Journal of Organizational Behavior, 22*(4), 347-366.

Baron, R. A., & Neuman, J. A. (1996). Workplace violence and workplace aggression: Evidence on their relative frequency and potential causes. *Aggressive Behavior, 22*, 161-173.

Bolino, M. C. (1999). Citizenship and impression management: Good soldiers or good actors? *Academy of Management Review, 24*(1), 82-98.

Bolino, M. C., & Turnley, W. H. (2003). Going the extra mile: Cultivating and managing employee citizenship behavior. *Academy of Management Executive, 17*(3), 60-71.

Bolino, M. C., Turnley, W. H., & Niehoff, B. P. (2004). The other side of the story: Reexamining prevailing assumptions about organizational citizenship behavior. *Human Resource Management Review, 14*, 229-246.

Borman, W. C., & Motowidlo, S. J. (1993). Expanding the criterion domain to include elements of contextual performance. In N. Schmitt, W. C. Borman, & Associates (Eds.), *Personnel selection in organizations* (pp. 71-98). San Francisco: Jossey-Bass.

Borman, W. C., & Motowidlo, S. J. (1997). Task performance and contextual performance: The meaning for personnel selection research. *Human Performance, 10*, 99-109.

Borman, W. C., White, L. A., & Dorsey, D. W. (1995). Effects of rater task performance and interpersonal factors on supervisor and peer performance ratings. *Journal of Applied Psychology, 80*, 168-177.

Bourke, A. J., III. (1994). Get smart about getting ripped off. *HR Focus, 71*,18.

Braverman, M. (1993, December, 12). The newest worry on the job. *New York Times*, p. 11.

Brief, A. P., & Motowidlo, S. J. (1986). Prosocial organizational behaviors. *Academy of Management Review, 11*, 710-725.

Bulkeley, W. M. (1992). Study finds hidden costs of computing. *Wall Street Journal* p. 4 (Section B).

Coleman, V. L. & Borman, W. C. (2000). Investigating the underlying structure of the citizenship performance domain. *Human Resource Management Review, 10*, 25-44.

Deutsch, M. (1985). *Distributive justice: A social-psychological perspective*. New Haven, CT: Yale University Press.

Diefendorff, J. M., Brown, D. J., Kamin, A. M., & Lord, R. G. (2002). Examining the roles of job involvement and work centrality in predicting organizational citizenship behaviors and job performance. *Journal of Organizational Behavior, 23*, 93-108.

Dulebohn, J. H., Muray, B., & Ferris, G. R. (2004). The vicious and virtuous cycles of influence tactic use and performance evaluation outcomes. *Organizational Analysis, 12*(1), 53-74.

Dunlop, P. D., & Lee, K. (2004). Workplace deviance, organizational citizenship behavior, and business unit performance: The bad apples do spoil the whole barrel. *Journal of Organizational Behavior, 25*, 67-80.

Ferris, G. R., Perrewé, P. L., Anthony, W. P., & Gilmore, D. C. (2000). Political skill at work. *Organizational Dynamics, 28*(4), 25-37.

Filipczak, B. (1993, July). Armed and dangerous at work. *Training, 7*, 29-43.

Folger, R., & Baron, R. A. (1996). Violence and hostility at work: A model of reactions to perceived injustice. In G. R. VandenBos & E. Q. Bulatao, (Eds.), *Violence on the job: Identifying risks and developing solutions* (pp. 51-85). Washington, DC: American Psychological Association.

Giacalone, R. A., & Knouse, S. B. (1990). Justifying wrongful employee behavior: The role of personality in organizational sabotage. *Journal of Business Ethics, 9*, 55-61.

George, J. M. (1990). Personality, affect, and behavior in groups. *Journal of Applied Psychology. 75*, 107-116.

George, J. M. (1991). State or trait: Effects of positive mood on prosocial behavior at work. *Journal of Applied Psychology, 76*, 299-307.

George, J. M., & Bettenhausen, K. (1990). Understanding prosocial behavior, sales performance, and turnover: A group-level analysis in a service context. *Journal of Applied Psychology, 75*, 698-709.

George, J. M., & Brief, A. P. (1992). Feeling good-doing good: A conceptual analysis of the mood at work-organizational spontaneity relationship. *Psychological Bulletin, 112*, 310-329.

George, J. M., & Jones, G. R. (1997). Organizational spontaneity in context. *Human Performance, 10*, 153-170.

Graham, J. W. (1995). Leadership, moral development, and citizenship behavior. *Business Ethics Quarterly, 55*, 43-55.

Greenberg, J. (1990). Employee theft as a reaction to underpayment inequity: The hidden cost of paycuts. *Journal of Applied Psychology, 75*, 561-568.

Greenberg, J. (1993). Stealing in the name of justice: Informational and interpersonal moderators of theft reactions to underpayment equity. *Organizational Behavior and Human Decision Processes, 54*, 81-103.

Greenberg, J. (1997). A social influence model of employee theft: Beyond the fraud triangle. In R. J. Lewicki, R. J. Bies, & B. H. Sheppard (Eds.), *Research on negotiation in organizations* (Vol. 6, pp. 29-51) Greenwich, CT: JAI Press.

Homans, G. C. (1961). *Social behavior: its elementary forms. Under the general editorship of Robert K. Merton.* New York: Harcourt, Brace & World.

Hubbard, R., Vetter, D. E., & Little, E. L. (1998). Replication in strategic management: Scientific testing for validity. *Strategic Management Journal, 19*(3), 243-254.

Kacmar, K. M., & Baron, R. A. (1999). Organizational politics: the state of the field, links to related processes, and an agenda for future research. In G. R. Ferris (Ed.), *Research in personnel and human resources management* (Vol. 17, pp. 1-39). Greenwich, CT: JAI Press.

Kedjijian, C. B. (1993, October). Is anyplace safe? *Safety and Health, 148*(4), 79-84.

Kelloway, E. K., Loughlin, C., Barling, J., & Nault, A. (2002). Self-reported counterproductive behaviors and organizational citizenship behaviors: Separate but related constructs. *International Journal of Selection and Assessment, 10*, 143-151.

Kidwell, R. E., & Bennett, N. (1993). Employee propensity to withhold effort: A conceptual model to intersect three avenues of research. *Academy of Management Review, 18*, 429-456.

Kurland, O. M. (1993). Workplace violence. *Risk Management, 40*, 76-77.

Lee, K., & Allen, N. J. (2002). Organizational citizenship behavior and workplace deviance: The role of affect and cognitions. *Journal of Applied Psychology, 87*, 131-142.

Lee, K., Ashton, M. C., & Shin, K-H. (2005). Personality correlate of workplace anti-social behavior. *Applied Psychology: An International Review.*

LePine, J. A., Erez, A., & Johnson, D. E. (2002). The nature and dimensionality of organizational citizenship behavior: A critical review and meta-analysis. *Journal of Applied Psychology, 87*(1), 52-65.

Liden, R., Wayne, S. J., Jaworski, R. A., & Bennett, N. (2004). Social loafing a field investigation. *Journal of Management, 30*(2), 285-304.

MacKenzie, S. B., Podsakoff, P. M., & Fetter, R. (1991). Organizational citizenship behavior and objective productivity as determinants of managerial evaluations of salespersons' performance. *Organizational Behavior and Human Decision Processes, 50*, 123-150.

MacKenzie, S. B., Podsakoff, P. M., & Fetter, R. (1993). The impact of organizational citizenship behavior on evaluations of sales performance. *Journal of Marketing*, 57, 70-80.

MacKenzie, S. B., Podsakoff, P. M., & Rich, G. A. (2001). Transformational and transactional leadership and salesperson performance. *Journal of the Academy of Marketing Sciences*, 29, 115-134.

Miner, J. B. (2003). The rated importance, scientific validity, and practical usefulness of organizational behavior theories: A quantitative review. *Academy of Management Learning and Education*, 2(3), 250-268.

Mitchell, T. R., & James, L. R. (2001). Building better theory: Time and the specification of when things happen. *Academy of Management Review*, 26, 530-547.

Moberg, D. (1998). On employee vice. *Business Ethics Quarterly*, 7(4), 41-60.

Moorman, R. H., & Harland, L. K. (2002). Temporary employees as good citizens: Factors influencing their OCBs performance. *Journal of Business and Psychology*, 17(2), 171-187.

Morrison, E. W. (1994). Role definitions and organizational citizenship behavior: The importance of the employee's perspective. *Academy of Management Journal*, 37, 1543-1567.

Motowidlo, S. J., & Van Scotter, J. R. (1994). Evidence that task performance should be distinguished from contextual performance. *Journal of Applied Psychology*, 79, 475-480.

Murphy, K. R. (1993). *Honesty in the workplace*. Belmont, CA: Brooks/Cole.

Nye, L. G., & Witt, L. A. (1993). Dimensionality and construct validity of the perceptions of organizational politics scale (POPS). *Educational and Psychological Measurement*, 53, 821-829.

O'Leary-Kelly, A. M., Griffin, R. W. & Glew, D. J. (1996). Organization-motivated aggression: A research framework. *Academy of Management Review*, 21, 225-253.

O'Reilly, C., & Chatman, J. (1986). Organizational commitment and psychological attachment: The effects of compliance, identification and internalization on prosocial behavior. *Journal of Applied Psychology*, 71, 492-499.

Organ D. W. (1988). *Organizational citizenship behavior: The good soldier syndrome*. Lexington, MA: Lexington Books.

Organ, D. W. (1990). The motivational basis of organizational citizenship behavior. In B. M. Staw & L. L. Cummings (Eds.), *Research in organizational behavior* (Vol. 12, pp. 43-72). Greenwich, CT: JAI Press.

Organ, D. W. (1997). Organizational citizenship behavior: It's construct clean-up time. *Human Performance*, 10, 85-97.

Podsakoff, P. M., Ahearne, M., & MacKenzie, S. B. (1997). Organizational citizenship behavior and the quantity and quality of work group performance. *Journal of Applied Psychology*, 82, 262-270.

Podsakoff, P. M., & MacKenzie, S. B. (1994). Organizational citizenship behaviors and sales unit effectiveness. *Journal of Marketing Research*, 3(1), 351-363.

Podsakoff, P. M., & MacKenzie, S. B. (1997). The impact of organizational citizenship behavior on organizational performance: A review and suggestions for future research. *Human Performance*, 10, 133-151.

Podsakoff, P. M., MacKenzie, S. B., Moorman, R. H. & Fetter, R. (1990). Transformational leader behaviors and their effects on followers' trust in leader, satisfaction, and organizational citizenship behaviors. *Leadership Quarterly, 1*(2), 107-142.

Podsakoff, P. M., MacKenzie, S. B., Paine, J. B., & Bachrach, D. G. (2000). Organizational citizenship behaviors: A critical review of the theoretical and empirical literature and suggestions for future research. *Journal of Management, 26*(3), 513-563.

Puffer, S. M. (1987). Prosocial behavior, noncompliant behavior, and work performance among commission salespeople. *Journal of Applied Psychology, 72*, 615-621.

Randall, M. L., Cropanzano, R., Bormann, C. A. & Birjulin, A. (1999). Organizational politics and organizational support as predictors of work attitudes, job performance, and organizational citizenship behavior. *Journal of Organizational Behavior, 20*(2), 159-174.

Rioux, S. M., & Penner, L. A. (2001). The causes of organizational citizenship behavior: A motivational analysis. *Journal of Applied Psychology, 86*, 1306-1314.

Robinson, S. L. & Bennett, R. J. (1995). A typology of deviant workplace behaviors: A multidimensional scaling study. *Academy of Management Journal, 38*, 555-572.

Robinson, S. L., & Greenberg, J. (1998). Employees behaving badly: Dimensions, determinants, and dilemmas in the study of workplace deviance. *Journal of Organizational Behavior, 5*, 1-30.

Robinson, S. L., & O'Leary-Kelly, A. M. (1998). Monkey see monkey do: The influence of workgroups on antisocial behavior of employees. *Academy of Management Journal, 41*, 658-672.

Ryan, J. J. (2001). Moral reasoning as a determinant of organizational citizenship behaviors: A study in the public accounting profession. *Journal of Business Ethics, 33*(3), 233-244.

Ryan, J. J. (2002). Work values and organizational citizenship behaviors: Values that work for employees and organizations. *Journal of Business and Psychology, 17*(1), 123-132.

Schnake, M. (1991). Organizational citizenship: A review, proposed model, and research agenda. *Human Relations, 44*, 735-759.

Schnake, M., & Dumler, M. P. (1997). Organizational citizenship behavior: The impact of rewards and reward practices. *Journal of Managerial Issues, 9*(2), 216-229.

Schnake, M., & Dumler, M. P. (2003). Levels of measurement and analysis issues in organizational citizenship behavior research. *Journal of Occupational and Organizational Psychology, 76*, 283-301.

Skarlicki, D. P., & Folger, R. (1997). Retaliation in the workplace: The roles of distributive, procedural, and interactional justice. *Journal of Applied Psychology, 82*, 416-425.

Slora, K. B., Joy, D. S., & Terris, W. (1991). Personnel selection to control employee violence. *Journal of Business and Psychology, 5*, 417-426.

Solomon, R. C. (1992). Corporate roles, personal virtues: An Aristotelian approach to business ethics. *Business Ethics Quarterly, 2*, 317-339.

Tarpey, L. X., Sr. (1974). A brand loyalty concept—A comment. *Journal of Marketing Research, 11*, 214-217.

Van Dyne, L., Cummings, L. L., & Parks, J. M. (1995). Extra-role behaviors: In pursuit of construct and definitional clarity (A bridge over muddied waters). In L. L. Cummings & B. M. Staw (Eds.), *Research in organizational behavior* (Vol. 17, pp. 215-285). Greenwich, CT: JAI Press.

Van Dyne, L., Graham, J. W., & Dienesch, R. M. (1994). Organizational citizenship behavior: Construct redefinition, measurement and validation. *Academy of Management Journal, 37*, 765-802.

Vardi, Y. & Weiner, Y. (1996). Misbehavior in organizations: A motivational framework. *Organization Science, 7*, 151-165.

Walz, S. M. & Niehoff, B. P. (2000). Organizational citizenship behaviors: Their relationship to organizational effectiveness. *Journal of Hospitality and Tourism Research, 24*, 108-126.

Werner, J. M. (1994). Dimensions that make a difference: Examining the impact of in-role and extra-role behaviors on supervisory ratings. *Journal of Applied Psychology, 79*, 98-107.

Williams, L. J., & Anderson, S. E. (1991). Job satisfaction and organizational commitment as predictors of organizational citizenship and in-role behaviors. *Journal of Management, 17*, 601-617.

Zellars, K. L., Bennett, J. T., & Duffy, M. K. (2002). Abusive supervision and subordinates' organizational citizenship behavior. *Journal of Applied Psychology, 87*(6), 1068-1076.

CHAPTER 14

SELF-CONCEPT-JOB FIT

Expanding the Person-Job Fit Construct and Implications for Retention Management

Wesley A. Scroggins and Philip G. Benson

> This paper proposes a new approach to person-job fit, based upon the match between individual self-concept and job tasks. Person-job fit is conceptualized as a multidimensional construct consisting of different types of fit (demand-abilities fit, supply-value fit, self-concept-job fit). Self-concept-job fit is defined and conceptually distinguished from other types of person-job fit. It is proposed that different types of person-job fit are differentially related to attitudinal and performance variables. A model is developed that relates self-concept-job fit to experienced meaningful work, which is argued to relate to various outcome variables related to employee retention. It is proposed that organizations should focus on self-concept-job fit in order to increase applicant attraction and employee retention. Implications and issues for future research are discussed.

The issue of person-job fit has received considerable attention in the literature in recent years (Bretz & Judge, 1994; Cable & Judge, 1997; Edwards, 1996; Judge & Cable, 1997; Kristof, 1996; Kristof-Brown,

2000). Research on person-job fit concerns the degree of compatibility between a person and a specific job. Recent interest in the issue may be due to the growing number of studies that support a relationship between person-job fit and outcome and process variables valued by organizations. For example, Saks and Ashforth (1997) found that job applicants' perceptions of fit with job and organization impacted their choices of organizations. Recruiters make hiring decisions on the basis of their perceptions of the degree to which applicants fit jobs (Kristof-Brown, 2000). Employees' perceptions of fit impact their turnover intentions (Cable & Judge, 1996) as well as many attitudinal variables (Cable & Derue, 2002).

One important attitudinal variable that has not received much attention in the literature is meaningful work. Work is of central significance to the lives of most people. Recently, an increasing number of individuals have begun to reevaluate their lives, work, and the organizations in which they are employed. As a result, attitudes toward work have shifted. Individuals are searching for qualitatively different outcomes from work as compared to past generations. People want jobs that have significance and provide them with a sense of internal satisfaction and meaning (Caudron, 1997). According to Conger (1994), both the desire for personal fulfillment in work and the creation of workplace environments that promote a sense of higher purpose have been gaining momentum since the time of Maslow and McGregor. Compared with workers of past generations, today's workers have a growing sense of entitlement to meaningful work and are increasingly expecting such work from their employers.

Because of the importance of meaningful work to many individuals, it is believed that meaningful work is an important determinant of employee retention. Turnover and retention are major concerns for many organizations today. Tight labor markets, competition for qualified, skilled employees and the costs associated with turnover have made retention a major challenge for human resource professionals. Mitchell, Holtom, and Lee (2001) state that retention may be the hottest topic in human resource management today.

It is imperative that any strategic human resource initiative aimed at attracting and retaining good employees and reducing turnover addresses the issue of meaningful work. The challenge to human resource management is the role that human resource practices must play in helping the organization create meaningful work for employees. One such area in which human resource professionals can make a contribution is in the area of selection, where the goal traditionally has been to create a match or fit between the job and employee. The concept of fit holds promise for creating meaningful work for individuals in organizations and impacting employee retention.

Schneider (1987) proposed the attraction-selection-attrition model that emphasizes the concept of fit in the attraction, selection and attrition of employees. According to this model, individuals find organizations attractive as a function of their perceptions of the congruence of their own characteristics and the attributes of the organization. The attrition process refers to the idea that individuals will leave an organization they do not fit. However, the model does not specify the personal and organizational characteristics that comprise good fit nor the best type of fit that will be related to higher levels of attraction and lower levels of attrition (Schneider, 1987; Schneider, Goldstein, & Smith, 1995).

A recently proposed theory of meaningful work and work motivation emphasizes the fit between the individual and the job and provides a theoretical foundation for the relationships between person-job fit, meaningful work, and retention. The self-concept based theory of work and motivation (Shamir, 1991) highlights the role of the self-concept in meaningful work and work motivation. The theory states that meaningful work and job motivation are a function of the interaction between work tasks, the context in which the work is performed, and the individual's self-concept. Shamir's theory holds promise for the creation of meaningful work for individuals through human resource management functions such as selection. The implication is that meaningful work can be created through the selection of applicants whose self-concept matches the tasks of the job. Shamir (1991) states that this is a general theory of meaningful work and motivation. Meaningful work and general work motivation are related to the degree of investment in the role of work. They are common elements that underlie attendance, tardiness, work effort, and donating personal time to work.

It is the argument of this paper that personnel selection can benefit from an expanded conceptualization of person-job fit to include a self-concept-job task fit. This means expanding the concept of person-job fit beyond the demand/ability match and the supply/value match that has been the primary focus of person-job fit research. By focusing on matching individual self-concepts and job tasks, human resource professionals are more likely to recruit and select individuals into the organization and particular positions who will experience higher levels of meaningful work, which will be related to higher levels of attachment to the organization and lower levels of turnover. This will enable human resource professionals make a contribution to the creation of meaningful work in the organization that can help organizations achieve goals of attracting top applicants and increasing employee retention.

This paper is divided into three sections. In the first section, self-concept-job task fit is defined and a distinction is made between this type of fit and other conceptualizations of person-job fit. Second, a model is proposed that relates self-concept-job task fit to meaningful work and retention. It is proposed that self-concept-job task fit is a better predictor of meaningful work than other types of person-job fit. It is further proposed that meaningful work is related to certain attitudinal variables that are related to turnover variables. Finally, implications of the proposed type of person-job fit and model are discussed as well as issues for future research.

CONCEPTUALIZATIONS OF PERSON-JOB FIT

Before an argument can be made regarding the relationships between self-concept-job task fit, meaningful work, and turnover variables, it is necessary to distinguish between this proposed type of fit and other conceptualizations of person-job fit in the literature. Person-job fit is considered to be a multidimensional construct that consists of at least three distinct but possibly related types of fit. The multidimensionality of the person-job fit construct has received both theoretical and empirical support. This paper proposes that self-concept-job task fit is a distinct type of fit that comprises one dimension of the person-job fit construct.

Two approaches to person-job fit have been identified in the literature: supply-value fit and demand-ability fit. Supply-value fit (S-V fit) exists to the extent that the motives or needs of the person fit or match the supplies in the environment or job for those motives or needs (Edwards, 1996). Supply-value fit involves the individual's evaluation of the environment or job, based upon personal needs or values (Livingstone, Nelson, & Barr, 1997; Van Vianen, 2000). Kristof (1996) conceptualizes and describes this type of fit as a needs/supplies match where the desires of the employee match the attributes of the job.

Demand-ability fit (D-A fit) involves the extent to which a person's abilities meet the demands of the job (Edwards, 1996; Werbel & Johnson, 2001). A person's knowledge, skills and abilities are emphasized in this approach in terms of how well he or she can perform the tasks required of the job (Livingstone et al., 1997). Similarly, Kristof (1996) defines this type of fit as the fit between the abilities of the person and the demands or requirements of the job.

Muchinsky and Monahan (1987) use different terminology to refer to these types of fit. They refer to both of these types of fit as complementary fit, where the characteristics of the individual complement the characteristics of the environment. The environment is seen as requiring an individual with certain characteristics in order for that individual to be effective. In the complementary model, the environment is described in terms of its demands and requirements and the individual's abilities and characteristics are matched to those demands, or vice versa. In the context of personnel selection, achieving fit between individuals and jobs has focused on these two types of fit, with most consideration placed on the achievement of demand-abilities fit.

This paper proposes a new concept of fit/match for personnel selection based on Shamir's (1991) self-concept based theory of work. Individuals should be matched to jobs on the basis of the degree to which their individual self-concept matches the tasks and requirements of the job or the behaviors that must be performed for task accomplishment. We call this proposed type of fit self-concept-job fit (SC-J fit). In order to gain an understanding of this type of fit, it is necessary to discuss the nature and content of the self-concept.

Research on the self-concept has a long history in psychology and numerous problems exist regarding the definition and conceptualization of the self-concept among researchers. Many of the problems stem from a lack of a universally accepted definition of self-concept, the assumed synonymity of self terms (self-concept, self-identity, self-perception, self-image), an unclear distinction between self-concept and self-esteem and self-concept and self-efficacy, and from the fact that many self-concept researchers fail to provide theoretical definition of what they are measuring because of the belief that everyone knows what self-concept is (Byrne, 1996). The consequence of this conceptual ambiguity is that numerous definitions and conceptualizations of the self-concept exist in the social psychological literature and the definition of the self-concept is to some degree dependent upon the researcher whose work is being consulted.

Rathus and Nevid (1980) identify several aspects of the self-concept. They define the self-concept as an individual's perception of self, including personal traits and the evaluation of those traits. Self-concept includes self-esteem, self-identity and conceptions of the ideal self. They state that self-esteem refers to self-approval, one's regard, respect or favorable opinion of oneself. The ideal self refers to the perception of what one ought to be or should be.

Early researchers conceptualized the self-concept as a unitary, generalized view of the self (Byrne, 1996). Current research in the self-concept literature appears to be similar to the conceptualization of Rathus and Nevid (1980). There is general agreement among contemporary researchers that the self-concept is a multidimensional construct defined in terms of an organized knowledge structure containing traits, values and beliefs about the self (content component) and which controls the processing of information relevant to the self (structural component) (Byrne, 1996; Campbell, Assanand, & Di Paula, 2000; Campbell, Trapnell, Heine, Katz, Lavallee, & Lehman, 1996). The content component can be divided into declarative self-knowledge and an evaluative component. Declarative self-knowledge is traditionally what researchers have referred to as the self-concept, and includes beliefs about one's specific attributes (traits, characteristics) as well as values, roles and personal goals (Campbell et al., 2000; Hoyle, Kernis, Leary, & Baldwin, 1999). Declarative self-knowledge consists of a coherent set of beliefs about the self. The evaluative component consists of an evaluation of the self and includes the positivity or negativity of specific self-beliefs and self-esteem, which is a more general, global evaluation of self (Campbell et al., 2000). Byrne (1996) states that although there has been ambiguity between the terms self-concept and self-esteem, most researchers today agree that the two constructs represent different aspects of the self system, with self-esteem being a more limited evaluative component of the broader self-concept construct.

Although there is general agreement among researchers regarding the multidimensionality of the self-concept, numerous multidimensional models of the self-concept have been proposed (Byrne, 1996). A substantial amount of construct validity research (Marsh & Hattie, 1996) seems to indicate support for the construct validity of a hierarchical model of the self-concept (Byrne, 1996; Shavelson, Hubner, & Stanton, 1976). The hierarchical model conceptualizes the self-concept as consisting of a general self-concept that is a second order factor having multiple, specific facets. These facets or dimensions are proposed to be separate, independent but related constructs. The multiple dimensions of the general self-concept consist of the content of the self-content discussed above. One dimension is likely to consist of the beliefs an individual possesses regarding personal characteristics and traits. A second and third dimension may consist of values or different roles the individual considers himself or herself to perform. Another dimension will include the evaluative component or self-esteem, and reflects the manner in which the individual evaluates the self. The measurement of the self-concept, according to the hierarchical model, would require the development of items that tap or measure each of the specific facets or constructs comprising general self-concept (Byrne, 1996). Construct validity research on the different multidimensional models of the self-concept appear to provide the greatest support for the validity of this conceptualization of the self-concept (Bryne, 1996; Marsh & Hattie, 1996).

Using this conceptualization of the self-concept, self-concept-job fit is proposed to occur when the performance of job tasks produces perceptions and feelings within the individuals that are congruent with the individuals' perceptions of who they are (self perceptions) and/or the kind of person they desire to be (ideal self). The performance of job tasks provides the individual with self-confirming or validating information regarding the self. The individual perceives the knowledge, skills, abilities, and behaviors involved in task performance, as well as job outcomes

Self-Concept-Job Fit 217

resulting from performance, to be consistent with his or her self-declarative knowledge, confirming the characteristics, beliefs, values, and roles the individual perceives to be characteristic of the self. In this way, the individual's sense of self is confirmed through the performance of job tasks and the consequences of task performance.

Self-concept-job fit can also be said to occur when the performance of job tasks provides the individual with perceptions and feelings consistent with self-esteem. Since self-esteem is the evaluative component of the self-concept (Campbell et al., 1996; Campbell et al., 2000), fit will be achieved when task performance and consequences enable the individual to view self in a manner consistent with the evaluation of self that comprises the self-concept.

Given the above conceptualizations of the different types of person-job fit, it can be argued that the fit types are distinct constructs that represent dimensions of the person-job fit construct. The distinctiveness of the fit types lies in the factors that are focused on and that form the basis for the type of fit. In demand-abilities fit, the focus is on the degree of congruence between the task requirements of the job and the knowledge, skills, and abilities possessed by the individual. In supply-value fit, the focus is on job outcomes and the needs, values and desires the individual expects to have satisfied through the job. In self-concept-job fit the focus is on yet another set of factors. The focus is on the congruence between perceptions of self and the nature of job tasks and essential job behaviors. Each type of fit focuses upon different aspects of the individual and job, which makes it likely that each fit type is distinct and represents different aspects of the greater person-job fit construct. It is also likely that individuals can possess high levels of one type of person-job fit and possess low levels of a different type. For example, it is possible that an individual can have the necessary qualifications to perform the requirements of the job at an above average level of performance. The individual would possess a high level of demand-abilities fit. However, the same individual may not receive valued outcomes from the job that satisfies their needs and desires (i.e., a high level of income or certain job benefits, a high degree of affiliation or interaction). This individual would have a low level of supply-value fit. Another example would be an individual trained to be a teacher, but who cannot find a teaching position in the area. The individual finds a job as a loan officer, approving loans for customers. The individual might have the necessary skill and ability to perform the job well and have a high level of demand-abilities fit. The job may also provide the level of compensation and other benefits that are expected from the job, and the level of interaction with others that are desired. The individual would therefore have a high level of supply-value fit as well. But the individual might have a low level of self-concept-job fit because the tasks they perform do nothing to affirm the image of self that they have as a teacher who helps others to learn and develop as individuals. Therefore, such individuals might find little meaning in their work although they possess the needed skill to perform the job well and the job supplies rewards that satisfy certain needs. The same individual may fit the job in some ways but not in others. It depends upon which aspects of the individual and job are under consideration.

Researchers have long considered demand-abilities fit and supply-value fit to be distinct types of fit (Kristof, 1996; Muchinsky & Monahan, 1987). Livingstone et al. (1997) state that these two versions of person-job fit can be viewed as separate and distinct constructs and found that they are differentially related to creativity, supporting the discriminant validity of the two types of fit. Cable and Derue (2002) performed confirmatory factor analysis on perceptual measures of demand-abilities and supply-value fit and found support for the distinctiveness of perceptions of the two types of fit. It is believed that self-concept-job fit is distinct from these two types of fit and forms a third dimension of the person-job fit construct. The result is a three-factor conceptualization of person-job fit that consists of the three types of person-job fit discussed above.

Proposition 1: Self-concept-job fit is a distinct type of person job fit from demand-abilities and supply-value fit and represents a separate dimension in a three-factor conceptualization of person-job fit.

If the fit types are distinct constructs, we can expect that the three types of person-job fit will be differentially related to certain outcome variables, establishing the convergent and discriminant validity of the three fit types. It has been suggested that demand-abilities fit should be related to job performance (Kristof, 1996, Livingstone et al., 1997). However, little support for the relationship between demand-abilities fit and performance has been found, especially when using perceptual measures of fit (Cable & Derue, 2002; Lauver & Kristof-Brown, 2001). Various reasons could explain the lack of support for this relationship. It is possible that individuals are motivated to inflate their demand-abilities fit ratings. It is also possible that there are range restriction problems in the performance measure. It is possible that perceptions of demand-abilities fit may be related to competence variables such as self-efficacy (Cable & Derue, 2002).

Supply-value fit would be expected to be related to job attitudes such as job satisfaction (Livingstone et al., 1997) and discretionary behaviors such as organizational citizenship behaviors. Discrepancy theories of job satisfaction would support the relationship between supply-value fit and job satisfaction. The higher the perceptions of supply-value fit the lower the discrepancy between what individuals desire and what they receive from the job, resulting in higher job satisfaction. Social exchange theory (Organ, 1990; Organ & Paine, 1999) provides a rationale for the relationship between supply-value fit and organizational citizenship behaviors. Individuals reciprocate with organizational citizenship behaviors for positive work experiences provided by the organization. When the job supplies what the individual expects and wants in the way of job outcomes, positive experiences should result and the individual be more likely to reciprocate with organizational citizenship behaviors in exchange for their needs and desires being fulfilled.

It is expected that self-concept-job fit will be related to experienced meaningfulness. According to Shamir (1991), self-concept-job congruence will lead to high levels of meaningful work, which will be related to outcome variables relevant to retention and attrition.

The social psychological literature on the self-concept provides support for the proposition that factors that verify the self-concept will be experienced as meaningful. Social psychological research suggests that individuals are motivated toward self-consistency. People have a need to maintain a consistent self-image of themselves and prefer information that is consistent with their existing self-concepts. Individuals will also engage in behaviors that help them maintain a sense of consistency (Hoyle et al., 1999).

Self-verification theory (Swann, 1983, 1990) provides one perspective on how individuals seek to maintain self-consistency. According to this theory, individuals are motivated to verify, validate and sustain existing conceptions of the self (Hoyle et al., 1999). Self-consistency increases the degree to which individuals feel that they can control and manipulate circumstances in their environment. A stable self-concept enables individuals to negotiate social reality and understand how to behave effectively in a given social situation. For this reason, individuals prefer information that is consistent with their self-concepts and dislike information that is inconsistent with their conception of self (Hoyle et al.). Therefore, it follows that information, roles or behaviors that are consistent with the individual's self-concept will be experienced as meaningful. Whatever the factor is that verifies the person's sense of self (job, hobby, social group), it will be experienced as meaningful because it provides the individual with consistency and self-verification.

> **Proposition 2:** Self-concept-job fit, demand-abilities fit and supply-value fit are differentially related to different outcome variables.

A MODEL OF FIT, MEANINGFUL WORK, AND RETENTION

It has been argued that person-job fit is a multidimensional construct consisting of three dimensions or types of fit. It has also been argued that these fit types are predictive of different variables that organizations may value. It is now possible to present a model that emphasizes the role of self-concept-job fit in creating meaningful work and impacting valued job attitudes and turnover related behaviors. Figure 14.1 shows the proposed model and relationships among the variables. It is believed that self-concept-job fit is the best type of fit for creating meaningful work and impacting job attitudes and retention.

Relationship Between SC-J Fit and Meaningful Work

It was discussed above that individuals seek consistency and self-verification and find meaning in those things that verify their sense of self. Therefore, when job tasks provide the individual with feedback or allow the individual to engage in roles or behaviors consistent with individual self-concept, verifying the sense of self, work should be experienced as meaningful. Self-verification theory (Swann, 1983, 1990) provides support for Shamir's (1990) self-concept based theory of work motivation and the proposition that self-concept-job fit will be more strongly related to meaningful work than demand-abilities or supply-value fit.

Because individuals behave in ways that verify their self-concepts, self-verification theory states that they will seek out and interact with other individuals in situations that enable them to perceive themselves in a manner consistent with their self-concept. Individuals prefer other individuals and situations that confirm their self-views. This provides support for the attraction-selection-attrition model (Schneider, 1987; Schneider, Goldstein & Smith, 1995) when considering self-concept-job fit, in that individuals will be attracted to and seek out jobs and organizations that provide them with self-confirming information and will likely continue in the job as long as self-confirming information is received and a high level of self-concept-job fit is perceived. If future research finds support for the validity of this argument, specificity may be added to the attraction-selection-attrition model by identifying self-concept-job fit as the type of person-job fit related to the highest levels of attraction and retention.

> **Proposition 3:** Because self-concept-job fit involves self-verification, self-concept-job fit is more strongly related to meaningful work than demand-abilities and supply-value fit.

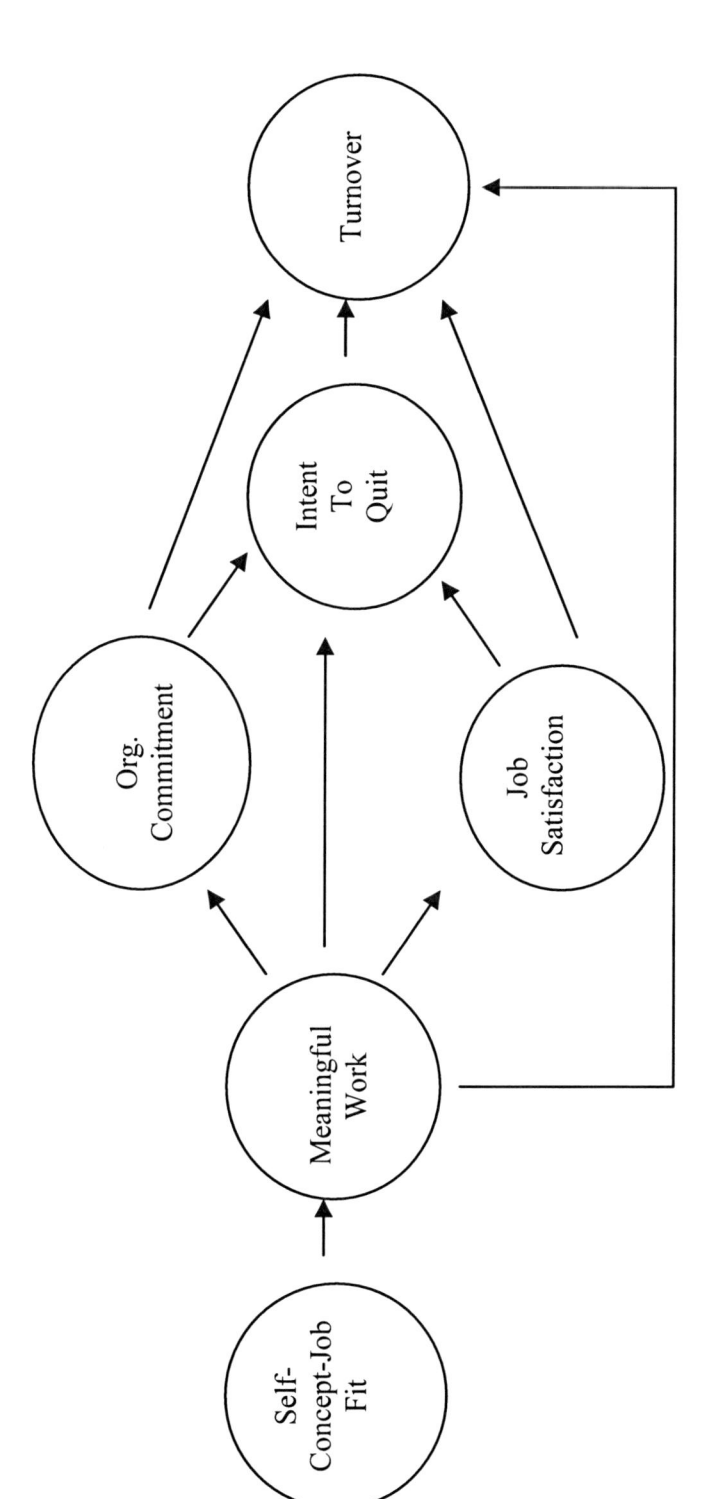

Figure 14.1. Proposed retention model.

Relationship Among Meaningful Work and Job Attitudes

It is believed that meaningful work is related to important job attitudes such as job satisfaction and organizational commitment. Although no studies are known that directly assess the relationship between meaningful work and these job attitudes, theory and research would suggest that a relationship should exist. The job characteristics model (Hackman & Oldham, 1976) theorizes that experienced meaningfulness created by job characteristics results in high job satisfaction. Furthermore, need and discrepancy theories of job satisfaction (Locke, 1976) suggest that individuals experience high levels of job satisfaction as a result of having salient needs fulfilled or experiencing little discrepancy between what they desire and actually receive from their work. If individuals need or desire meaningful work as argued in the introduction, then job satisfaction should result when meaningful work is experienced and received through work. It is also believed that individuals will have high levels of job satisfaction due to meaningful work that verifies the self-concept. This alone should make the work satisfying.

Theory and research also support a proposed relationship between meaningful work and organizational commitment. Shamir's (1991) theory maintains that meaningful work will be related to levels of absenteeism, tardiness, and donating personal time to work. All of these variables seem to be associated with organizational commitment, so it is likely that meaningful work will be related to organizational commitment as well. Empirical studies have found that high levels of perceived shared values between employee and organization are related to higher levels of organizational commitment (Box, Odom, & Dunn, 1991; Harris & Mossholder, 1996; Posner, Kouzes, & Schmidt, 1985). Research also suggests that unmet expectations of employees are related to lower levels of organizational commitment (Rosin & Korabik, 1991). Since many employees have expectations of meaningful work, levels of organizational commitment may decrease in employees whose expectations are not met. Furthermore, self-verification theory (Swann, 1983, 1990) states that individuals seek out and are more likely to remain in situations that verify their self-concepts. When self-concept-job fit is high resulting in meaningful work, the individual is more likely to be committed to staying in the job because of the meaningful self-verifying information received through the work. Therefore, there appears to be both theoretical and empirical support for the hypothesis that meaningful work will be related to organizational commitment.

> **Proposition 4:** Meaningful work will be related to both job satisfaction and organizational commitment.

Meaningful Work, Job Attitudes, and Retention Variables

Turnover intention has been defined as the conscious and deliberate willingness to leave the organization and has been described as the last in a sequence of withdrawal cognitions that also includes thinking of quitting and searching for alternative employment (Tett & Meyer, 1993). The proposed model shows that meaningful work is proposed to be both directly related to turnover intentions and indirectly related to turnover intentions through job attitudes. This allows for the assessment of the total effects of meaningful work on turnover intentions. Shamir's (1991) theory and Schneider's (1987) attraction-selection-attrition model supports the proposition that individuals who do not experience self-concept-job fit nor have expectations regarding meaningful work met will more likely perceive a lack of fit between themselves and the organization. The lack of perceived fit will be related to higher levels of intention to quit as individuals select themselves out of organizations that do not match their self-concepts. Therefore, Shamir and Schneider provide theoretical support for the proposition that meaningful work will be directly related to lower levels of intentions to quit.

Empirical research supports the relationships between job satisfaction, organizational commitment, and intentions to quit (Allen & Meyer, 1996; Jaros, 1995; Jaros, Jermier, Koehler, & Sincich, 1993; Pinder, 1998). These relationships have been well established in the research literature. Although these relationships are contained in the model, no propositions will be made regarding them because they already have been tested and supported in the literature.

Proposition 5: Meaningful work will be related to intentions to quit. It will have indirect effects on intentions to quit through job attitudes.

Turnover is defined as the voluntary termination of an individual's employment with an organization (Tett & Meyer, 1993). As discussed above, Shamir (1991) and Schneider (1987) provide conceptual support for the relationship between meaningful work and intent to quit. For the same reasons, it is believed that they also provide support for the relationship between meaningful work and actual voluntary turnover. Individuals who do not perceive a fit or match with the job or organization because of unmet expectations will select themselves out of the organization. Tett and Meyer (1993) state that research has generally supported the hypothesized linkages between organizational commitment, intent to quit and actual turnover. Therefore, it is also possible that meaningful work will be indirectly related to turnover through organizational commitment and intentions to quit.

Proposition 6: Meaningful work will be directly related to voluntary turnover. It will also have indirect effects on voluntary turnover through organizational commitment and intentions to quit.

In this section, a model of employee retention has been proposed that is based on self-concept-job fit and meaningful work. A theoretical rationale has been provided to support the relationships proposed in the model. It is believed that the proposed fit-meaningful work-retention model holds promise for the management of retention in organizations. The position of this paper is that self-concept-job fit is the most promising type of fit/match for creating meaningful work and impacting employee retention and attrition rates.

IMPLICATIONS AND FUTURE RESEARCH

A new type of person-job fit has been proposed that fits individuals to jobs on the basis of the match between individual self-concept and job tasks. This represents a new approach to person-job fit that is different from the traditional demand-abilities and supply-value fit approaches that have dominated person-job fit research and have formed the basis for matching individuals to jobs in personnel selection practices. Person-job fit is a multidimensional construct and demand-abilities and supply-value fit perspectives represent a limited number of ways that individuals can be matched to jobs. It is proposed that self-concept-job fit represents an additional dimension of the person-job fit construct. This represents additional criteria by which to fit individuals to jobs and should allow for a more complete person-job match. Matching individuals to jobs across multiple dimensions of the construct should allow for a more complete fit between individuals and jobs. Future research should examine the construct validity of the fit types and the additive effects of these types of person-job fit on overall fit between the individual and job.

It was also proposed that self-concept-job fit is related to different outcome variables than demand-abilities and supply-value fit. Therefore, an additional reason to focus on self-concept-job fit is that it may be related to valued job attitudes and behaviors that organizations need for competitive advantage and strategy implementation. This paper has argued that self-concept-job fit is related to meaningful work and employee retention. This type of fit might be important to organizations in which client relations and satisfaction are important for competitive advantage and survival. Employee retention is important for maintaining client relationships and satisfaction. Self-concept-job fit might be the type of fit that such an organization should focus on for high retention that would facilitate the development and maintenance of good client relationships.

One implication for the proposed differential prediction of the fit types is that organizations need to focus on the type of fit that will have the greatest impact on attitudes and behaviors consistent with the particular organization's strategic initiative. If retention is important, then self-concept-job fit may be the type of fit upon which to focus. If high performance in the short-term is important, with little need for the development of relationships, then demand-abilities fit may be the fit type that needs the most attention. It is also possible that different types of fit may be more critical to certain jobs in the organization than to others, depending on the nature of the job and the manner in which the job contributes value to the organization. Future research needs to examine the differential relations of the fit types with the proposed variables and other variables of interest and value to organizations.

The paper also presents a new model of employee retention. The model differs from other retention models because of the proposed antecedents of the job attitudes and turnover variables. According to this model, employees stay with an organization due to self-concept-job fit and experienced meaningful work. The model has important implications for the management of retention in organizations. If meaningful work is related to the proposed outcome variables, it is important for human resource professionals to create meaningful work for employees if they are to help the organization retain quality employees and reduce attrition rates. The concept of self-concept-job fit in the context of employee selection is one method in which human resource professionals may facilitate the development of meaningful work in employees. This is the implication of the self-concept theory of work and motivation (Shamir, 1991) for selection in organizations. Organizations can attempt to increase levels of meaningful work among employees by seeking to match job tasks with individual self-concepts during the recruitment and selection process. Organizations often attempt to impact retention by offering extrinsic factors that individuals value and that might increase individuals' sense of continuance organizational commitment (Allen & Meyer, 1996), in which the individuals perceive the costs of leaving the organization as too high. The proposed retention model focuses attention on intrinsic factors that motivate individuals to stay. Individuals stay with the organization because they perceive they fit and experience meaning through the performance of job tasks.

Although it is argued that self-concept-job fit has the greatest efficacy of the person-job fit types for affecting meaningfulness and retention, it must be noted that it is likely that certain factors moderate the relationship between these variables due to the affect these factors may have on the value that individuals attach to various job outcomes. Economic conditions, market conditions and world events likely influence the value employees place on various job outcomes. Receiving valued job outcomes influences individual decisions to turnover or remain an organizational member. A 2005 Job Satisfaction Survey (Society for Human Resource Management [SHRM], 2005) indicates that employee preferences for job outcomes have changed somewhat from 2002 to 2005. Compensation, pay and benefits are the job outcomes employees report are the most important for job satisfaction. Most notably, the percentage of individuals reporting that feeling safe in the work environment increased from 36% in 2002 to 62% and 55% in 2004 and 2005, respectively. Furthermore the percentage of individuals reporting that meaningful work was important decreased from 52% in 2002 to 37% in both 2004 and 2005. These recent shifts in employee preferences are probably due in part to terrorism, the outsourcing and offshoring of jobs, and the fact that many organizations are either abandoning benefits programs or are shifting a greater part of the burden and cost of health care to the employee. As we experience these types of shifts in employee preferences for job outcomes, it is possible that supply-value fit could predict meaningful work or retention better than self-concept-job fit. Needs-based motivation theories such as Maslow's hierarchy of needs would predict this. As basic safety and security needs become more salient to employees, it is possible that higher-order needs such as the meaningfulness of work could become less important. Under these conditions, organizations may need to focus on other types of fit for better retention.

Another issue likely to attenuate the relationships between self-concept-job fit and meaningful work and retention is the clarity of the self-concept. In the absence of self-concept clarity or a well defined identity, it may be very difficult, if not impossible, to achieve self-concept-job fit. This may have implications for the generalizability of the model, possibly on the basis of age. In general, it is possible that older workers will have more established and well-defined self-concepts than younger workers. Due to the developmental stage in life, older workers may also value meaningfulness to a greater degree than younger workers who often place more value on compensation and career opportunities. Therefore, the model may be more predictive for some groups than others due to differences in needs and values. Future research is needed to investigate these issues. Obviously, workers with well defined self-concepts will be needed in order to establish the construct validity of the self-concept-job construct and investigate it relationship to meaningfulness and retention.

Future research should focus on the development of self-concept-job fit perceptions in existing employees or maintaining these perceptions in employees after they have been selected into particular jobs. Socioanalytic theory provides a framework for the management of self-concept-job fit perceptions in individuals in organizations (Hogan & Roberts, 2000). According to the theory, managers and supervisor largely define situations for and shape the perceptions of subordinates through interactions with them. It is possible that managers can develop high self-concept-job fit perceptions in employees by designing a job for an individual or assigning job tasks that that they know fit the individual employee's self-concept. It is also possible that managers can create high fit perceptions through the feedback they provide and communications they have with employees. High self-concept-job fit perceptions might also be created by assigning goals that the individual can achieve. This can impact efficacy perceptions and enhance self-esteem, which would satisfy the need for positive self-esteem and be consistent with the positive evaluative component of the self-concept. Future research needs to explore management behaviors and practices that facilitate the development of valued fit perceptions.

Future research must also focus on the measurement of self-concept-job fit. The measurement of fit in research has been controversial (Edwards, 1993; Kristof, 1996; Schneider et al., 1995) and has proceeded along two lines: indirect measures of fit and direct, perceptual measures of fit. Indirect measures involve the comparison of profiles and use the D^2 statistic as a measure of the difference between the profiles. An indirect method of measurement would involve the use of a self-concept scale to create a profile of the individual self-concept and the use of a job analytic method to create a profile of the job. The two profiles would then be compared and the D^2 statistic would be a measure of the degree of difference (fit) in the two profiles. This method of calculating fit has received considerable criticism (Edwards, 1993) but is one manner in which self-concept-job fit could be measured.

Direct, perceptual measures offer another method of measuring fit. This method would involve the individual reporting the degree to which they perceive that their job tasks match their self-concepts. Items would need to be developed for measuring the self-concept-job fit construct and the construct validity of the measure established through construct validation procedures. Perceptual measures of fit are beginning to receive more attention in the research literature (Cable & Derue, 2002; Lauver & Kristof-Brown, 2001), in part because it is known that perceptions have a strong impact upon attitudes and behaviors and may be more predictive of behavior than indirect measures of fit that are not based upon individual perception.

Last, future research should investigate the structure of fit perceptions (Cable & Derue, 2002). This paper has proposed that self-concept-job fit is distinct from demand-abilities and supply-value fit. However, it is possible the individuals' fit perceptions are structured differently. An individual's perception of their abilities, values, needs, and desires could impact or be a large part of that individual's self-concept. Therefore, it is possible that fitting the self-concept to a job involves demand-abilities and supply-value fit and that these two types of fit are included in self-concept-job fit. Future research needs to examine these possibilities and the implications for fitting individuals to jobs.

REFERENCES

Allen, N., & Meyer, J. (1996). Affective, continuance, and normative commitment to the organization: An examination of construct validity. *Journal of Vocational Behavior, 49*(3), 252-276.

Boxx, R., Odom, R. Y., & Dunn, M. G. (1991). Organizational values and value congruency and their impact on satisfaction, commitment, and cohesion: An empirical examination within the public sector. *Public Personnel Management, 20*(1), 195-205.

Bretz, R. D., & Judge, T. A. (1994). Person-organization fit and the theory of work adjustment: Implications for satisfaction, tenure, and career success. *Journal of Vocational Behavior, 44*, 32-54.

Byrne, B. M. (1996). *Measuring self-concept across the life span: Issues and instrumentation*. Washington DC: American Psychological Association.

Cable, D. M., & Derue, D. S. (2002). The convergent and discriminant validity of subjective fit perceptions. *Journal of Applied Psychology, 87*, 875-883.

Cable, D. M., & Judge, T. A. (1996). Person-organization fit, job choice decisions, and organizational entry. *Organizational Behavior and Human Decision Processes, 67*, 294-311.

Cable, D. M., & Judge, T. A. (1997). Interviewers' perceptions of person-organization fit and organizational selection decisions. *Journal of Applied Psychology, 82*, 546-561.

Campbell, J. D., Assanand, S., & Di Paula, A. (2000). Structural features of the self-concept and adjustment. In A. Tesser, R. B. Felson & J. M. Suls (Eds.), *Psychological perspectives of self and identity* (pp. 67-87). Washington DC: American Psychological Association.

Campbell, J. D., Trapnell, P. D., Heine, S. J., Katz, I. M., Lavallee, L. F., & Lehman, D. R. (1996). Self-concept clarity: Measurement, personality correlates, and cultural boundaries. *Journal of Personality and Social Psychology, 70*(1), 141-156.

Caudron, S. (1997). The search for meaning at work. *Training and Development, 51*(9), 24-27.
Conger, J. A. (1994). *Spirit at work: Discovering the spirituality of leadership*. San Francisco: Jossey-Bass.
Edwards, J. R. (1993). Problems with the use of profile similarity indices in the study of congruence in organizational research. *Personnel Psychology, 46*, 641-665.
Edwards, J. R. (1996). An examination of competing versions of the person-environment fit approach to stress. *Academy of Management Journal, 39*(2), 292-339.
Hackman, J. R., & Oldham, G. R. (1976). Motivation through the design of work: Test of a theory. *Organizational Behavior and Human Performance, 16*, 250-279.
Harris, S. G., & Mossholder, K. W. (1996). The affective implications of perceived congruence with culture dimensions during organizational transformation. *Journal of Management, 22*(4), 527-547.
Hogan, R., & Roberts, B. W. (2000). A socioanalytic perspective on person-environment interaction. In W. B. Walsh, K. H. Craik, & R. H. Price (Eds.), *Person-environment psychology: New directions and perspectives* (2nd ed., pp. 1-23). Mahwah, NJ: Erlbaum.
Hoyle, R. H., Kernis, M. H., Leary, M. R., & Baldwin, M. R. (1999). *Selfhood: Identity, esteem, regulation*. Boulder, CO: Westview Press.
Jaros, S. J. (1995). An assessment of Meyer and Allen's (1991) three-component model of organizational commitment and turnover intentions. *Best Papers Proceedings of the Academy of Management Journal, USA*, 317-325.
Jaros, S .J., Jermier, J. M., Koehler, J. W., & Sincich, T. (1993). Effects of continuance, affective and moral commitment on the withdrawal process: An evaluation of eight structural equation models. *Academy of Management Journal, 36*(5), 951-995.
Judge, T. A., & Cable, D. M. (1997). Applicant personality, organizational culture, and organization attraction. *Personnel Psychology, 50*(2), 359-395.
Kristof, A. L. (1996). Person-organization fit: An integrative review of its conceptualizations, measurement, and implications. *Personnel Psychology, 49*, 1-49.
Kristof-Brown, A. L. (2000). Perceived applicant fit: Distinguishing between recruiters' perceptions of person-job and person-organization fit. *Personnel Psychology, 53*(3), 643-671.
Lauver, K. J., & Kristof-Brown, A. (2001). Distinguishing between employees' perceptions of person-job and person-organization fit. *Journal of Vocational Behavior, 59*(3), 454-470.
Livingstone, L. P., Nelson, D. L., & Barr, S. H. (1997). Person-environment fit and creativity: An examination of supply-value and demand-ability versions of fit. *Journal of Management, 23*(2), 119-146.
Locke, E. A. (1976). The nature and causes of job satisfaction. In M. D. Dunnette (Ed.), *Handbook of industrial and organizational psychology* (pp. 1297-1349). Chicago: Rand McNally.
Marsh, H. W., & Hattie, J. (1996). Theoretical perspectives on the structure of self-concept. In B. A. Bracken (Ed.), *Handbook of self-concept: Developmental, social, and clinical considerations* (pp. 38-90). New York: Wiley.

Mitchell, T. R., Holtom, B. C., & Lee, T. W. (2001). How to keep your best employees: Developing an effective retention policy. *Academy of Management Executive, 15*(4), 96-109.

Muchinsky, P. M., & Monahan, C. J. (1987). What is person-environment congruence? Supplementary versus complementary models of fit. *Journal of Vocational Behavior, 31*, 268-277.

Organ, D. W. (1990). The motivational basis of organizational citizenship behavior. In B. M. Staw & L. L. Cummings (Eds.), *Research in organizational behavior* (Vol. 12, pp. 43-72). Greenwich, CT: JAI Press.

Organ, D. W., & Paine, J. B. (1999). A new kind of performance for industrial and organizational psychology: Recent contributions to the study of organizational citizenship behavior. In C. L. Cooper & I. T. Robertson (Eds.), *International review of industrial and organizational psychology* (pp. 337-368). New York: Wiley.

Pinder, C. (1998). Beliefs, attitudes and emotions at work. In C. C. Pinder (Ed.), *Work motivation in organizational behavior* (pp. 241-284). Upper Saddle River, NJ: Prentice-Hall.

Posner, B. Z., Kouzes, J. M., & Schmidt, W. H. (1985). Shared values make a difference: An empirical test of corporate culture. *Human Resource Management, 24*, 293-309.

Rathus, S A., & Nevid, J. S. (1980). *Adjustment and growth: The challenges of life.* New York: Holt, Rinehart and Winston.

Rosin, H. M., & Korabik, K. (1991). Workplace variables, affective responses, and intention to leave among women managers. *Journal of Occupational Psychology, 64*, 317-330.

Saks, A. M., & Ashforth, B. E. (1997). A longitudinal investigation of the relationships between job information sources, applicant perceptions of fit, and work outcomes. *Personnel Psychology, 50*, 395-426.

Schneider, B. (1987). The people make the place. *Personnel Psychology, 40*, 437-453.

Schneider, B.,Goldstein, H. W., & Smith, D. B. (1995). The ASA framework: An update. *Personnel Psychology, 48*, 747-773.

Shamir, B. (1991). Meaning, self, and motivation in organizations. *Organization Studies, 12*(3), 405-424.

Shavelson, R. J., Hubner, J. J., & Stanton, G. C. (1976). Self-concept: Validation of construct interpretations. *Review of Educational Research, 46*, 407-441.

Society for Human Resource Management. (2005, June). *SHRM job satisfaction series: 2005 job satisfaction survey report.* Retrieved November 11, 2005, from http://www.shrm.org/hrresources/surveys_published/SHRM%20job%20satisfaction

Swann, W. B., Jr. (1983). Self-verification: Bringing social reality into harmony with the self. In J. Suls & A. G. Greenwald (Eds.), *Psychological perspectives on the self* (Vol. 4, pp. 33-66). Hillsdale, NJ: Erlbaum.

Swann, W. B., Jr. (1990). To be adored or to be known? The interplay of self-enhancement and self-verification. In R. M. Sorrentino & E. T. Higgins (Eds.), *Motivation and cognition* (Vol. 4, pp. 408-448). New York: Guilford.

Tett, R. P., & Meyer J. P. (1993). Job satisfaction, organizational commitment, turnover intention, and turnover: Path analyses based on meta-analytic findings. *Personnel Psychology, 46*(2), 259-280.

Van Vianen, A. E. M. (2000). Person-organization fit: The match between newcomer's and recruiter's preferences for organizational cultures. *Personnel Psychology, 53*(1), 113-149.

Werbel, J. D., & Johnson, D. J. (2001). The use of person-group fit for employment selection: A missing link in person-environment fit. *Human Resource Management, 40*(3), 227-240.

CHAPTER 15

PERSON-ORGANIZATION FIT AND JOB SATISFACTION

An Interactional Approach

Daniel J. Svyantek, Kristin. L. Cullen,
Brian L. Perdomo, and Scott A. Goodman

Person-organization (PO) fit is a complex conceptualization of the congruence between an employee and their organization's environment. The following paper investigates two different approaches to looking at this relationship. PO fit is assessed (1) using recognized statistical measures of PO fit and (2) using measures of employee and organizational characteristics and assessing their interactions. An empirical study of the relationship between PO fit and job satisfaction is presented. The organizational implications of the relationship between PO fit and job satisfaction are discussed using Schneider's (1987) ASA framework to integrate the results of the study. The implications of this study support the importance of PO fit. The relationship of PO fit varies depending on the facet of job satisfaction used as the dependent variable of interest. This research is used to assess whether either of the two approaches have more utility for organizations seeking to use PO fit to improve on important organizational criteria.

Refining Familiar Constructs: Alternative Views in OB, HR, and I/O, pp. 233–259
Copyright © 2007 by Information Age Publishing
All rights of reproduction in any form reserved.

The explanation of complex human behavior requires the consideration of person, contextual, and behavioral variables (Funder, 2001). The behaviors exhibited in a situation have an adaptive function (Morris, 1988). The degree to which behavior is adaptive, however, is defined relative to the situational requirements and individual differences of the people in the situation. The mission of personality psychology is to account for the characteristic patterns of thoughts, emotions, behaviors and the psychological mechanisms that generate these adaptive patterns of behavior (Funder, 2001). The primary theoretical approach to personality today is the interactional model of personality (Fleeson, 2004; Mischel, 2004).

THE INTERACTIONAL MODEL OF PERSONALITY

The interactional approach to understanding and predicting behavior requires that the effects of both dispositional and situational elements are assessed by the researcher. This approach is exemplified by the social-cognitive approach to personality (Mischel & Shoda, 1998). The social cognitive approach construes personality as a system of mediating units (e.g., encodings, expectancies, and goals) and psychological processes that interact with the situation in which an individual resides. These psychological processes, or cognitive-affective dynamics, can be either conscious or unconscious. The key element of this model is that both situational and dispositional factors must be incorporated to understand how behavior is determined.

New research is showing that individuals exhibit stable patterns of cross-situational variability which characterize the individuals when behavior is examined in relation to situations in which this behavior occurs (Mischel, 2004). These stable patterns of person-situation interactions, in turn, hint at the organization of the underlying system that generates them. The focus of research shifts from search for broad, situation-free trait descriptors (e.g., conscientiousness) to more situation-qualified characterizations of persons in contexts (e.g., conscientious people in the workplace). This means that dispositions must be understood as conditional and interactive with the situations in which they are expressed.

This view proposes that different situations will acquire different meanings for the same individual and the same situation may have different meanings for different people (cf. Mischel, 2004). Therefore, there is no theoretical reason to expect individuals to display similar behavior in relation to different psychological situations unless they are functionally equivalent in meaning for them. The route to finding the invariance in personality requires taking account of the situation and its meaning for the individual and finding stable interactions illustrating the interplay between individuals and the situations.

Interactional Models in Organizational Research

The person, situation, and the behaviors being performed in a situation must be defined for a clear understanding of human behavior (Funder, 2001). This is particularly important for research on behavior in organizational contexts. Organizational research, by definition, is the study of individuals in a particular type of context: the workplace. Therefore, while this is a simple point, organizational research into the determinants of workplace behavior must include both situational and dispositional variables to truly begin to understand the causes of important job behaviors such as task performance, organizational commitment, and contextual performance (sometimes also called organizational citizenship (OCB)). Understanding organizational behavior, therefore, requires an interactional approach to personality to be used in research in organizations.

We propose that there are two basic research approaches which may be used to conduct interactional studies of personality and situational effects in organizations. These are (1) person-organization fit studies and (2) the conduct of studies which explicitly incorporate measures of personality and the situation to assess the main effects of each type of variable and to assess the interactions between these variables.

Person-Organization Fit as an Interactional Variable

Person-organization fit has been defined as "the congruence between patterns of organizational values and patterns of individual values, defined here as what an individual values in an organization, such as being team-oriented or innovative" (Chatman, 1991, p. 459). The emphasis here is on the match of an individual's values, when considered along with the value system in a specific organizational context, and the potential effects that this match (or lack of this match) has on that individual's subsequent behavior and attitudes. Therefore, both situational and dispositional aspects are combined into one measure which, conceptually, represents an interaction between the two classes of situational and dispositional variables.

Person-organization fit has been shown to be related to a number of organizational variables including (1) job choice decisions by organizational applicants (Cable & Judge, 1996); (2) organizational attraction of applicants (Judge & Cable, 1997); (3) selection decisions made by recruitment interviewers (Cable & Judge, 1997); (4) employee job satisfaction, job tenure and career success (Bretz & Judge, 1994); and (5) employee's level of task and organizational citizenship performance (Goodman & Svyantek, 1999). Person-organization fit has been defined as "the congruence between patterns of organizational values and patterns of individual values, defined here as what an individual values in an organization, such as being team-oriented or innovative" (Chatman, 1991, p. 459). The emphasis here is on the match of an individual's values, when considered along with the value system in a specific organizational context, and the potential effects that match (or lack of match) has on that individual's subsequent behavior and attitudes. Therefore, both situational and dispositional aspects are combined into one measure which, conceptually, represents an interaction between the two classes of situational and dispositional variables.

Researchers must decide how to measure person-organization fit. There are two related methods of doing this. Person-organization fit assessment involves collapsing two constructs into one measure as a predictor of some outcome. The vast majority of person-organization fit studies have operationalized congruency by collapsing two or more measures into a single index. These profile similarity indices (PSIs) combine two sets of measures, or profiles, from corresponding entities (e.g., the ideal state and organization) into a single score intended to represent overall congruence (Cronbach & Glesser, 1953). Examples of this include the use of discrepancy scores and the use of correlations between observed culture and personal values (cf. O'Reilly, Chatman, & Caldwell, 1991).

Edwards (1993, 1994, 1995), however, suggests that PSIs should no longer be used in congruence research, such as person-organization fit. Instead, researchers should use polynomial equations containing measures of both entities (here the actual and ideal culture measurements) that typically are collapsed in PSIs (cf. Edwards, 1993, 1994; Edwards & Cooper, 1990; Edwards & Harrison, 1993; Edwards & Parry, 1993). The general approach suggested by Edwards (1993, 1994) offers several advantages over congruence indices currently in use. First, polynomial regression maintains the interpretability of the original component measures. Second, polynomial regression yields separate estimates of the relationships between component measures and the outcome. Third, polynomial regression provides a complete test of models underlying congruence indices, focusing not only on the overall magnitude of the relationship, but also on the significance of individual effects, the validity of implied constraints, and the significance of higher-order terms. Finally, the approach proposed by Edwards (1993, 1994) may yield considerable increases in explained variance.

Goodman and Svyantek's (1999) findings were based on the use of Edwards' (1993, 1994) approach. The use of this method allowed interpretable patterns of results to be found for both actual and ideal measure of organizational climate as predictors of employee task and organizational citizenship performance. Therefore, we recommend that Edward's approach be used when addressing issues of person-organization fit when investigating the interaction of situational and dispositional factors as defined by the construct of person-organization fit.

Measuring *Both* Situational and Dispositional Variables

One question to consider when conducting research based on an interactional model of personality is whether perceptions of organizational climate and measured dispositional variables *or* the match between individuals' perceptions of the current and ideal states (e.g., person-organization fit as assessed above) is more helpful in predicting organizational behavior. At this point, the answer to this question is still unknown. Therefore, it may be appropriate to explicitly include both situational and dispositional variables in research studies to assess how these variables affect organizational criteria.

Research studies incorporating both dispositional and situational variables have been conducted. For example, Schein and Diamonte (1988) found a relationship between three different personality variables and organizational characteristics. People who rated themselves as high on a personality characteristic were more likely to be attracted to an organization that was described as reflecting that characteristic. Similarly, it was found that organizational climate information and personality variables interact in a recruitment situation (Furlong & Svyantek, 1998). Personality variables were found to prime individuals to perceive and select organizational climates in which they will have a high probability of succeeding. Beatty, Cleveland, and Murphy (2001) studied the relationship between strong and weak situations and the Big Five personality variables. Their findings were that while Big Five personality variables did predict organizational citizenship performance variables, the variable with the highest R^2 value was the situation. Miles, Borman, Spector, and Fox (2002) used both situational and dispositional variables and found that situational variables and dispositional variables accounted for nearly the same amount of variance.

It has been hypothesized that actual measures of organizational climate may be more predictive of performance measures than are perceived fit measures (Kristof, 1996). Therefore, it may be appropriate to explicitly include both situational and dispositional variables in research studies to assess how these variables affect organizational criteria. This is the second method of studying the interactional model's value for predicting important organizational criteria. The organizational criterion of interest in this chapter is job satisfaction.

Job Satisfaction and Person-Organization Interactions

Job satisfaction has been defined in many ways. For example, job satisfaction may be thought of as a pleasurable or positive emotional state resulting from the appraisal of a person's job or job experiences (Locke, 1976). Perhaps the simplest definition is "Job satisfaction is the degree to which people like their jobs" (Spector, 1997, p. vii). Job satisfaction is the most studied construct in organizational behavior research (Spector, 1997). Job satisfaction is hypothesized to have the potential to improve job performance and organizational citizenship behavior; to decrease withdrawal behaviors such as absenteeism and turnover; to decrease counterproductive behaviors on the job; and improve the psychological well-being of employees (Spector, 1997). Conversely, job dissatisfaction is hypothesized to have the opposite effects on these criteria.

Job satisfaction (and its opposite, job dissatisfaction) may be considered global feelings about the job or may be related to specific facets of jobs. The primary difference is that, while global models may provide information to company's about whether departments or other organizational units (e.g., teams) differ in job satisfaction levels, facet models of job satisfaction and job dissatisfaction provide organizations with clues for where interventions may be made to increase employee job satisfaction. The facet approach, therefore, may be a more appropriate way to research job satisfaction if there is a practical application to the research being conducted.

Two primary classes of variables are held to be predictors of job satisfaction (Spector, 1997). These are personal dispositional variables (e.g., personality differences) and organizational variables (e.g., job characteristics and/ or organizational variables). Much of job satisfaction research has considered these two classes of variables separately. Person-job fit research, however, has been proposed as a model of how job satisfaction is caused. Person-job fit allows the interaction between job and person factors to be investigated. This model proposes that job satisfaction will be the result of a match between the characteristics of the employee in a job and the characteristics of the job. However, research has shown that person-organization fit and job satisfaction are strongly related.

The largest correlations between PO fit and dependent measures occur with job satisfaction, OCBs, commitment, turnover, and job search and choice in Tables 15.1 and 15.2. Performance outcomes are less related as there are many other mediating factors, including the job type, limitations of technology, and factors present in the external environment. Even with these moderators, Bretz and Judge (1994) still found that PO fit relates to job promotions and salary level, which are indicators of performance.

Job satisfaction is the individual worker's subjective evaluation of the degree to which his or her needs are meet by the organization. Bretz and Judge (1994) proposed the theory of work adjustment (TWA), in which they stated that job satisfaction, tenure, and rewards moderate the relationship between person-environment fit. If there is congruence between an employee's needs and what the organization provides then both job satisfaction and job tenure will follow.

Job satisfaction correlations are .40 person-organization fit; and .39 with person-job fit while intentions to quit correlates −.47 with person-organization fit and and −.22 with person-job fit (Lauver & Kristof-Brown, 2001). These findings imply that each of the types of fit measured contribute equally to job satisfaction, however employees' perceptions of their person-organization fit has the largest impact on their intention to quit. Tett and Meyer (1993) hoped to address the issue of predictive direc-

Table 15.1. Correlation Between Individual Outcomes and Fit Operationalization (from Kristof-Brown, Zimmerman, & Johnson, 2005)

Outcome	Person-Job Fit	Person-Organization Fit	Person-Group Fit	Person-Supervisor Fit
Job satisfaction	.56	.44	.31	.44
Organizational satisfaction		.65		
Coworker satisfaction	.32	.39	.42	
Supervisor satisfaction	.33	.33	.28	.46
Overall performance	.20	.07	.19	.18
Contextual performance		.27	.23	
Indicators of strain	−.28	−.27		
Organizational commitment	.47	.51	.19	.09
Intention to quit	−.46	−.35	−.22	
Tenure	.18	.03	.06	.09
Turnover	−.08	−.14		
Withdrawal		−.05		

Table 15.2. Correlations between Individual Outcomes and Perceived Fit Operationalization (from Cable & DeRue (2002))

Individual Outcomes	Person-Organization Fit	Demands-Abilities Fit	Need-Supplies Fit
Organizational identification	.48	.23	.34
POS	.53	.34	.40
OCB	.22	.01	.16
Turnover	−.17	−.11	−.10
Occupational commitment	.33	.24	.43
Job performance	.11	.00	−.02
Pay raises	.13	.13	.20
Job satisfaction	.53	.33	.61
Career satisfaction	.17	.27	.38

tion between commitment and satisfaction and eventual turnover intentions. They found satisfaction and commitment to be distinguishable, yet moderately related constructs that contribute uniquely to turnover intentions.

Summary

Person-organization fit research has shown that the discrepancy between actual and ideal organizational culture (i.e., discrepancies between what the organization and the individual values) can influence important organizational criteria (Chatman, 1991). The present study used a facet model of job satisfaction to address two research questions with both practical and academic importance. First, the relative influence of dispositional and organizational characteristics on facets of job satisfaction was investigated. Second, the effects of person-organization fit on the facets of job satisfaction were investigated.

METHODS

Setting and Subjects

A survey was administered on-site to 356 organizational members, encompassing a wide variety of jobs across 11 departments of a major Midwestern manufacturing organization to assess the current state of the organizational culture and employee satisfaction. Participation in the survey was voluntary. Two hundred and twenty one of the 356 respondents had useable surveys (a return rate of 62.1%). Of the 221 incumbents, 161 (72.90%) were male and 60 (27.10%) were female.

Procedure

Incumbents received a packet of materials along with an instruction sheet. The packet included self-report measures of job satisfaction, organizational climate, and personality. The administration time for each session was approximately 1 hour. Subordinates were informed their responses would be kept confidential and results were to be analyzed at the group level for purposes of feedback to the organization.

Measures

Job Satisfaction

Job satisfaction was measured with the Job Descriptive Index (JDI) developed by Smith, Kendall, and Hulin (1969). The JDI uses a combination of an adjective checklist and Likert format to yield satisfaction scores in five different areas: the job itself, pay and benefits, promotion, supervision, and coworkers. In addition to the five separate scores for the various aspects of job satisfaction, it has also been suggested that the JDI can be used as a measure of general job satisfaction (Hulin, Drasgow, & Komocar, 1982; Parsons & Hulin, 1982). The JDI contains a total of 72 items and takes approximately 15 minutes to complete. The JDI is widely accepted in satisfaction research (Landy, 1989). It has been described by many as the most carefully constructed measure of job satisfaction (cf. Vroom, 1964). The reliability and validity of the JDI have been reconfirmed in the literature (cf. Johnson, Smith, & Tucker, 1982; Schneider & Dachler, 1978). The JDI scales have been used extensively over a 20 year period and commonly have shown internal consistency estimates of .80 or more (Taber, 1991). The response format for the JDI is a 3-point Likert scale with the following options: Yes, ?, or No. Johnson et al. (1982) compared this traditional response format with a 5-point Likert-type scale. Results showed that both methods yielded acceptable reliabilities and validities; differences were trivial. These researchers recommend continued use of the original format and hence the 3-point response option was employed in this study. Interestingly, there has been much debate about scoring the ? option for JDI items. Traditionally, the scoring system for the adjective-like items is as follows: Agreement (yes) responses to positive items and disagreement (no) responses to negative items receive a score of 3; disagreement (no) responses to positive items and agreement (yes) responses to negative items receive a score of 0; and the ? response is given a score of 1 (Smith et al., 1969). This scoring system, in which the ? receives a score that reflects a more negative than positive response (1 rather than 1.5, which is the midpoint of the 0-3 scale) was recently evaluated to see if it is still appropriate. Hanisch (1992) confirmed that the ? option should be scored as a more negative than positive response. The present study relied on the traditional scoring system.

Organizational Climate

Organizational climate was assessed using the Organizational Climate Questionnaire (OCQ) developed by Litwin and Stringer (1968). Schein (1990) suggests that organizational climate is what we perceive when we observe the way a company functions, whereas organizational culture relates to the causes of an organization's operating style. This suggests that organizational climate refers to individual psychological perceptions of the characteristics of an organization's practices whereas culture is regarded as an emergent property of group interactions. Litwin and Stringer's measure assesses the shared beliefs and values of organizational members that constitute the perceived work environment. The OCQ is one of the better known surveys of its kind (Payne & Pugh, 1976). It consists of 50 items that assess nine dimensions of climate: structure, responsibility, reward, risk, warmth, support, standards, conflict, and identity. Table 15.3 describes the OCQ in greater detail.

Personality

Saville and Holdsworth's (1993) 56-item personality inventory IMAGES was used to measure personality. IMAGES reduces personality to six broad, general factors: **I**maginative, **M**ethodical, **A**chieving, **G**regarious, **E**motional, and **S**ympathetic. Table 15.4 shows how the labels attached to the six IMAGES scales coincide with Norman's (1963) traditional Big Five categories. These factors have been given different names by different psychologists, but the behaviors they represent are very similar. The internal consistency of the IMAGES dimensions are quite acceptable. The technical manual/user's guide reports alpha coefficients for the six scales as follows: Imaginative (.80), Methodical (.83), Achieving (.76), Gregarious (.85), Emotional (.88), and Sympathetic (.79) (Saville & Holdsworth, 1993). Evidence for the validity of IMAGES was derived using a sample of 222 managers who completed the personality inventory. The managers' superiors rated them on a range of criteria (or competencies). It was found that the IMAGES scales proved to be statistically significant predictors of several competencies.

Table 15.3. Organizational Climate Questionnaire (OCQ) Scale Descriptions

Scale	Description
Structure	The feeling that employees have about the constraints in the group, how many rules, regulations, procedures there are; is there an emphasis on "red tape" and going through channels, or is there a loose and informal atmosphere.
Responsibility	The feeling of being your own boss; not having to double-check all your decisions; when you have a job to do, knowing that it is your job.
Reward	The feeling of being rewarded for a job well done; emphasizing positive rewards rather than punishment; the perceived fairness of the pay and promotion policies.
Risk	The sense of riskiness and challenge in the job and in the organization; is there an emphasis on taking calculated risks, or is playing it safe the best way to operate.
Warmth	The feeling of general good fellowship that prevails in the work group atmosphere; the emphasis of being well liked; the prevalence of friendly and informal social groups.
Support	The perceived helpfulness of the managers and other employees in the group; emphasis on mutual support from above and below.
Standards	The perceived importance of implicit and explicit goals and performance standards; the emphasis on doing a good job; the challenge presented in personal and group goals.
Conflict	The feeling that managers and other workers want to hear different opinions; the emphasis placed on getting problems out in the open rather than smoothing them over or ignoring them.
Identity	The feeling that you belong to a company and you are a valuable member of a working team; the importance placed on this kind of spirit.

Table 15.4. Correspondence Between the IMAGES Labels and Big Five Labels

Images Label	Big Five Label
Imaginative	Culture, Openness to experience, intellect
Methodical	Dependability, Conscientiousness
Achieving	—
Gregarious	Surgency, extroversion
Emotional	Emotional stability, Neuroticism
Sympathetic	Agreeableness, Affiliation, Compliance

RESULTS

The present study used a facet model of job satisfaction to address two research questions with both practical and academic importance. First, the relative influence of dispositional and organizational characteristics on facets of job satisfaction was investigated. Second, the effects of person-organization fit on the facets of job satisfaction were investigated. The results of these analyses are presented in the next two sections.

Joint Influence of Dispositional and Organizational Characteristics on Job Satisfaction

Hierarchical regression was used to assess the influence of personality variables based on the Big Five approach and organizational climate variables on facets of job satisfaction. Table 15.5 presents the results of these analyses. The F, significance level, df, and R-squared columns show the results for the entry of personality variables in Step 1 and the entry of the organizational climate variables which were entered in Step 2. The final

Table 15.5. Regression Results for the Five Facets of Job Satisfaction from the JDI

Dependent Variable	Predictor Variables	F	Sig	df	R-Squared	Significant Predictors in Step 2
Present job and work	Personality	2.69	.022	5, 211	.060	Achievement
	Climate	9.482	.000	14, 202	.397	Structure; Reward; Warmth; Identity
Pay benefits	Personality	1.638	.151	5, 211	.037	—
	Climate	9.375	.000	14, 202	.394	Reward; Warmth; Standards; Identity
Promotion opportunity	Personality	2.595	.027	5, 211	.058	—
	Climate	7.287	.000	14, 202	.335	Reward
Supervisors	Personality	2.32	.045	5, 211	.052	—
	Climate	10.72	.000	14, 202	.426	Structure; Reward; Risk; Warmth; Standards; Identity
Coworkers	Personality	2.101	.067	5, 211	.047	Sympathetic
	Climate	8.009	.000	14, 202	.357	Warmth; Identity

column provides the individual predictors with significant t values in Step 2.

Personality variables were significant predictors of (a) present job and work; (b) promotion opportunities; and supervisor facets of job satisfaction. Organizational climate variables were significant predictors of all five facets of job satisfaction. The relative influence of the two classes of predictor variables was such that the organizational climate variables accounted for a much larger percentage of variance than did the personality variables.

Person-Organization Fit and Job Satisfaction

Numerous studies in organizational behavior research have examined congruence between two constructs (here person-organization fit) as a predictor of some outcome. The vast majority of these studies have operationalized congruency by collapsing two or more measures into a single index. These profile similarity indices (PSIs) combine two sets of measures, or profiles, from corresponding entities (e.g., the person and organization) into a single score intended to represent overall congruence (Cronbach & Glesser, 1953). Edwards (1993, 1994) suggests that PSIs should no longer be used in congruence research. Instead, researchers should use polynomial equations containing measures of both entities (here the actual and ideal culture measurements) that typically are collapsed in PSIs (cf. Edwards, 1993, 1994; Edwards & Cooper, 1990; Edwards & Harrison, 1993; Edwards & Parry, 1993). The Edwards (1993, 1994) approach was employed in the present study.

To examine whether people's values and the organization's values (i.e., climate) are important in determining job satisfaction, the research question was phrased as follows: Does an employee's ideal climate determine job satisfaction above and beyond the organizational climate? This question can be examined via hierarchical regression to test the effect of the discrepancy on the dependent variable without creating a discrepancy score using Edwards' (1993, 1994) polynomial regression method.

To investigate research question two, separate hierarchical regression analyses (one for each climate dimension) using the five facets of job satisfaction in the JDI as dependent variables were conducted. Within each of these three-step, three-predictor regressions, perceived culture was entered at Step 1. Step 1 of each regression equation tested the effect of perceptions of actual climate on a facet of job satisfaction. Ideal climate perceptions were entered at Step 2. Evidence for the proposal that person-organization fit influences job satisfaction can be demonstrated by results showing ideal climate possesses some incremental ability to predict job satisfaction after statistically controlling for perceived climate. Here the incremental R^2 at Step 2 must be significant. This order was used because it is the most conservative for testing Hypothesis 2. The interaction created by multiplying perceived and ideal climate scores for each respondent was entered in Step 3 to assess whether this factor predicted a facet of job satisfaction.

Present Job and Work Facet

Table 16.6 shows the results of the hierarchical regression analyses used to predict the job satisfaction facet, present job and work, from perceived and ideal climate. When this facet, present job and work, served as the DV of interest, the R^2 at Step 1 was significant for six of the nine culture dimensions. At Step 2, the increments in R^2 were only significant for one of the nine culture dimensions. This provides only weak support for the proposal that PO fit influences job satisfaction. Last, the cross product of the perceived and ideal ratings of climate dimensions were entered into the prediction equations as a final step. Results showed there were no significant increments in R^2 from Step 2 to Step 3.

Table 15.6. R^2 Values for Hierarchical Regression Analyses Predicting Present Job and Work Facet From Perceived and Ideal Climates

Dimension	Step 1[1]	Step 2[2]	Step 3[3]	Total[4]
Warmth	.273**	.002	.001	.276
Reward	.245**	.000	.003	.248
Risk	.000	.001	.008	.008
Conflict	.017	.000	.002	.019
Support	.113**	.001	.000	.115
Standards	.000	.014	.005	.019
Identity	.252**	.002	.000	.254
Responsibility	.043*	.019*	.011	.073
Structure	.064**	.000	.044	.069

*$p < .05$
**$p < .01$
1. R^2 value for Step 1 predictor, perceived culture
2. Incremental R^2 value for Step 2 predictor, ideal culture
3. Incremental R^2 value for Step 3 predictor, the interaction of perceived and ideal culture
4. Total R^2 for all three predictors

Table 16.7. R^2 Values for Hierarchical Regression Analyses Predicting Pay and Benefit Facet from Perceived and Ideal Climates

Dimension	Step 1[1]	Step 2[2]	Step 3[3]	Total[4]
Warmth	.258**	.001	.002	.261
Reward	.274**	.004	.002	.280
Risk	.017	.009	.011	.038
Conflict	.008	.001	.001	.010
Support	.109*	.007	.002	.118
Standards	.017	.008	.008	.032
Identity	.177**	.009	.005	.191
Responsibility	.033*	.010	.000	.044
Structure	.007	.044*	.027*	.078

$*p < .05$
$**p < .01$
1. R^2 value for Step 1 predictor, perceived culture
2. Incremental R^2 value for Step 2 predictor, ideal culture
3. Incremental R^2 value for Step 3 predictor, the interaction of perceived and ideal culture
4. Total R^2 for all three predictors

Pay and Benefits

Table 15.7 shows the results of the hierarchical regression analyses used to predict the job satisfaction facet, present job and work, from perceived and ideal climate. When this facet, present job and work, served as the DV of interest, the R^2 at Step 1 was significant for five of the nine culture dimensions. At Step 2, the increments in R^2 were only significant for one of the nine climate dimensions. This provides only weak support for the proposal that PO fit influences job satisfaction. Last, the cross product of the ratings of the perceived and ideal climate dimensions were entered into the prediction equations as a final step. Here the increments in R^2 were only significant for one of the nine climate dimensions. Once again, this provides only weak support for the proposal that PO fit influences job satisfaction.

Promotion Opportunities

Table 15.8 shows the results of the hierarchical regression analyses used to predict the job satisfaction facet, present job and work, from perceived and ideal climate. When this facet, present job and work, served as the DV of interest, the R^2 at step 1 was significant for seven of the nine culture dimensions. At step 2, the increments in R^2 was not significant for any of the nine climate dimensions. Last, the cross prod-

Table 15.8. R^2 Values for Hierarchical Regression Analyses Predicting Promotion Opportunities From Perceived and Ideal Climates

Dimension	Step 1[1]	Step 2[2]	Step 3[3]	Total[4]
Warmth	.170**	.000	.000	.170
Reward	.267**	.000	.003	.270
Risk	.007	.007	.004	.019
Conflict	.040*	.005	.012	.056
Support	.173**	.006	.000	.179
Standards	.000**	.017	.011	.028
Identity	.163**	.002	.000	.165
Responsibility	.024*	.000	.000	.025
Structure	.029*	.004	.018*	.051

*$p < .05$
**$p < .01$
1. R^2 value for Step 1 predictor, perceived culture
2. Incremental R^2 value for Step 2 predictor, ideal culture
3. Incremental R^2 value for Step 3 predictor, the interaction of perceived and ideal culture
4. Total R^2 for all three predictors

uct of the ratings of the perceived and ideal climate dimensions were entered into the prediction equations as a final step. Here the increments in R^2 were only significant for one of the nine climate dimensions. Once again, this provides only weak support for the proposal that PO fit influences job satisfaction.

Supervision

Table 15.9 shows the results of the hierarchical regression analyses used to predict the job satisfaction facet, present job and work, from perceived and ideal climate. When this facet, present job and work, served as the DV of interest, the R^2 at Step 1 was significant for eight of the nine culture dimensions. At Step 2, the increments in R^2 was not significant for any of the nine climate dimensions. Last, the cross product of the ratings of the perceived and ideal climate dimensions were entered into the prediction equations as a final step. Here the increments in R^2 were only significant for one of the nine climate dimensions. Once again, this provides only weak support for the proposal that PO fit influences job satisfaction.

Coworkers

Table 15.10 shows the results of the hierarchical regression analyses used to predict the job satisfaction facet, present job and work, from per-

Table 15.9. R^2 Values for Hierarchical Regression Analyses Predicting Supervision Facet from Perceived and Ideal Climates

Dimension	Step 1[1]	Step 2[2]	Step 3[3]	Total[4]
Warmth	.298**	.000	.011	.309
Reward	.263**	.000	.003	.266
Risk	.045*	.007	.000	.052
Conflict	.021*	.015	.012	.048
Support	.168**	.018*	.001	.187
Standards	.003**	.005	.015	.023
Identity	.230**	.003	.015	.248
Responsibility	.057*	.008	.001	.067
Structure	.067**	.004	.022*	.093

*$p < .05$
**$p < .01$
1. R^2 value for Step 1 predictor, perceived culture
2. Incremental R^2 value for Step 2 predictor, ideal culture
3. Incremental R^2 value for Step 3 predictor, the interaction of perceived and ideal culture
4. Total R^2 for all three predictors

Table 15.10. R^2 Values for Hierarchical Regression Analyses Predicting Co-workers Facet From Perceived and Ideal Climates

Dimension	Step 1[1]	Step 2[2]	Step 3[3]	Total[4]
Warmth	.224**	.000	.225	.225
Reward	.169**	.006	.175	.175
Risk	.013	.007	.007	.027
Conflict	.017	.001	.010	.020
Support	.148**	.009	.007	.164
Standards	.020*	.003	.000	.023
Identity	.281**	.007	.001	.289
Responsibility	.036*	.013	.008	.057
Structure	.061**	.010	.034	.105

*$p < .05$
**$p < .01$
1. R^2 value for Step 1 predictor, perceived culture
2. Incremental R^2 value for Step 2 predictor, ideal culture
3. Incremental R^2 value for Step 3 predictor, the interaction of perceived and ideal culture
4. Total R^2 for all three predictors

ceived and ideal climate. When this facet, present job and work, served as the DV of interest, the R^2 at step 1 was significant for seven of the nine culture dimensions. At step 2 and step 3, the increments in R^2 were not significant for any of the nine climate dimensions. This provides no support for the proposal that PO fit influences job satisfaction.

DISCUSSION

The results of this study provide data for drawing some conclusions about the relationship between person-organization fit and job satisfaction. The present study used a facet model of job satisfaction to address two research questions with both practical and academic importance. First, the relative influence of dispositional and organizational characteristics on facets of job satisfaction was investigated. Second, the effects of person-organization fit on the facets of job satisfaction were investigated. The remainder of the discussion will focus on (1) interpreting the results of this study and integrating the results of this study into the general body of literature on person-organization fit; (2) discussing the limitations of these results and offering recommendations for future research; and (3) offering some tentative conclusions for the practitioner.

Relationship Between Job Satisfaction and Organizational and Personality Variables

First, we investigated the relative influence of situational and individual difference variables on job satisfaction. Table 15.5 presents these results. There were two primary findings in this analysis. First, situational variables accounted for a higher proportion of variance than did the individual difference variables. Second, the individual predictors of the facets of job satisfaction differ across the facets. Inspection of the final column in Table 5 shows that the effects of personality variables differed across facets of job satisfaction. Achievement was a significant predictor of feelings toward the present job and work facet. Gregariousness (Extroversion) was a significant predictor of feelings about the Promotion Opportunities facet. Sympathetic (Agreeableness) was a significant predictor of feeling on the Coworker facet. There was more consistency for the effects of the organizational climate variables. Warmth was a predictor of four facets (all except Promotion Opportunities). Reward was a predictor of four facets (all except Coworkers). Identity was a predictor of four facets (all except Promotion Opportunities). Structure predicted two facets, Present Job and Work and Supervisors. Standards was a significant predictor of the Pay Benefits facet and Risk was a significant predictor of the Supervisor facet as well.

Patterns of Prediction Across the Dependent Variables for PO Fit

Second, we were interested in the degree to which standard measures of PO fit predict facets of job satisfaction. The issue remains whether actual or ideal ratings of climate are more important in predicting contextual and task performance. The results of the inspection of the patterns of significance among the predictors in Tables 15-6–15.11 provides some insight into this issue. The primary predictors of job satisfaction are the employee's ratings of the actual state of the organization on the climate dimensions.

A closer inspection of Tables 15.6–15.10 provide insight into the relationship between person-organization fit and facets of job satisfaction. First, the organizational climate dimensions may be sorted into two classes of predictors, strong and weak, in relation to their respective value for predicting facets of job satisfaction. The organizational climate dimensions, Warmth, Reward, Identity, and Support, may be assigned to the strong class of predictors for facets of job satisfaction. Table 15.11 compares the R^2 values for each of the nine perceived climate dimension for each of the five job facets. These four organizational climate dimen-

Table 15.11. Comparison of R^2 Values for Perceived Climate Dimensions Relationships With All Job Satisfaction Facets From

Dimension	Present Job and Work	Pay and Benefits	Promotion Opportunities	Supervision	Coworkers
Warmth	.273**	.258**	.170**	.298**	.224**
Reward	.245**	.274**	.267**	.263**	.169**
Identity	.252**	.177**	.163**	.230**	.281**
Support	.113**	.109**	.173**	.168**	.148**
Structure	.064**	—	.029*	.067**	.061**
Responsibility	.043*	.033*	.024*	.057*	.036**
Risk	—	—	—	.045*	—
Standards	—	—	—	—	.020*
Conflict	—	—	.040*	.021*	—

*$p < .05$
**$p < .01$

sions are significant predictors of each of the five predictors. Moreover, these predictors each account for a substantial amount of variance, as assessed by R^2, as well. The amount of variance accounted for by these four dimensions is, individually, over 10% for each of the job facets.

The other five organizational climate dimensions (Structure, Responsibility, Risk, Standards, and Conflict) may be classified as weaker predictors of the facets of job satisfaction. These predictors dimensions, while having some statistically significant relationships with facets of job satisfaction, do not have account for the same amount of variance as the predictors in the same category.

Second, for all organizational climate dimensions, the primary step in which these variables had their effect was in Step 1 in which ratings of the actual organizational culture were entered. Table 15.11 contains the amount of variance accounted for by each dimension in Step 1. Step 1 prediction accounted for almost all the significant relationships found in this study.

Third, Table 15.11 also shows that there was a slightly different pattern of prediction of the individual facets of job satisfaction for the organizational climate dimensions classified as strong predictors. For example, the strongest predictor of the facets, Present Job and Work and Supervision, was the Warmth dimension. The strongest predictor of the facets, Pay and Benefits and Promotion Opportunities, was the Reward Dimension. The strongest predictor of the Coworker facet was the Identity Dimension. This provides support for the proposal that there is differential prediction of job facets by the organizational climate dimensions being evaluated in this study.

Integrating the Results

Kristof's (1996) hypothesized that actual measures of organizational climate and culture may be more predictive of performance measures than are perceived fit measures. This may be true for measures such as job satisfaction as well. Both forms of analyses revealed that the evaluation of situational variables provided the greatest degree of prediction for the facets of job satisfaction. However, both individual difference variables and person-organization fit measures did predict some facets of job satisfaction.

Person-job fit research, is often, proposed as a model of how job satisfaction is caused (cf. Spector, 1997). The results of the study support a broadening of this view of the predictors of job satisfaction to include PO fit measures. The results show that job satisfaction is also predicted by the result of a match between the characteristics the employee perceives to be present in the organization and facets of job satisfaction for at least some facets of job satisfaction.

Person-organization fit is essentially the idea that the extent to which the individual and the organization "match" has important consequences. The results of this study are consistent with, and extend, the findings of other researchers interested in person-organization fit. The findings provide support for the ASA model proposed by Schneider (1983). It has been shown that person-organization fit is an important determinant of organizational attraction (Judge & Cable, 1997); job choice (Cable & Judge, 1996); and hiring decisions (Cable & Judge, 1997). These variables are all related to the Attraction and Selection phases of the ASA model (Schneider, 1983). There are few studies of the later phase, Attrition, in Schneider's (1983) model. One study by Bretz and Judge (1994) have shown that person-organization fit is an important predictor of job satisfaction, salary, and success in the organization. This study show that person-organization fit can affect the ratings of job satisfaction by employees. This means that PO fit may be a very critical component of job satisfaction, and hence, retention of employees by companies.

Limitations of the Present Research

There are several limitations to the present research. Important limitations in this study include limitations in the measurement of job satisfaction and limitations on the external validity of the findings. First, the present study relied on employees' self-ratings of personality, organizational climate and job satisfaction in a single survey. This may be a major problem: However, this problem may be lessened by the fact that the variables assessed in this study are typically assessed by self-ratings.

Second, there may be other third variables which affect the ratings of both climate and job satisfaction which were not measured in this study. For example, personality variables (e.g., a more specific individual difference variable such as Negative Affectivity) may be manifested in the ratings of both climate and job satisfaction. Someone high on negative affectivity, for example, might be describing the climate negatively and providing ratings of low job satisfaction. This idea of searching for more specific individual predictors should be pursued in future research.

Third, the present study used only one organization with a common type of job. As a result, generalizations as to which components of climate are likely to predict job satisfaction elsewhere are problematic. This study examined individual's perceptions of climate. Therefore, the present study does not directly imply that a change in organizational climate will result in a change in job satisfaction. Rather, the study supports the view that discrepancies between what the individual and organization values are account for increased variance in job satisfaction. However, employees in different organization may value different things. Therefore, while discrepancies should still be important in determining job satisfaction, the relative contribution of each climate dimension may play out differently across organizations. Therefore, future research should be done using the person-organization fit methodologies in multiple organizations. This research should seek to include (1) organizations of comparable size; (2) organizations from the same geographic area and (3) organizations from the same industry to provide better conclusions as to the generalizability of these findings.

Practical Implications

Research surrounding PO fit and its resultant outcomes is important for organizations to understand as this research applies in the workplace. This study's results provide avenues for future research.

It is essential to distinguish PO fit from the various other conceptualizations of person-environment congruence (e.g., PJ fit), because even though these constructs are related, they are also distinctly different and influence employee behavior in organizations indifferent manners. The use of each conceptualization of fit should vary depending on the variable being considered and the level of analysis required.

For example, perceived fit of values and personality is likely most important to an organization's applicants decisions to join an organization. However the actual fit of the applicants concerning their values, goals, and KSAs to both the job and organization is what matters to the organization. Thus, if the organization is the differentiating factor then it only makes sense that job seekers would place more emphasis on PO fit. Employment interviews are an opportunity for the company and the applicant to assess their respective fit with each other. Specifically, this gives the applicant an opportunity to learn more about the culture and values of the organization after having previously received preliminary job information. PO fit research implies that job satisfaction develops through self-selection based on fit with the company (e.g. Bowen, Ledforth, & Nathan, 1991; Schneider, 1987). Based on these findings that vocational counseling should emphasize job selection based on knowledge, skills, and abilities (KSAs) and the culture of the organization. Positive outcomes of person-organization fit include more commitment, more satisfaction, and less intention to quit (Bretz & Judge, 1994; Chatman, 1989; Meglino, Ravlin, & Adkins, 1989; O'Reilly et al., 1991).

These findings all support the notion of fit as a very complex phenomenon. The predictors of organizational criteria will not, necessarily, be the same across these different criteria. Managing fit will require that managers concretely state what criteria they wish to affect and analyze the specific organizational and individual difference variables which impact that criteria. citizenship behavior, organizational commitment, decreased intention to leave, and turnover.

The present study highlights the importance of person-organization fit in understanding job satisfaction and offers some insights into how to increase and support job satisfaction of employees. An interesting pattern was found in which four dimensions assessing the general state of the organization, Warmth, Reward, Support, and Identity, were the largest predictors of all facets of job satisfaction measured in this study. Therefore, the most likely finding that would be consistent across settings is that these four dimensions will continue to be important in determining job satisfaction. Managers and organizational consultants seeking to increase the levels of job satisfaction shown by employees should diagnose the general state of their organization. Expectations for job satisfaction contextual performance should be consistent with the organization's climate: Changes in the organization's general climate may be required to achieve increased levels of job satisfaction.

The most likely climate dimension to target for change, at least in the initial stages of such a change intervention, is the Reward dimension. The Reward dimension was a strong predictor for all facets of job satisfaction. The finding that Reward is a significant predictor of job satisfaction shows that increases in job satisfaction may not be free. Organizations would be wise to remember the old saying "You get what you pay for." The reward system of an organization should support job satisfaction by providing some mechanism for showing employees that there is a reciprocal relationship between their behavior (most likely performance) and rewards. Reward systems which do not have this reciprocity are unlikely to find high levels of job satisfaction among their employees. Today, with the onset of the Information Age, there may be a revolutionary change occurring in the human resource management (HRM) principles which guide business organizations as economic forces in the world change models of organizations emphasizing long-term employment and employee loyalty to those emphasizing short-term employment and rapid turnover of employees. Person-organization fit issues will only be come more important as these new HRM principles are developed. This study provides a starting point for understanding how person-organization fit issues will affect the development of these new HRM practices for the twenty-first century.

Conclusion

The growing consensus in personality psychology that the appropriate model for understanding how dispositional and situational variables act to determine behavior is an interactional model (Fleeson, 2004). The person-situation debate, concerning whether consistencies in individuals' behavior are pervasive or broad enough to be meaningfully described in terms of personality traits can at last be declared about 98% over (Funder, 2001). The long-standing dichotomy between the effect of the situation and the person on behavior is a false dichotomy. Rather, the study of the causes of behavior requires an understanding of the "personality triad" (Funder, 2001). The empirical study of personality properly has three elements: the person, the situation, and the behavior of interest. This is the personality triad referred to by Funder. Organizational research should be conducted which assesses all three aspects of this triad. We, therefore, call for always using an interactional approach to understanding organizational behavior. Without studying both the employee and the context in which he or she resides, we will always have less understanding of why some individuals are high performers or good organizational citizens and others are poor performers and poor organizational citizens than we could. We believe that the more complex studies necessitated by the interactional approach to personality offers a fascinating and interesting way of understanding the performance of individuals in the workplace which should be the guiding force of organizational research into the effects of personality on workplace behavior in the future.

AUTHOR'S NOTE

The order of the second and third authors was determined alphabetically. Please direct all correspondence to: Daniel J. Svyantek, PhD Psychology Department Auburn University Auburn, AL 38932 svyandj@auburn.edu

REFERENCES

Beatty, J. C. Jr., Cleveland, J. N., & Murphy, K. R. (2001). The relation between personality and contextual performance in "strong" versus "weak" situations. *Human Performance, 14*, 125-148.

Bowen, D. E., Ledford, G. E., & Nathan, B. R. (1991). Hiring for the organization, not the job. *Academy of Management Executive, 4*, 35-51.

Bretz, R. D., & Judge, T. A. (1994). Person-organization fit and the theory of work adjustment: Implications for satisfaction, tenure, and career success. *Journal of Vocational Behavior, 44*, 32-54.

Cable, D. M., & DeRue, D. S. (2002). The convergent and discriminant validity of subjective fit perceptions. *Journal of Applied Psychology, 87*, 1-17.

Cable, D. M., & Judge, T. A. (1996). Person-organization fit, job choice decisions, and organizational entry. *Organizational Behavior and Human Decision Processes, 67*, 294-311.

Cable, D. M., Judge, T. A. (1997). Interviewer's perceptions of person-organization fit and organizational selection decisions. *Journal of Applied Psychology, 82*, 546-561.

Chatman, J. A. (1989). Improving interactional organizational research: A model of person-organization fit. *Academy of Management Review, 14*, 333-349.

Chatman, J. A. (1991). Matching people and organizations: Selection and socialization in public accounting firms. *Administrative Science Quarterly, 36*, 459-484.

Cronbach, L. J., & Glesser, G. C. (1953). Assessing the similarity between profiles. *Psychological Bulletin, 50*, 456-473.

Edwards, J. R. (1993). Problems with the use of profile similarity indices in the study of congruence in organizational research. *Personnel Psychology, 46*, 641-665.

Edwards, J. R. (1994). The study of congruence in organizational behavior research: Critique and a proposed alternative. *Organizational Behavior and Human Decision Processes, 58*, 51-100.

Edwards, J. R. (1995). Alternatives to difference scores as dependent variables in the study of congruence in organizational research. *Personnel Psychology, 64*, 307-324.

Edwards, J. R., & Cooper, C.L. (1990). The person-environment fit approach to stress: Recurring problems and some suggested solutions. *Journal of Organizational Behavior, 11*, 293-307.

Edwards, J. R., & Harrison, R. V. (1993). Job demands and worker health: Three-Dimensional reexamination of the relationship between person-environment fit and strain. *Journal of Applied Psychology, 78*, 628-648.

Edwards, J. R., & Parry, M. E. (1993). On the use of polynomial regression equations as alternatives to difference scores in organizational research. *Academy of Management Journal, 36*, 1577-1613.

Fleeson, W. (2004). Moving personality beyond the person-situation debate: The challenge and the opportunity of within-person variability. *Current Directions in Psychological Science, 13*, 83-87.

Funder, D. C. (2001). Personality. *Annual Review of Psychology, 52*, 197-221.

Furlong, M. A. & Svyantek, D. J. (1998). The relationship between organizational climate and personality: A contextualist perspective. *Journal of Psychology and Behavioral Sciences, 12*, 43-53.

Goodman, S. A., & Svyantek, D. J. (1999). Person-organization fit and conceptual performance: Do shared values matter? *Journal of Vocational Behavior, 55*, 254-275.

Hanisch, K. A. (1992). The Job Descriptive Index revisited: Questions about the question mark. *Journal of Applied Psychology, 77*, 377-382.

Hulin, C. L., Drasgow, F., & Komocar, J. (1982). Applications of item response theory to analysis of attitude scale translations. *Journal of Applied Psychology, 67*, 818-825.

Johnson, S. M., Smith, P. C., & Tucker, S. M. (1982). Response format of the JDI: Assessment of reliability and validity by the multitrait-multimethod matrix. *Journal of Applied Psychology, 67*, 500-505.

Judge, T. A. & Cable, D. M. (1997). Applicant personality, organizational culture and organizational attraction. *Personnel Psychology, 50*, 359-394.

Kristof, A. L. (1996). Person-organization fit: An integrative review of its conceptualization, measurement, and implications. *Personnel Psychology, 49*, 1-49.

Kristof-Brown, A. L., Zimmerman, R. D., & Johnson, E. C. (2005). Consequences of individuals' fit at work: A meta-analysis of person-job, person organization, person-group and person-supervisor fit. *Personnel Psychology, 58*, 281-342.

Landy, F. J. (1989). *Psychology of work behavior*. Belmont, CA: Brooks/Cole.

Lauver, K. J., & Kristof-Brown, A. (2001). Distinguishing between employees' perceptions of person-job and person-organization fit. *Journal of Vocational Behavior, 59*, 454-470.

Litwin, G. H., & Stringer, R. A. (1968). *Motivation and organizational climate*. Cambridge, MA: Harvard University Press.

Locke, E. A. (1976). The nature and causes of job satisfaction. In M. D. Dunnette (Ed.), *Handbook of Industrial and organizational psychology* (pp. 1297-1350). Chicago: Rand McNally.

Meglino, B. M., Ravlin, E. C., & Adkins, C. L. (1989) A work values approach to corporate culture: A field test of the values congruence process and its relationship to individual outcomes. *Journal of Applied Psychology, 74*(3), 424-432.

Miles, D. E., Borman, W. E., Spector, P. E., & Fox, S. (2002). Building an integrative model of extra role work behaviors: A comparison of counterproductive work behavior with organizational citizenship behavior. *International Journal of Selection and Assessment, 10*, 51-57.

Mischel, W. (2004). Toward an integrative science of the person. *Annual Review of Psychology, 55*, 1-22.

Mischel, W., & Shoda, Y. (1998). Reconciling processing dynamics and personality dispositions. *Annual Review of Psychology, 49*, 229-258.

Morris, E. K. (1988). Contextualism: The world view of behavior analysis. *Journal of Experimental Child Psychology, 46*, 289-323.

O'Reilly, C. A., III, Chatman, J., & Caldwell, D. F. (1991). People and organizational culture: A profile comparison approach to assessing person-organization fit. *Academy of Management Journal, 34*, 487-516.

Parsons, C. K., & Hulin, C. L. (1982). An empirical comparison of item response theory and hierarchical factor analysis in the applications to the measurement of job satisfaction. *Journal of Applied Psychology, 67*, 826-834.

Payne, P., & Pugh, D. S. (1976). Organizational structure and climate. In M. Dunnette (Ed.), *Handbook of industrial and organizational psychology*. New York: Wiley.

Schneider, B. (1987). The people make the place. *Personnel Psychology, 40*, 437-453.
Saville & Holdsworth Ltd. (1993). *OPQ Images Manual and User's Guide*. London: Author.
Schneider, B. (1983). Interactional psychology and organizational behavior. In B.M. Staw & L.L. Cummings (Eds.), *Research in organizational behavior, 5*, 1-31. Greenwich, CT: JAI Press.
Schneider, B. (1987). The people make the place. *Personnel Psychology, 40*, 437-453.
Schneider, B., & Dachler, H.P. (1978). A note on the stability of the Job Descriptive Index. *Journal of Applied Psychology, 63*, 650-653.
Schein, E. H. (1990). Organizational culture. *American Psychologist, 45*(2), 109-119.
Schein, V. E., & Diamonte, T. (1988). Organizational attraction and the person-environment fit. *Psychological Reports, 62*, 167-173.
Smith, P. C., Kendall, L. M., & Hulin, C. L. (1969). *The measurement of satisfaction in work and retirement: A strategy for the study of attitudes*. Skokie, IL: Rand-McNally.
Spector, P. E. (1997). *Job satisfaction: Application, assessment, causes, and consequences*. Thousand Oaks, CA: Sage.
Taber, T. (1991). Triangulating job attitudes with interpretive and positivist measurement methods. *Personnel Psychology, 44*, 577-600.
Tett, R. P., & Meyer, J. P. (1993). Job satisfaction, organizational commitment, turnover intention, and turnover: Path analyses based on meta-analytic findings. *Personnel Psychology, 46*, 259-293.
Vroom, V. H. (1964). *Work and motivation*. New York: Wiley.

CHAPTER 16

TECHNOLOGICAL DETERMINISM, SOCIOTECHNICAL SYSTEMS, AND CLASSICAL WARFARE

Social Innovation During a Period of Technological Stasis

Daniel J. Svyantek, Kevin T. Mahoney, and Kristin L. Cullen

This paper investigated the degree to which sociotechnical systems theory and technological determinism explain organizational effectiveness and efficiency. First, a brief review of technological determinism and sociotechnical systems was provided. Second, a description of warfare in the Mediterranean world over a 1,400 year period (1000 B.C to 400 A.D.) is given. Next, the degree to which technological change and social innovation affected organizational effectiveness during this period is analyzed. Finally, conclusions are offered about how to better understand the role of technology and social systems in organizational theory.

There is an enduring question in organizational theory. This question concerns the role of technological change as a driving force in the creation of organizational productivity and new organizational structures. This question has been answered in various ways. Those who support the idea of technological determinism believe that technology determines organizational structure (Jones, 1998). Those who support the sociotechnical systems idea believe that there are two independent, but correlated, systems (the social and technical) within an organization which reciprocally determine how work is organized and productivity determined in the organization (Cummings & Srivastva, 1977).

This paper will investigate the degree to which either sociotechnical systems theory or technological determinism may better explain organizational structure and organizational effectiveness. This question is based on Damanpour's (1991) definition of technological and administrative innovations. *Technological innovations* represent changes in products, services, and production technology. Changes in the means of production, for example, would be a technological innovation. *Administrative innovations* occur in the organizational structure and in the organizational processes supporting the structure. Changing from a functional to a product structure would be an example of the former type of administrative innovation. Altering the reward system from one based on individual incentives (e.g., a piece-rate system) to one based on group level incentives (e.g., gainsharing) would be an example of the latter type of administrative innovation.

Specifically, this paper investigated the degree to which technological and administrative innovations affect the performance of, and change, organizational systems using a case-study approach. First, a brief review of technological determinism and sociotechnical systems and an integration of the two viewpoints will be provided. Second, a description of warfare in the Mediterrean world over a 1,400 year period (1000 B.C to 400 A.D.) will be given. Next, the degree to which technological change and social innovation affected organizational effectiveness during this period will be analyzed. Finally, conclusions will be offered about how to better understand the role of technology and technological innovation and social systems and administrative innovation in organizational theory.

TECHNOLOGICAL DETERMINISM

Technological determinism is an outgrowth of the idea that, historically, technology has been a crucial agent of social and cultural change (Marx & Smith, 1994). This belief developed because of the salience of technological change in history. Technological determinism represents the belief that technological forces *determine* social and cultural changes (Winter & Taylor, 1996). This causal role of technology has been widely accepted in Western culture. The emphasis of such analysis is on the new technology and the change it causes without dealing with the forces that lead to the invention of this technological innovation.

Some Premises of Technological Determinism

Technological determinism has used two theoretical assumptions on how technology affects organizations. First, technological determinism implies that technological change leads to fundamental changes in how goods are produced or services provided by changing the set of organizations providing these goods and services. Organizations which do not change their technology become less and less effective until the new technology, and new organizations, replace the old. This is illustrated by the literature on punctuated movements in technology (cf. Anderson & Tushman, 1990 ; Rosenkopf & Tushman, 1994; Tushman & Anderson, 1986).

Second, within organizational theory, the first assumption is supported by Woodward's work with technology and structure (Jones, 1998). This work suggests that if a company operates with a certain technology, then that company needs to adopt a certain kind of structure to be effective. Steiner's (1972) work on the relationship between group process and productivity further illustrates these assumptions.

Steiner (1972) defines three primary determinants of productivity. These are task demands, resources, and process.

Task demands include all prescriptions in a job manual and include requirements imposed on individual or group by task; or by the rules under which a task must be performed. Resources include all relevant knowledges, skills, abilities, and tools possessed by the group that are relevant to the productivity of the group. Steiner proposed that task demands and participants' resources determine the maximum level of productivity that can be achieved. This maximum level of productivity is the potential productivity.

Actual productivity, however, does not always equal potential productivity. This is due to process loss.

Process consists of the actual steps taken by an individual or group when confronted by a task. Process includes all those intrapersonal and interpersonal actions by which people transform resources into a product. Process consists of the individual or collective actions of the people who have been assigned to perform a task.

Actual productivity equals potential productivity minus losses due to faulty process. Steiner's model is one where the potential productivity is always greater than actual productivity. Therefore, the human element in this model is a source of error. As such, we believe that Steiner's view reflects the two assumptions for technological determinism proposed here.

One potential problem with the technological determinism approach is that this approach emphasizes the internal efficiency of the group or organization (Jones, 1998). Therefore, the reliable conversion of skills and resources into goods and services is more emphasized than other measures of organizational effectiveness such as the organization's ability to control its environment or to be adaptive and innovative within a changing environment.

Assessing Support for the Technological Determinism Imperative

The popular version of technological innovation as the sole determinant of change in organizations is inadequate. Social, political, economic, and cultural forces powerfully shape both technological changes and the organization of work. The salience of technological change has led analysts to ignore the importance of accompanying socioeconomic, political, cultural, and ideological forces associated with the technological change (Marx & Smith, 1994). The challenge for advocates of technological determinism, therefore, has been to demonstrate that technology exerts its effects on organizations and societies in unique and generalizable ways (Heilbroner, 1994a). Newer views on technological determinism, therefore, reflect the idea that the effect of technological determinism on a society or organization exists on a continuum (Smith, 1994). At one end of the continuum, technological change leads to structural and social changes inevitably: This is the strong technological determinism view (Bimber, 1994). Strong advocates of technological determinism face a dilemma. Under closer scrutiny, almost all technological changes provided as examples of their views are associated with social and cultural changes (Heilbroner, 1994b). At the other end of the continuum, technology is socially constructed (Scott, 1992). Here the consistency seen in how work is structured in common technologies is the result of assumptions about humans and human behavior held by the designers of work systems (Scott, 1992). In between, these endpoints, technology and social elements interact to determine both structure and effectiveness for organizations and societies.

SOCIOTECHNICAL SYSTEMS

This interpretation of the continuum of technological determinism complements the theoretical premises of the sociotechnical systems approach. A sociotechnical system is an organized collection of people and technology structured to produce a specified outcome (Cummings & Srivastava, 1977). The achievement of this outcome depends upon the appropriate joint operation of both social and technological components. The social system is concerned with the relationship between people who interact with each other in a given environment for the basic purpose of achieving an agreed upon task or goal. Human interactions are (1) mechanisms of human influence on human beings; (2) used to develop common values; (3) as mechanisms for social and group integration. Human beings are in constant exchange with environment. Exchanges (1) are mechanisms for manipulation and control of environment; (2) mechanisms for creation of new environments; and (3) mechanisms for the development of new technology. The technological system is the tools, techniques, and methods of doing a task that are employed for task performance. However, the technological system only exists when social groups bring it into existence and bestow meaning upon it. The technological system, therefore, is an artifact, created by human purposes to serve human purposes. The technological system can be characterized by (1) characteristics of materials being produced; (2) the physical work setting; (3) a spatio-temporal dimension; (4) the level of mechanization used in the technology; (5) unit operations; and/ or (6) the degree of centrality.

The sociotechnical systems approach has two fundamental premises (Cummings & Srivastva, 1977). These are (1) the production of a good or service requires the joint operation of two independent, but correlated, social and technical systems and (2) that the interaction between the social and technical system must relate to the environment if the organization is to function effectively. The "softer" portions of the technological determinism continuum (other than the strong endpoint) represent the interaction of social and technological elements.

Sociotechnical systems also are hypothesized to produce two kinds of outcomes (Cummings & Worley, 1993). These outcomes are (1) the goods manufactured and/or services provided by the organization and (2) social and psychological consequences of work for employees (e.g., job satisfaction and organizational commitment). These outcomes are related to the internal functioning of the organization. This may be a failing of the sociotechnical approach as it is for the technological determinism approach. This approach tends to emphasize organizational efficiency and work attitudes as the primary determinants of a good functioning organization. It ignores organizational effectiveness issues (Mathews, 1997).

WARFARE AND TECHNOLOGY

The role of technological determinism in military effectiveness has been studied thoroughly (Raudzens, 1990). There are few, if any, clear examples of the war-winning weapons (Raudzens, 1990). Across time, there is little evidence to show that casualties proportional to soldiers engaged have been much influenced by technological change. Casualties have gone up and down with the numbers of combatants involved in a battle rather than the effectiveness of the weapons technology used to kill combatants. Historians still seek for the "decisive weapon." The use of such weapons, however, always emerges from unique cultural contexts, and is associated with dozens of lesser developments and devices. Institutional superiority, not technological advantage, may be the dominant factor in success in battle.

One thing to remember, however, is that all such superiority has a limited "shelf-life." This superiority is based on either technological or administrative innovations occurring within one organizational system (an internal, efficiency based response). However, the drive for change is based on response to competitor's (an effectiveness based response). This creates a cycle of change in which today's dominant weapon system becomes tomorrow's quaint antique.

The literature fails to show clear effects of technological change on the practice of warfare. Rather, such analyses support a viewpoint that requires the integration of technological determinism and sociotechnical systems to explain military effectiveness. This paper attempts to assess the degree to which sociotechnical systems and technological determinism may be integrated in organizational theory using a study of the styles of battles and soldiers found in the classical Mediterrean world (1000 B.C. to 400 A.D.).

Developments in Classical Western Warfare (680 B.C. to 378 A.D.)

Western warfare is characterized by battles between opposing heavy infantry units during a 1,000 year period lasting from 680 B.C. to 378 A.D. In both Greece and Rome (and one of their primary enemies, Carthage), the core of the army was formed by heavy infantry protected by metal body armor, helmets, and shields carrying spears and swords (van Creveld, 1991). The primary Greek offensive weapon was the thrusting spear or pike: The primary Roman offensive weapon was the short sword. Much of Western warfare during this period is concerned with battles fought between countries and city-states with approximately equal technology level. The Mediterranean peoples (Greeks, Romans, and Carthaginians) had very similar technology levels (van Creveld, 1991).

The complexity of ancient warfare combat and the key to victory was less a question of obtaining technological superiority than of coordinating the elements of technology available to all in such a way as to mask weaknesses, and bring out strengths, of these elements (van Creveld, 1991). The means by which this is done can be followed throughout this 1,000 year period as different armies seek how best to use the common technological elements available to all. There are three broad phases to this process. These are (1) early classical warfare in which heroes fight for glory (Heroic warfare); (2) the development and perfection of the Greek phalanx (Phalanx warfare); and (3) the development and perfection of the Roman legion (Legion warfare). An analysis of this period shows that common technologies may be used in different ways. In addition, the concept of dominant design in technology (i.e., the technological innovation) does not change across a stable period of technological development, but the use of this dominant design does change as new structures and organizational processes (i.e., administrative innovations) are developed to utilize the dominant design of the technology being used.

Phase I: Heroic Warfare

The warfare of this era is best illustrated by the fighting described in the *Iliad*. The warrior in Homeric warfare used bronze body armor and carried a body length shield of wood and leather that was suspended from a strap worn around the warrior's neck to protect himself (Warry, 1980). The offensive weapons of the heroic warrior were throwing spears and long, bronze cutting swords. Armor usually was directly related to wealth: Wealthier warriors had better armor and were more effective.

Battle during this period was a "free-for-all" in which the warriors of the opposing sides fought as individual, not disciplined units (Connolly, 1981). The typical battle of this period had several characteristics (Warry, 1980). Warrior chieftains would ride to battle in chariots and then dismount to fight on foot. They would then do battle with identified opponents from the opposing side. These battles were more similar to duels than organized warfare as known today.

Their followers would trail them onto the battlefield in loose formations (Warry, 1980). The formations used throwing spears and bows to

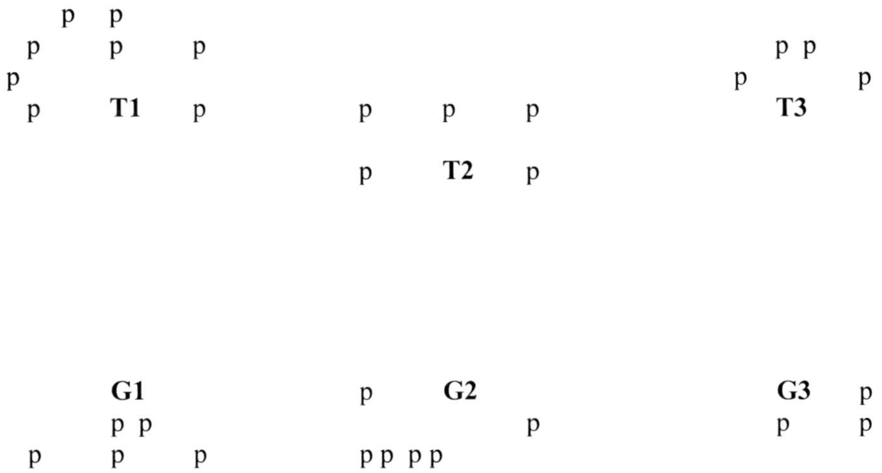

```
     p  p
  p  p    p                                    p p
p                                            p     p
  p  T1   p        p   p   p                   T3
                      p  T2  p
```

```
      G1           p   G2                      G3  p
      p p                   p                  p   p
   p  p  p           p p p p
```

Note: **G1-G3** are Greek heroes; **T1-T3** are Trojan heroes; p = light armed supporting troops.

Figure 16.1. An illustration of heroic warfare.

provide missile support for their chieftains. These formations easily dissolved in battle (especially if the chieftain of a unit was killed). Figure 16.1 provides an example of this type of warfare.

Collaboration between chieftains and their followers was more by personal acquaintance than by training. Friends might jointly work together to defeat a common enemy. King Nestor in *The Iliad* noted that when two friends worked side-by-side, one or the other might spot an opening and kill their enemy more easily than would either warrior fighting by himself (Tsouras, 1992). There was, however, no army-wide system of discipline and/or cohesiveness. Individuals fought as individuals within opposing sides on the battlefield.

Phase II: Phalanx Warfare

A technological development in about 1200 B.C. led to a change in the nature of warfare in the classical world. This development was the invention of a cheap method of making iron (Raudzens, 1990). This development changed the nature of warfare, not by creating new types of weaponry, but by making the offensive and defensive weapons used more widely available to the individuals of the time. More individuals could be armed with the weapons. The result was a gradual change in how battles were fought and the development of hoplite warfare and the use of the phalanx (Connolly, 1980). Warfare during this period occurs in five basic styles. These are (1) the traditional hoplite phalanx; (2) the Spartan phalanx; (3); the counter-responses of the Theban phalanx and the peltast; and (4) the Macedonian phalanx.

The Traditional Hoplite Phalanx

The hoplite was the typical individual soldier in Greece. The Greek hoplite wore body armor of bronze or reinforced linen in later periods as the need for speed increased (Connolly, 1981; Warry, 1980). Their offensive weapons were a thrusting spear and a short, cutting sword. Each hoplite carried a heavy shield, the *hoplon*, that was three feet in diameter.

This shield allowed warfare to change from an individual affair (as in heroic warfare) to a disciplined battle. The shield was too heavy and unwieldy to be used effectively for protection by an individual fighting by himself (Hanson, 1989). The only effective use of this shield was if a group of men fought together as a unit. This unit was known as the phalanx.

The phalanx took the loose formations of the followers seen in heroic warfare and made the individuals in these units a disciplined formation. This formation became the dominant influence on the battlefield in the late eighth century B.C (Connolly, 1980). By 680 B.C, clear descriptions of phalanx battles are available (Hanson, 1989).

The phalanx was a disciplined system: The phalanx created a battle line that was several ranks (files) deep and broader than deep (Connolly, 1980). The Greek phalanx was built of subunits. The most common subunits were usually units of men taking a formation that was three men in a row in columns of eight totaling 24 men, the *enonotiai* (Connolly, 1980). This unit would be under the command of an officer. Two of these units made up a *pentekostyes* of 48 men and four *pentekostyes* made up the *lochos* of 196 men. The organization of a *pentekostyes* is seen in Figure 16.2. The primary tactical unit was the *lochos*. This formation consisted of eight *enonotiai*s combined together. The *lochos* was the smallest unit that might operate independently in most battles. Several *lochoi* would be combined to form the larger phalanx for a battle (Connolly, 1980).

Greek warfare was based on the decisive, pitched battle (Hanson, 1989). This model of warfare became the basic theory of war in Western civilization for 2,500 years. This model of warfare requires both heavy offensive and heavy defensive armament. Greek warfare required both the ability and the desire to deliver fatal blows to enemies while enduring, without retreating, any counterresponse by the enemy. The hoplite class chose to disdain the bow or javelin in preference for the spear and bronze armor (Hanson, 1989). This armament required the elimination

```
              Pentekostyes= 48 men

Enonotiai= 24 men            Enonotiai= 24 men
     HHH                           HHH
     HHH                           HHH
     HHH                           HHH
     HHH                           HHH
     HHH                           HHH
     HHH                           HHH
     HHH                           HHH
     HHH                           HHH
```

A Greek Hoplite Battle Formation (4 pentekostyes= 196 men)

```
HHHHHHHHHHHH HHHHHHHHHHHH
HHHHHHHHHHHH HHHHHHHHHHHH
HHHHHHHHHHHH HHHHHHHHHHHH
HHHHHHHHHHHH HHHHHHHHHHHH
HHHHHHHHHHHH HHHHHHHHHHHH
HHHHHHHHHHHH HHHHHHHHHHHH
HHHHHHHHHHHH HHHHHHHHHHHH
HHHHHHHHHHHH HHHHHHHHHHHH
```

Figure 16.2. The Greek phalanx system.

of the critical distance (about 15 to 20 feet) that usually separated men in battle. Men in the Greek phalanx drew themselves up in dense formation, charged each other, and killed and died (Hanson, 1989). At some point, one phalanx collapsed and the men in the collapsing phalanx suffered great casualties. Figure 16.3 illustrates how a phalanx battle developed.

A side effect of the development of the phalanx was a decrease in the importance of leadership. Phalanx warfare is relatively simple and requires little direction from a leader after the order to attack is given. Leadership became more a matter of maintaining morale in the phalanx than in making complicated tactical plans. The leader was a member of the phalanx. Hanson (1989) notes that in Greek literature, there is a criticism of any leader who is not one of the men, who by nature of his dress or conduct sought to elevate himself above the rank and file of the phalanx and fostered the impression he did not share the same dangers or interests. Hanson quotes the seventh century poet Archilochos—

```
LLLLLLLLLLLLLLLLLLLLLLLLLLLLLLLLLLLLLLLLLL
LLLLLLLLLLLLLLLLLLLLLLLLLLLLLLLLLLLLLLLLLL
LLLLLLLLLLLLLLLLLLLLLLLLLLLLLLLLLLLLLLLLLL
LLLLLLLLLLLLLLLLLLLLLLLLLLLLLLLLLLLLLLLLLL


AAAAAAAAAAAAAAAAAAAAAAAAAAAAAAAAAAAA
AAAAAAAAAAAAAAAAAAAAAAAAAAAAAAAAAAAA
AAAAAAAAAAAAAAAAAAAAAAAAAAAAAAAAAAAA
AAAAAAAAAAAAAAAAAAAAAAAAAAAAAAAAAAAA
```

Figure 16.3A. Opening phases of a Greek phalanx battle.

```
AAAAAAAAAAAAAAAAAAAAAAAAAAAAAAAAAAA
AAAAAAAAAAAAAAAAAAAAAAAAAAAAAAAAAAA
AAAAAAAAAAAAAAAAAAAAAAAAAAAAAAAAAAA
AAAAAAAAAAAAAAAAAAAAAAAAAAAAAAAAAAA
LLLLLLLLLLLLLLLLLLLLLLLLLLLLLLLLLLLLLLLL
LLLLLLLLLLLLLLLLLLLLLLLLLLLLLLLLLLLLLLLL
LLLLLLLLLLLLLLLLLLLLLLLLLLLLLLLLLLLLLLLL
LLLLLLLLLLLLLLLLLLLLLLLLLLLLLLLLLLLLLLLL
```

Figure 16.3B. End of a stalemated Greek phalanx battle.

```
                  AAAAAAAAAAAAAAAAAAAAAAAAAAAAAAAA
                  AAAAAAAAAAAAAAAAAAAAAAAAAAAAAAAA
                  AAAAAAAAAAAAAAAAAAAAAAAAAAAAAAAA
                  AAAAAAAAAAAAAAAAAAAAAAAAAAAAAAAA

                  LLLLLLLLL      LLLLLLLLLLLLLLLLLLLLLLL
                  LLLLLLLLLLLLLLL    LLLLLLLLLLLL
                  LLL            LLLLLLLLLLLLLLLLLLLLLLLLL
                  LLLLLLLLLLL                  LLLLLLLLL

L L               LLLL      LLLL LL       LLL
     LL                LL            LL            LLLL
L                 L             L             L         L
```

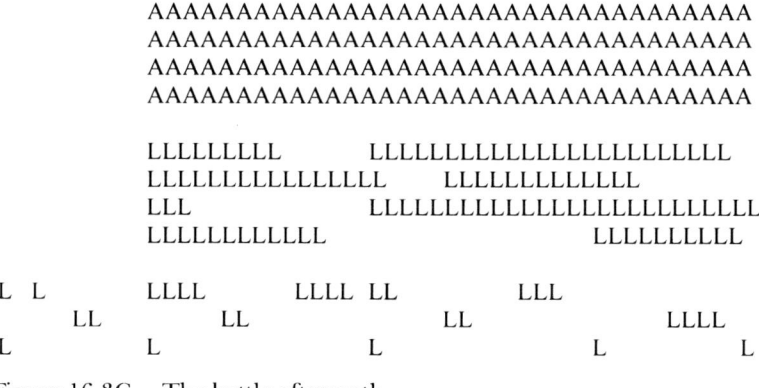

Figure 16.3C. The battle aftermath.

I don't like the towering captain with the spraddly length of leg, one who swaggers in his lovelocks and clean shaves beneath his chin. Give me a man short and squarely set upon his legs, a man full of heart, not to be shaken from the place he plants his feet. (Hanson, 1989, p. 110)

The leader was, therefore, expected to share in the fighting and dangers of phalanx warfare.

Each man in the phalanx was dependent on the individual on his right for protection. This led to an interesting phenomenon in the battle. Individual hoplites tended to sidestep right to keep their unprotected side within the area of protection offered by shield of the individual on their right (Hanson, 1989). Greek phalanx battles, thus, were characterized by both phalanxes moving right which meant during the battle opposing phalanxes might revolve on the battlefield and the battle might be stalemated (See Figure 16.3b for an illustration of this tendency).

As long as the phalanx formation was maintained, casualties were relatively light. The typical battle was the "push" in which ranks of opposing phalanxes pushed on the opposing one till one collapsed (Warry, 1980). It was during the pursuit afterward that most casualties occurred (Hanson, 1989) (See Figure 16.3c for an illustration of this outcome).

Greek hoplite tactics may be regarded as the either the outcome or the determinant of hoplite arms and armor (Warry, 1980). The Greek hoplite was a citizen of a Greek city-state who could afford to arm himself with hoplite armor. All adult males in a city-state essentially served in a citizen militia. Except for a brief period connected to transition to adult life and citizenship, most Greek states gave little or no military training to citizens (Sage, 1996). Athens, for example, required no formal training of the citizens who served as hoplites. Some rudimentary training was probably given in how to march and change formation (Sage, 1996). This lack of formal training led to the simplicity of tactics seen in phalanx battles. The classical phalanx battle occurred without reserves or coordination of specialized troops (Hanson, 1989). The Greeks relegated cavalry and missile troops to secondary roles.

The cohesiveness that allowed the phalanx battle to occur was based on the close relationship of the hoplites to each other in the phalanx (Hanson, 1989). The phalanx was comprised of hoplites from small Greek city-states. Hoplites knew and were related to each other.

The Spartan Phalanx

Sparta followed a different model of phalanx warfare than did other Greek city-states. Sparta became an example of a totalitarian state based on the Spartan army (Lazenby, 1985). The Spartan male trained for war from the age of 7 to 20. The Spartans became full-time professional soldiers (Lazenby, 1985). The purpose of this life-long training was to produce unit cohesion, not individual skill (unless in pursuit or flight). The Spartans were trained to move and respond to commands during battle.

They, for example, could feign the collapse of their phalanx and retreat (Lazenby, 1985). When the opposing phalanx would break apart as it pursued the Spartans, the Spartans could reform their phalanx and turn and crush their enemy who was now in disarray.

Spartan training produced morale and steadiness in battle. This training was seen as the key to Spartan success by Thucydides who noted that it was the Spartan training, not the exhortations of leaders, prior to battle that led to victory (Tsouras, 1992). This training was what allowed them to have a long record of success against Greek enemies (which as noted above were primarily part-time, citizen militias). Such an approach, the emphasis on training and morale, clearly is an example of an administrative innovation.

The Spartans also organized their phalanx into larger units (Connolly, 1981). The *enonotiai* was 36 men (3 men wide by 12 men deep); the *pentekostyes* was 72 men; and the *lochos* was 288 men (See Figure 16.4). These men, however, were organized in a shallower formation (6 men) than the traditional Greek phalanx (8 men deep). This allowed the Spartan army to present a broader front than the normal phalanx. This provided a tactical advantage to the Spartans (See Figure 16.5). Six *lochoi* made up a *mora* and their were six *mora* in the Spartan army. In addition, a special unit of 300 men, the *hippeis* was formed to fight on the right of the Spartan army (Connolly, 1981; Lazenby, 1985). These were the Spartan army's elite and formed the Spartan king's bodyguard. Their elite status made it less likely that they would revolve when meeting another phalanx (as shown in Figure 16.3b). The Spartan right, which was traditionally the weak link in the Greek phalanx, would overcome their enemy's left (the strongest portion of the traditional Greek phalanx army) in most battles.

The Spartan army trained in marching and changing formation quickly (Connolly, 1981). For example, the *enontiai* could change quickly from a 3 men wide by 12 men deep formation to a formation of 6 men wide by 6 men deep as shown in Figure 16.4. This formation retained enough depth to withstand the push of the opposing phalanx while extending the Spartan formation so that it would (a) outflank the enemy phalanx and/ or (b) make each individual in the front rank of the opposing phalanx face two Spartans in battle (See Figure 16.5).

The Spartan army also used missile troops in the initial parts of a phalanx battle to begin the process of disruption of the enemy phalanx (Connolly, 1981; Lazenby, 1985). These missile troops were not Spartan. Rather, they were comprised of the Spartans' serfs (*helots*). The role of these troops was to use missiles before the phalanxes met and then retire behind the Spartan phalanx when the phalanx battle began.

Pentekostyes= 72 men

Enonotiai= 36 men		Enonotiai= 36 men	
HHH	HHH	HHH	HHH
HHH	HHH	HHH	HHH
HHH	HHH	HHH	HHH
HHH	HHH	HHH	HHH
HHH	HHH	HHH	HHH
HHH	HHH	HHH	HHH
HHH	HHH	HHH	HHH
HHH	HHH	HHH	HHH
HHH	HHH	HHH	HHH
HHH	HHH	HHH	HHH
HHH	HHH	HHH	HHH
HHH	HHH	HHH	HHH

A Spartan Battle Formation (4 pentekostyes= 288 men)

```
HHHHHHHHHHHHHHHHHHHHHHHHHHH HHHHHHHHHHHHHHHHHHHHHHHHHHH
HHHHHHHHHHHHHHHHHHHHHHHHHHH HHHHHHHHHHHHHHHHHHHHHHHHHHH
HHHHHHHHHHHHHHHHHHHHHHHHHHH HHHHHHHHHHHHHHHHHHHHHHHHHHH
HHHHHHHHHHHHHHHHHHHHHHHHHHH HHHHHHHHHHHHHHHHHHHHHHHHHHH
IIIIIIIIIIIIHHHHHHHHHHHHHHH HHHHHHHHHHHHHHHHHHHHHHHHHHH
HHHHHHHHHHHHHHHHHHHHHHHHHHH HHHHHHHHHHHHHHHHHHHHHHHHHHH
HHHHHHHHHHHHHHHHHHHHHHHHHHH HHHHHHHHHHHHHHHHHHHHHHHHHHH
```

Figure 16.4. The Spartan phalanx system.

Traditional Greek City-State Army (One *lochos*)

```
HHHHHHHHHHHHHHHHHHHHHHHHHHH
HHHHHHHHHHHHHHHHHHHHHHHHHHH
HHHHHHHHHHHHHHHHHHHHHHHHHHH
HHHHHHHHHHHHHHHHHHHHHHHHHHH
HHHHHHHHHHHHHHHHHHHHHHHHHHH
HHHHHHHHHHHHHHHHHHHHHHHHHHH
HHHHHHHHHHHHHHHHHHHHHHHHHHH
HHHHHHHHHHHHHHHHHHHHHHHHHHH
```

```
HHHHHHHHHHHHHHHHHHHHHHHHHHH HHHHHHHHHHHHHHHHHHHHHHHHHHH
HHHHHHHHHHHHHHHHHHHHHHHHHHH HHHHHHHHHHHHHHHHHHHHHHHHHHH
HHHHHHHHHHHHHHHHHHHHHHHHHHH HHHHHHHHHHHHHHHHHHHHHHHHHHH
HHHHHHHHHHHHHHHHHHHHHHHHHHH HHHHHHHHHHHHHHHHHHHHHHHHHHH
HHHHHHHHHHHHHHHHHHHHHHHHHHH HHHHHHHHHHHHHHHHHHHHHHHHHHH
HHHHHHHHHHHHHHHHHHHHHHHHHHH HHHHHHHHHHHHHHHHHHHHHHHHHHH
HHHHHHHHHHHHHHHHHHHHHHHHHHH HHHHHHHHHHHHHHHHHHHHHHHHHHH
```

The Spartan Army (One *lochos*)

Figure 16.5. The Spartan advantage.

The Greek Counterresponses to the Spartan Phalanx

The Greeks faced a difficult problem. The Spartan army and phalanx could defeat the phalanxes comprised of the militia of their city-states easily. This was because only the Sparta economic, political, and cultural system was established to support a professional army. The rest of the Greek armies were only part-time amateurs (Sage, 1996). Therefore, any battle fought would only lead to losses for these city-states. This led to a period of Spartan hegemony in Greece from about 490 B.C. to 390 B.C. (cf. Connolly, 1981; Lazenby, 1985). Two responses (i.e., administrative innovations) to Spartan superiority were developed: These were the Theban phalanx tactics and the peltast military system. Each of these systems were able to defeat the Spartan phalanx but they were not widely adopted in Greece.

The Theban Phalanx Tactics

The Theban phalanx represented an organizational innovation that did not change the basic relationship of the arms used in the phalanx. The goal of this innovation was to maximize the force of the phalanx at the decisive point of a battle. The Theban phalanx was made very deep on its left side (50 men deep) (Connolly, 1981) and shallower in the center and on the right (See Figure 16.4). In addition, the Thebans developed an elite unit, the Sacred Band, of 300 men to serve as the front ranks of the phalanx's left (Warry, 1980). The sole purpose of this depth was to quickly crush the right of the enemy phalanx. The tactics were developed to defeat the Spartan phalanx. This tactical innovation led to the first victories of a Greek city-state phalanx over a Spartan phalanx in almost 300 years between the years of 380 B.C. and 360 B.C. The use of these tactics, however, declined in Greece after the death of their originator, Epaminondas, in battle against the Spartans (cf. Lazenby, 1985). Figure 16.6 provides an illustration of this tactic.

The Peltasts

The development of the peltast was another response to the superiority of the Spartan phalanx. Peltasts were lighter armed troops who wore a linen corselet to protect their body and carried a wicker shield and longer, throwing spears (Warry, 1980). Peltasts would surround a phalanx and throw javelins at the hoplites within it to disrupt the phalanx's formation (See Figure 16.5). The peltast was most effective in rough ground where it was hard to maintain the phalanx. They would dash in and out until the phalanx collapsed. Their lighter armor made is easier to take on individual hoplites after this collapse.

An Athenian general, Iphicrates, is credited with the development of the peltasts as an effective military system (Sage, 1996). He developed the

The Spartan Army

SSSSSSSSSSSS
SSSSSSSSSSSS
SSSSSSSSSSSS
SSSSSSSSSSSS
SSSSSSSSSSSS
SSSSSSSSSSS

HHHHHHHHH
HHHHHHHHH
HHHHHHHHH
HHH
HHH
HHH
HHH
HHH
HHH
HHH
...
...
HH (50 deep)

The Theban Army

Note: S = Spartan Hoplite; H = Theban Hoplite.

Figure 16.6. The Theban solution.

peltast units from professional mercenaries: These individuals could be given more extensive training than the citizen militia. The peltast was made a lightly armed hoplite with a longer spear as well as the javelin by Iphicrates. The peltasts were used to address the basic problem that the Athenian phalanx, by itself, could not defeat the Spartan phalanx. The peltasts, in combination with traditional Athenian hoplites in the phalanx, were, however, able to defeat the Spartan phalanx in battle (Lazenby, 1985; Sage, 1996). The peltast system could also defeat the Spartan phalanx without the aid of traditional hoplites if the ground on which the battle was fought was very rough (Sage, 1996). Figure 16.7 provides an illustration of the use of peltasts in battle against the Spartan phalanx.

Summary

The Greek city-states were able to develop two responses to Spartan superiority. These were the Theban phalanx tactics and the peltast mili-

The Spartan Army

```
P    SSSSSSSSSSS    P
P    SSSSSSSSSSS    P
P    SSSSSSSSSSS    P
P    SSSSSSSSSSS    P
P    SSSSSSSSSSS    P
P    SSSSSSSSSSS    P

     HHHHHHHHH
     HHHHHHHHH
     HHHHHHHHH
```

Note: P = Peltast; H = Hoplite; S = Spartan Hoplite

Figure 16.7. The Athenian peltasts.

tary system. Each of these systems were able to defeat the Spartan phalanx but were not widely adopted. Both systems violated the Greek norms of equality. The Theban phalanx required the development of an elite unit, the Sacred Band, and the peltast system required the use of mercenaries. Moreover, in both cases, the effective use of these innovations relied on the leadership of creative geniuses (Epaminondas and Iphicrates). When these individuals were not present, their innovations were not effective. The end result was that neither system displaced the Spartan phalanx. They only offered possible alternatives to the Spartan system. The system that would replace the Spartan system, however, was being developed in northern Greece in Macedon.

The Macedonian Phalanx

The Macedonian army represented the culmination of the phalanx military system. Its success was due to the change in emphasis given the phalanx in battle. The phalanx remained a dominant component of the Macedonian army but it was no longer the only important unit: The Macedonians had discovered the combined arms concept (Tsouras, 1992). Different elements were used in combination to both enhance their strengths and decrease their weaknesses.

Philip II is credited with developing the training regime which transformed a barbarian army not based on hoplites to the ultimate phalanx system (Connolly, 1981). His son, Alexander the Great, would use this system to conquer most of the known world (Sekunda & Warry, 1998). The Macedonian soldier's armor was different from traditional hoplite armor.

It was based on the use of the *sarissa* (a 16 foot spear) which required use of two hands (Connolly, 1981). Soldiers, therefore, could not carry both the *hoplon* shield and the *sarissa*. Soldiers wore a metal helmet and linen corselet like the hoplite but carried a smaller shield (about 25 inches round). They carried a short cutting sword as their secondary offensive weapon. This decrease in defensive armor (body armor and shield) was the culmination of a trend in Greek warfare designed to increase the tactical speed of Greek armies on the battlefield (Sekunda & Warry, 1998).

The Macedonian phalanx was based on the best elements from the various Greek phalanx systems. First, the Macedonian phalanx was based on the Theban idea of depth to the phalanx (Connolly, 1981). The Macedonian phalanx was organized to fight normally in a depth of 16 men. This was deeper than even the Spartan phalanx. Second, the Macedonian phalanx was well-trained in formation changes as the Spartan phalanx (Connolly, 1981). The Macedonian phalanx could shorten its front and fight in a depth of 32 men or extend its front and fight in a depth of eight men. Third, a new unit was developed. This unit was the *hypasists* (Connolly, 1981). The role of the *hypasists* was to protect flanks of the slower phalanx and link phalanx to the Macedonian cavalry. The *hypasist* was armed similarly to Iphicrates's *peltasts*. They were more lightly armored to increase the speed with which they could move on the battlefield. In addition, the hypasists were considered an elite unit and received more training than Macedonian phalangites (Sage, 1996).

Finally, the Macedonian army developed a large cavalry component (Connolly, 1981). The cavalry component was an elite unit and seen as an offensive, striking unit. Philip created this force of heavy cavalry to destroy an enemy that had been pinned in place by the Macedonian phalanx (Sekunda & Warry, 1998). The cavalry wore heavy armor and used specially developed tactical formations (wedge and diamond): This allowed cavalry to play an important role in the early history of the Macedonian army (e.g., at Chaeronea, Issus, and Gaugemela). This cavalry component was very large relative to other armies using the phalanx (Connolly, 1981). For example, when Alexander the Great's invaded Persia, his army was composed of 25,000 infantry and 5,000 cavalry (a 1:6 ratio of cavalry to infantry).

The end result was a military system that could beat any other system based on the traditional or Spartan phalanx. The Macedonian phalanx became the dominant military system in the Greek world for about 180 years (350 B.C. to 168 B.C.). Figure 16.8 shows how the Macedonian army could utilize its different elements in combination to crush other phalanx formations.

The Macedonian system as developed by Philip II and his son, Alexander the Great, was costly to maintain. Its use required outlays for training of the hypasists and maintenance of the cavalry component. Over time, for example, the ratio of cavalry to infantry decreased from 1:6 to 1:20 in response to these costs (Connolly, 1981). In addition, the training costs associated with the hypasists slowly changed them from a specialized, elite unit to a unit similar to the elites of the Theban and Spartan phalanx (e.g., the hippeis and Sacred Band) (cf. Sekunda & Warry, 1998). These factors led to a reliance on, and increase in size of, the phalanx component in later armies based on the Macedonian system (Sage, 1996). This led to increased rigidity in battle and a loss of the flexibility seen in the original Macedonian system.

Summary

The Macedonian system represented the culmination of a 500 year long development process. The period from 680 B.C. to 168 B.C. represents the period in which the phalanx was the dominant military system used in the classical world. At its core, the phalanx was designed for a decisive battle in which the strength and morale of opponents was matched. The stronger phalanx won. All other arms became secondary: Light missile armed troops were developed to protect the phalanx from the enemy. All innovations were to protect the phalanx and its decisive role in battle (Connolly, 1981). The phalanx, however, required the right conditions for its effective use (Sage, 1996). The hoplite's armor was designed for use in a unit. In rough terrain, however, the phalanx was subject to disruption. When the phalanx was disrupted, individual hoplites were easy prey for individuals using different arms (e.g., peltasts or Macedonian cavalry).

The loss in flexibility of the Macedonian phalanx noted above came at a critical time in the development of Western warfare. The Macedonian phalanx system was about to meet the Roman legions in battle. The battles between the Macedonian phalanx system and the Roman legion system would be a transition period in warfare that would see the phalanx supplanted by the legion as the dominant military system.

Phase III: Legion Warfare

The Roman legion system, like the Greek phalanx system, was based on heavy infantry. The Roman legionnaire was armed similarly to the Greek hoplite. His armor, however, was designed to maximize individual defensive protection and the offensive power of the Roman tactical unit. The shield was the *scutum* (Connolly, 1981). The scutum was 2.5 feet wide by 4 feet long. It was made of laminated wood and curved around the body of the individual soldier. The scutum could be used as a weapon (Connolly, 1981). Romans were trained to hit enemy with the scutum in an initial charge and then to rest the scutum on the ground and fight behind it while crouched. Romans wore light body armor (small square metal breastplate over heart). In addition, one greave for leg protection was worn on the left leg which led into combat: The right was left bare to minimize the weight carried by the legionnaire. The primary offensive weapons were the short sword (designed for both cutting and thrusting) and two *pila* (javelins). The defensive armor would change during the different phases of development of the Roman legion but the pattern of offensive weaponry is basically consistent from about 350 B.C. to 378 A.D. (cf. Connolly, 1981; Warry, 1980).

The Roman system became very effective because it combined two elements of the Greek phalanx system in one soldier. The Romans used both javelins (e.g., as the peltast) combined with a primary weapon (here swords) (e.g., as a hoplite) in their system. This combination placed an enemy in an impossible position (van Creveld, 1991). It was dangerous to close ranks because the Romans would then throw javelins at this compact target: It was also dangerous to open ranks because the Roman sword was a more dangerous individual offensive weapon than the spear or sarissa used by members of a phalanx.

There are three basic phases in the development of the Roman legion system as a tactical system for use on the battlefield. These were the (1) Republican system; (2) the Imperial system and (3) the Late Imperial system.

The Republican System (350 B.C. to about 110 B.C.)

The Roman army was organized very differently from the phalanx (Connolly, 1981). The basic subunit of the legion was the maniple. Each maniple was comprised of about 60 troops organized to fight in broader, not deeper, formations. For example, a Greek phalanx subunit of 60 men might fight in a formation that was 6 men wide and 10 men deep: The Roman maniple would fight in a formation that was 10 men wide by 6 men deep (See Figure 16.9) (Connolly, 1981). Once again, this provide the Roman army with a tactical advantage particularly if the terrain was even slightly rough. The maniple formation provided the ideal combination for the use of the sword and pila. It maximized the firepower of the use of javelins by the Roman soldiers and provided the Roman legions with a flexibility not found in the phalanx.

Traditional Greek Phalanx

```
HHHHHHHHHHHHHHHHHHHHHHHHHHHHHHHHHHHHH
HHHHHHHHHHHHHHHHHHHHHHHHHHHHHHHHHHHHH   CCCCC
HHHHHHHHHHHHHHHHHHHHHHHHHHHHHHHHHHHHH   CCCCC
HHHHHHHHHHHHHHHHHHHHHHHHHHHHHHHHHHHHH   CCCCC
HHHHHHHHHHHHHHHHHHHHHHHHHHHHHHHHHHHHH
HHHHHHHHHHHHHHHHHHHHHHHHHHHHHHHHHHHHH   CCCCC
HHHHHHHHHHHHHHHHHHHHHHHHHHHHHHHHHHHHH   CCCCC
HHHHHHHHHHHHHHHHHHHHHHHHHHHHHHHHHHHHH   CCCCC


MMMMMMMMMMMMMMM    mmmmmmmmmmmmm    CCCCC
MMMMMMMMMMMMMMM    mmmmmmmmmmmmm    CCCCC
MMMMMMMMMMMMMMM    mmmmmmmmmmmmm    CCCCC
MMMMMMMMMMMMMMM    mmmmmmmmmmmmm
MMMMMMMMMMMMMMM
MMMMMMMMMMMMMMM
MMMMMMMMMMMMMMM
MMMMMMMMMMMMMMM
MMMMMMMMMMMMMMM
MMMMMMMMMMMMMMM
MMMMMMMMMMMMMMM
MMMMMMMMMMMMMMM
MMMMMMMMMMMMMMM
MMMMMMMMMMMMMMM
MMMMMMMMMMMMMMM
```

Note: M = Macedonia Phalanx; m = Hypasists; C = Cavalry.

Figure 16.8. The Macedonian army at work.

The maniples were also organized differently from a phalanx (Connolly, 1981). The Roman legion did not form a solid block of men as did phalanxes. Rather, the maniples comprising a legion were divided into four lines (Connolly, 1981). The front line was comprised of light troops whose purpose was to skirmish and harass the enemy. These troops were known as the velites by 160 B.C. There were 1,200 veltites acting as skirmishers in the 4,200 man legion of the time. Velites were lightly armed and young. Next, came the hastati maniples. Hastati were armed as described above with the short sword and two pila. These individuals were experienced and just coming into the prime of their adult life. The third line was the principi maniples. These individuals were armed in the same way as the hastati. These individuals were old enough to be very experienced but young enough to have stamina for battle. These units were the

A Greek Phalanx

HHHHHHHHHHHH
HHHHHHHHHHHH
HHHHHHHHHHHH
HHHHHHHHHHHH
HHHHHHHHHHHH
HHHHHHHHHHHH
HHHHHHHHHHHH
HHHHHHHHHHHH

LLLLLLLLLL   LLLLLLLLLL
LLLLLLLLLL   LLLLLLLLLL
LLLLLLLLLL   LLLLLLLLLL
LLLLLLLLLL   LLLLLLLLLL
LLLLLLLLLL   LLLLLLLLLL
LLLLLLLLLL   LLLLLLLLLL

The Roman Legion solution

Figure 16.9. The Roman Maniple versus the phalanx.

best units in the army. Finally, the last line was the triarii. These men carried hoplite spears, not pila. Their role was to serve as a rear guard during a defeat. They, if necessary could form a phalanx against a pursuing enemy. Each legion had a small cavalry unit attached: The standard size of the cavalry unit attached to a 4,200 man legion was 300 (a 1:14 ratio).

This version of the Roman army, therefore, represents a transition period between the phalanx and later legion organization because of the retention of the spears for the triari (Connolly, 1981). In addition, the Romans organized themselves in the quincunx order: Maniples of each line were staggered so that an enemy breaking through could be attacked from several sides. The Roman legion in this formation may be thought of as the dark squares on one half of a chess board. The light squares would represent the intervals between the maniples.

It is this military system which defeated the Macedonian phalanx system in a series of battles. These battles showed that the phalanx system could defeat the legion when the terrain was good for the phalanx (Warry, 1980). These defeats were not decisive, however. The legion, however, if able to draw the phalanx into rough terrain, could crush the phalanx (Warry, 1980). The end result was the legion became the predominant military system used in the western world.

The Imperial Legion (110 B.C. to 200 A.D.)

The beginnings of the Roman imperial army are found in the reforms of Marius. The Marian reforms were based on a change in the nature of the enemies faced by the Roman legions. Prior to this, the legions had faced more "civilized" enemies that used the phalanx military system. The manipular legion had proved its superiority against these enemies. Now, however, Roman armies faced barbarian enemies (e.g., the Cimbri and Germans) (Warry, 1980). These Germans were armed with iron breastplates, shields, two javelins and swords for their cavalry. The primary tactic used by these enemies was a charge in loose formation against the Romans. The Romans found they needed a return to the stability of the phalanx formation while retaining the flexibility of the manipular legion.

Therefore, the cohort legion system was developed (Warry, 1980). The cohort became the tactical unit of the Roman imperial army (Connolly, 1981). A cohort was larger than the maniple (about 372 men in a formation about 20 men wide by 18 men deep with 12 officers). There were 10 cohorts in a legion. All soldiers in the legion were now armed with the pila and swords: This change eliminated the triarii and velites. Finally, the first cohort of a legion was considered the elite of the legion. This cohort was double strength (approximately 750 men). By the end of the first century A.D., the cohort legion contained 5,500 men in 10 cohorts (900 men in the first cohort with 480 men in the other nine cohorts) (Connolly, 1981).

Two radical changes in the social structure of the legions are seen here. First, the entire legion was heavy infantry. This need for heavy infantry in the legions led to the professionalization of the Roman citizen army. The state provided arms to anyone who enlisted in the army (Warry, 1980). These arms were basically the same as seen in the manipular legion. The body armor, however, became heavier to provide more protection for the torso of the individual soldier (Warry, 1980). Second, the combined arms portions (e.g., the velites and cavalry) were no longer an integral portion of the legion. The Romans addressed this by recruiting auxilary troops from its subject provinces. These auxilary troops were attached to each legion to act as skirmishers, missile troops and cavalry (Warry, 1980). These auxiliaries were non-Roman citizens. In addition, there was a gradual change from the use of the quincunx order (with four cohorts in the front line, three in the second and three in the third) from the time of Julius Caesar (60 B.C. to 44 B.C.) to formations that provided greater flexibility and greater strength in meeting the barbarian enemy.

Professionalization allowed the Roman legion to develop the tactical flexibility to face different opponents. A similar approach to training and discipline had provided the Spartan army an advantage over other phalanx armies. The professionalization of the army provided the Roman army with superior training and discipline which allowed them to defeat barbarian enemies (Warry, 1980). These formations varied with the enemy and situation. For example, during the revolt in Britain against Roman rule in 60 A.D., the Roman general, Suetonius Paulinus, ordered his 10,000 legionairres and auxilaries to take wedge formations against the 60000 troops of Queen Boudica (Warry, 1980). The 60,000 Britons charged the Roman formation and were destroyed. There were 50,000 Britons killed in the battle. There were only 500 Romans casualties. Another formation was the pig's head. This was an attack formation in which the first cohort formed the tip of a wedge. This tip was followed by three lines of two, three, and four cohorts (Connolly, 1981).

Late Imperial Legion (200 A.D. to 378 A.D.)

After 200 A.D. the Roman Empire began to face new barbarian enemies on many fronts. There was a need for more rapid response to barbarian raids. This led to a decline in the value of infantry and a rise in the value of cavalry. The infantry slowly degenerated and cavalry increased in importance during this period as strategic speed became important (Connolly, 1981). Roman infantry slowly adopted barbarian armor and weapons. Their body armor decreased and their shield shrank (Connolly, 1981). The legion became the tactical unit during this period (Warry, 1980). The size of the legion ranged from 1,500 to 3,000 men who fought as one unit. The decline in Roman infantry continued until the battle of Adrianople in 378 A.D. A Roman army of 30,000 infantry and 10,000 cavalry was destroyed by Gothic army of 30,000 infantry and 20,000 cavalry (Warry, 1980). After this the value of infantry declined rapidly in the Western world and cavalry replaced it as the dominant military system of medieval Europe.

DISCUSSION

Which came first? The chicken or the egg? The discussion over the role of technology versus social, administrative innovations as a primary force in the determinant of organizational effectiveness appears to be a similar question. The example of classical Western warfare, when its beginning and end points are considered, as well as the period of stasis, offers some insights into the issue of the driving force of technology. These insights may be grouped into three broad areas. These are (1) the model of technological change that is most descriptive of this period of warfare; (2) the changes that occur in how technology is used during the period of stasis; and (3) the importance of other factors (e.g., the environment and leadership).

Technological Punctuations

The challenge for advocates of technological determinism is to demonstrate that technology exerts its effects in generalizable ways (Heilbroner, 1994a). There must be some lawlike properties which may be attributed to a technological change background and impose order on human behavior if the technological determinism view is to be supported. Therefore, technological determinism, if it is true, must show that technological change (1) affect norms of practice; (2) lead to only one possible future; or (3) creates unintended consequences and anticipated effects (Bimber, 1994).

The description of classical Western warfare provides some support for a technological determinist approach if one considers the beginnings and the ending of this period of warfare. First, the beginning of this period of warfare is associated with the development of new iron production methods in approximately 700 B.C. This led to a basic change in warfare in Western society. The heroic warfare phase ended. The development of these iron production methods meet the three criteria outlined by Bimber (1994). The style of warfare changed from a meeting of heroic leaders in duels to the clash of the phalanx and a change in the nature of leadership. The norms of the practice of warfare were changed. The 1,000 year period of the superiority of the heavy infantryman during this period supports the proposal that there was only one possible future, that of large groups of heavily armed soldiers fighting fixed battles to determine the course of history. In addition, there are unanticipated and unintended consequences of the development of these iron production methods. By making it more affordable for more citizens to arm themselves and fight, this technological change also may have been a major force in the development of Western democracy.

Second, the ending of the period of warfare shows similar support for a technological deterministic model. This period of warfare ends with the destruction of a Roman army by a Gothic cavalry force in 378 A.D. The change from a heavy infantry army to one based on cavalry has been attributed to several technological developments (van Creveld, 1991). These developments included the invention of the stirrup, high saddle, and horse shoes which helped both heavy cavalry (i.e., lancers) and light cavalry (i.e., horse archers) develop the stability as a weapons platform necessary to defeat a heavy infantry army.

The long middle period of classical Western warfare, however, supports a softer view of technological determinism which is closer to the sociotechnical system approach and shows the importance of social, administrative innovations. This period of warfare is associated with social, cultural, and managerial changes which affected the utilization of the heavily armed soldier of the period. During this middle period of warfare, these social changes became paramount. The key to victory was less a question of obtaining superiority in any single weapon or technological development, than it was of coordinating existing techologies in such a way as to mask these technologies respective weaknesses and bring out their respective strengths in relation to opponents (van Creveld, 1991). Over time, this tendency worked in favor of the more varied, complex use of the existing technology over simpler uses of the same technology.

A current model of technological change describes periods of rapid technological change and then long periods of stability (Anderson & Tushman, 1990; Basalla, 1993; Tushman & Anderson, 1986). The differing viewpoints on the role of technological change as a driving force are reconcilable if one considers a model of technology change which is based on saltatory, not linear, rates of change. Competence-destroying technological changes (cf. Anderson & Tushman, 1986; Tushman & Anderson, 1986) are changes which meet the criteria of hard technological determinism. The two competence-destroying changes in this analysis are the development of (1) new production methods for iron products and (2) changes in horse equipment (e.g., the stirrup). Competence-enhancing technological changes (cf. Anderson & Tushman, 1986; Tushman & Anderson, 1986), however, occur during periods of stability. These changes reflect the development of the phalanx and legion styles of warfare across time.

Developments During a Period of Stasis

A related issue is how, during periods of stability, the changes in social systems affect the utilization of technology. During the period of this case-study, the utilization of technology becomes an effect, not cause of developments.

The work of Thompson (1986a, 1986b) offers a framework for describing the changes witnessed across classical Western warfare. Thompson (1986a) proposes that there are three primary types of technology. Two long-linked technologies and intensive technologies, are of particular relevance for this discussion. Long-linked technologies have serial interdependence. Serial interdependence can be characterized as an assembly line in which steps occur in the same sequence over and over. This type of technology approaches perfection only when it produces a single product using a single technology repetitively. Coordination occurs through standardization of procedures (Thompson, 1986b). Intensive technologies have reciprocal interdependence. Here a variety of techniques is drawn upon in order to achieve a change in some specific object. The selection, combination, and order of application are determined by feedback from the actions of the object itself. Coordination here occurs by mutual adjustments of the elements of the technology in a dynamic environment (Thompson, 1986b).

The changes in classical Western warfare show that the utilization of military technology during this period underwent a process of elaboration. The use of the technology goes from serial to reciprocal interdependence across time. The early Greek phalanx system was used in a standard way and may be characterized by long-linked technology in its operation. Changes in effectiveness occur through training in the use of the primary weapon system, the heavy infantryman. However, across time, there is a change to reciprocal interdependence. For example, the Spartan army begins to use missile troops. This leads to the development of the peltast in Athens. The culmination of this is the Macedonian army under Alexander the Great where heavy and light infantry, artillery and cavalry are used as they are needed. This development is mirrored by the changes in the Roman legion that occur across the Republic and early empire periods.

Therefore, the utilization of technology is a developmental process. After the development of a new technology, organizations do not completely understand how to manage that technology. During this early period, simpler is better. As time passes, however, elaboration of the management processes occurs and more complex utilization of the technology can develop. An important note is that just because the utilization of a technology changes from simple to complex, is no guarantee that this elaboration will continue. The more complex use of technology takes both resources and skilled individuals. When these resources or skilled individual are gone, the utilization of the technology may become simpler. This is illustrated by the changes in the Macedonian phalanx system after the death of Alexander the Great.

Other Factors

One of the interesting things in the study of technological determinism and sociotechnical systems is the paucity of discussion on the role of leadership. For example, Taylor's (1993) discussion of sociotechnical systems there is no mention of leadership in the index. Leadership, however, is probably critical to the successful utilization of technology. Once again, there appear to be two primary aspects to this leadership that parallel the type of interdependence seen in these classical Western military systems. Leadership during the early period of this warfare emphasized the morale factor. As noted earlier, the role of the leader in the phalanx was to bravely fight at the front of the battle and serve as an example to others. This function never leaves in a military system. For example, Tsouras (1992) describe Julius Caesar in a battle with the Gauls. Tsouras proposes at a critical point the personal presence of the commander is necessary and in this instance Caesar saw that the situation was critical. There was no reserve to throw in. Caesar, therefore, snatched a shield from a soldier in the rear and moved to the front line. His coming inspired the men with hope and gave them new heart and the battle was won.

As the methods of utilization of a technology become more elaborate, however, the role of the leader changes. The leader becomes responsible for making the mutual adjustments necessary to meet unexpected environmental events.

The best leader combines both elements. Alexander the Great is an example of such a leader (Sage, 1996). His leadership was based on personal charisma and his acting in the tradition of Greek warfare that leader directly participate in battle. His military genius, however, allowed him to control his entire force and make the optimum combination of infantry, cavalry, and artillery to defeat opponents using widely different military systems.

Conclusions

Technological determinism and sociotechnical systems really seem to represent two sides of the same coin. Technological and institutional innovations reciprocally co-produce each (van de Ven, 1993). Whether one believes that technological or social elements drive change in the methods of production is more dependent on the time at which the effects of these developments are studied. The construct, technological momentum, offers a reconciliation of the effects of these forces. Technological momentum is based on the proposal that relationship between technological and social forces is reciprocal and time-dependent

(Hughes, 1994). Technological systems and social systems can both be causes and effects. Therefore, technological change may have causal effects during the initial period of its development. Changes in social systems become an effect here. However, during periods of stability, social change becomes the cause and the effect is change in way the technology is used.

AUTHOR'S NOTE

Please direct all correspondence to: Daniel J. Svyantek, Psychology Department Auburn University Auburn, AL 36849-5214 (334) 844-6478 svyandj@auburn.edu

REFERENCES

Anderson, P., & Tushman, M. L. (1990). Technological discontinuities and dominant designs: A cyclical model of technological change. *ASQ, 35*, 604-633.

Basalla, G. (1993). *The evolution of technology.* New York: Cambridge University Press.

Bimber, B. (1994). Three faces of technological determinism. In M. R. Smith & L. Marx (Eds.), *Does technology drive history: The dilemma of technological determinism* (pp. 79-100). Cambridge, MA: MIT Press.

Connolly, P. (1981). *Greece and Rome at war.* Englewood Cliffs, NJ: Prentice-Hall.

Cummings, T. G., & Srivastva, S. (1977). *Management of work: A socio-technical systems approach.* Kent, OH: Kent State University Press.

Cummings, T. G., & Worley, C.G. (1993). *Organization development and change* (6th ed.). Cincinnati, OH: South-Western College.

Damanpour, F. (1991). Organizational innovation: A meta-analysis of effects of determinants and moderators. *Academy of Management Journal, 34*, 555-590.

Hanson, V. D. (1989). *The western way of war.* New York: Alfred A. Knopf.

Heilbroner, R. (1994a). Technological determinism revisited. In M. R. Smith & L. Marx (Eds.), *Does technology drive history: The dilemma of technological determinism* (pp. 67-78.) Cambridge, MA: MIT Press.

Heilbroner, R. L. (1994b). Do machines make history. In M. R. Smith & L. Marx (Eds.), *Does technology drive history: The dilemma of technological determinism* (pp. 53-65). Cambridge, MA: MIT Press.

Hughes, T. P. (1994). Technological momentum. In M. R. Smith & L. Marx (Eds.), *Does technology drive history: The dilemma of technological determinism* (pp. 101-113). Cambridge, MA: MIT Press.

Jones, G. R. (1998). *Organizational theory* (2nd ed.). Reading, MA: Addison-Wesley.

Lazenby, J. F. (1985). *The Spartan army.* Chicago: Bolchazy-Carducci.

Marx, L., & Smith, M. R. (1994). Introduction. In M. R. Smith & L. Marx (Eds.), *Does technology drive history: The dilemma of technological determinism* (pp. ix-xv.) Cambridge, MA: MIT Press.

Mathews, J. A. (1997). Introduction to the special issue. *Human Relations, 50,* 487-496.

Raudzens, G. (1990). War-winning weapons: The measurement of technological determinism in military history. *Journal of Military History, 54,* 403-433.

Rosenkopf, L., & Tushman, M. L. (1994). The coevolution of technology and organization. In J. A. C .Baum & J. V. Singh, (Eds.), *Evolutionary dynamics of organizations* (pp. 403-424). New York: Oxford University Press.

Sage, M. M. (1996). *Warfare in ancient Greece.* New York: Routledge.

Scott, W. R. (1992). *Organizations: Rational, natural and open systems* (3rd ed.). Englewood Cliffs, NJ: Prentice-Hall.

Sekunda, N., & Warry, J. (1998). *Alexander the Great: His armies and campaigns 334-323 BC.* London: Osprey.

Smith, M. R. (1994). Technological determinism in American culture. In M. R. Smith & L. Marx (Eds.), *Does technology drive history: The dilemma of technological determinism* (pp. 1-35). Cambridge, MA: MIT Press.

Steiner, I. D. (1972). *Group process and productivity.* New York: Academic Press.

Taylor, J. C., & Felten, D. F. (1993). *Performance by design: Sociotechnical systems in North America.* Englewood Cliffs, NJ: Prentice-Hall.

Thompson, J. D. (1986a). Rationality in organizations. In M. Jelinek, J. A. Litterer, & R. E. Miles (Eds.), *Organizations by design: Theory and practice* (pp. 284-292). Homewood, IL: BPI/Irwin.

Thompson, J. D. (1986b). Technology and structure. In M. Jelinek, J. A. Litterer, & R. E. Miles (Eds.), *Organizations by design: Theory and practice* (pp. 292-302). Homewood, IL: BPI/Irwin.

Tsouras, P. G. (1992). *Warrior's words: A quotation book.* New York: Arms and Armour Press.

Tushman, M. L., & Anderson, P. (1986). Technological discontinuities and organizational environments. *ASQ, 31,* 439-485.

van Creveld, M. (1991). *Technology and war from 2000 B.C. to the present.* New York: Free Press.

Van de Ven, A. H. (1993). A community perspective on the emergence of innovations. *Journal of Engineering and Technology Management, 10,* 23-51.

Warry, J. (1980). *Warfare in the Classical world.* London: Salamander Books.

Winter, S. J., & Taylor, S. L. (1996). The role of IT in the transformation of work: A comparison of post-industrial, industrial, and proto-industrial organization. *Information systems research, 7,* 5-21.

CHAPTER 17

A NEW PERSPECTIVE ON LEADERSHIP

A Review of *Resonant Leadership: Renewing Yourself and Connecting With Others Through Mindfulness, Hope, and Compassion*, by Richard Boyatzis and Annie McKee

Loren R. Dyck

Resonant Leadership: Renewing Yourself and Connecting with Others Through Mindfulness, Hope, and Compassion, by Richard Boyatzis and Annie McKee. Boston, MA: Harvard Business School Press, 2005, 286 pp., $25.95, paper (ISBN: 1-59139-563-1)

Rich diversity of leadership applications, industry sectors, and cultural contexts supported by an inspiring theory and packed with helpful professional and self-development tools await readers from a multitude of audiences for *Resonant Leadership*. One of the most striking features of this leadership development and personal revitalization book is its large variety of compelling examples in multiple contexts. The reader gets to visit chief executive officers and other senior corporate leaders in dynamic and extremely challenging circumstances.

One such individual is the cochairman of Unilever. He slips from being a resonant leader which the authors explain is one who is inspirational, creates a positive emotional tone, and is in touch with others to being a dissonant or a disconnected leader and then returns to being the former while directing a controversial product launch. The authors refer to the leadership slip as the "Sacrifice Syndrome" which is characterized by losing sight of the important ingredients to effective leadership such as understanding and managing oneself and the need to understand and connect with others. Key elements of the "Cycle of Renewal" which is offered as the "antidote" to this leadership trap are mindfulness, hope, and compassion. Spinning out of the Sacrifice Syndrome and into renewal occurs when one hears the "wake-up call" or becomes aware of what one does not know and acts on it. By being deaf or inactive regarding this opportunity one ultimately traverses into dissonance. This process is depicted in Figure 4.2 and could be enhanced by labeling the arced dashed lines with hearing and missing the wake-up call, respectively.

The book also contains persuasive arguments for the development and sustainability of resonant relationships in numerous other leadership contexts besides the corporate sphere. Examples include a visionary leader who creates a South African primary school; an athletics and recreation director at a U.S. college who saved one of her athletic programs from being shut down by being aware of and attentive to the input from others; and a university professor from Kuwait who loses everything with the invasion of his country by Saddam Hussein's armies but gets traction on his larger dream of living and working in the United States by remaining hopeful and focusing on the future. The gender, cultural, and racial diversity of leaders depicted in *Resonant Leadership* will be of wide appeal to audiences such as senior corporate leaders who want to set a positive emotional tone in their organizations and organizational development practitioners who want to effect positive organizational change. Human resources directors will be informed of a strategic alternative to the revolving door of hiring and dehiring that can increase talent retention by helping to holistically develop leaders. Executive coaches will find an invigorating approach with practical yet impactful instruments to facilitate meaningful personal change with their clients. Researchers will be anxious to learn about "Intentional Change Theory" and then conceive of ways to further empirically test it and extend existing leadership development and individual change theories. Lastly, students will benefit by adding *Resonant Leadership* to their learning agenda that concerns building sustainable leadership. Audiences familiar with other writing by the authors on Emotional Intelligence (EI) will be very comfortable with this book as it builds on and goes beyond the need for emotionally intelligent leaders to suggest that "EI alone is not enough to sustain resonance" (p. 32).

Resonance is contagious and it is the leader's job to create this condition and to spread it. Understanding the role of intentionality in the individual change process is critical to effecting the personal transformation required of a leader to build resonance. Boyatzis' Intentional Change Theory provides the conceptual framework to understand how it can work. This refreshing approach to change involves five "discoveries" or discontinuities in one's self-knowledge. It typically starts by an individual identifying his or her ideal self or one's greatest personal aspiration. This is met with the discovery of one's real self or one's strengths where the ideal and real selves overlap and the individual's gaps where the ideal and real selves differ. The rest of the model is a reconciliation of what is desired versus what needs to change put into a learning agenda (discovery 3) where opportunities to experiment and practice (discovery 4) with the support of trusting relationships (discovery 5) are manifested.

To encourage movement among the discoveries and thereby facilitate resonance while avoiding dissonance, the authors offer numerous tools based on their conception that "hope is the driver, compassion enables its, and mindfulness makes the path smoother and more understandable" (p. 88). At the end of chapter 6 there are progressive exercises to build more mindfulness. Appendix B continues mindfulness skill-building with another six exercises. While at first review some exercises may appear simple and easy, the authors suggest that readers give themselves sufficient time to allow for incremental learning and reflection. Completing these exercises can really start to set the direction of one's personal change process. This is the case with "Exercise 2: Your Moral Code" (p. 82) at the end of chapter 4 which invites you to clarify your beliefs by reviewing a long list of desirable personal characteristics and then identifying and prioritizing your top five values. The result is the creation of a decision filter through which future decisions can be screened. For instance, how will taking that promotion impact your personal value of family happiness?

"Exercise 1: Insight into Your Operating Philosophy" in Appendix B (p. 215), is representative of the thoroughness that the authors take to learning and is a great complement to the values exercise. After completing this exercise readers come to understand how they value different experiences through one of three different views. A "Pragmatic" view suggests a concern for cost/benefit analysis. The "Intellectual" will value experiences based on their contribution to understanding something. The "Humanist" will determine the worthiness of an activity based on its impact on others. Knowing which of these you lean toward will help you in becoming more self-aware and to critically assess opportunities.

The authors contend that leadership is a tough job which can create "power stress" for the leader who can ultimately slip into dissonance. A new concept is offered that examines the reciprocal benefits of coaching with compassion. It is proposed that the coach also derives benefits from a coaching relationship in addition to the benefits that the coachee derives. This is a unique perspective on the traditional relationship. According to the authors, leaders become more other-focused, open and in touch with people which in turn serves as a prescription for "CEO disease" or the isolation symptoms that executives incur. Coaches experience regular renewal provided that they act for the coachee's benefit and not for purely the instrumental purposes of the organization. The focus of attention has to be on the person being coached not the problem that the person may bring to the relationship or the coaching process. Once again exercises are provided to apply this concept and extensive endnotes are offered for further reading on coaching and all of the other topics discussed.

The only inconsistency that I noticed in the logic of the authors' arguments was in their caution at the end of chapter 6 to not turn mindfulness into one's end goal for fear of becoming self-centered. However, in the chapter the authors note that mindfulness is the "practical application of self-awareness, self-management, and social awareness" (p. 137). How then could one become self-centered if one is truly paying attention to others, having empathy, and being service oriented? Perhaps the recommendation to the reader was meant to properly balance attention to self and to others so as to not have a lopsided awareness of what you are feeling while being oblivious to your impact on others.

CHAPTER 18

LEADERSHIP IN THE NEW MILLENNIUM

A Review of *Finding Our Way: Leadership for an Uncertain Time* by Margaret Wheatley

David L. Luechauer and William B. Locander

Margaret Wheatley has authored some of the most thoughtful and thought provoking books in the field of management. *Leadership and the New Science* (1993) explored how wisdom from biology, chemistry and quantum physics could inform managerial behavior. *A Simpler Way"* (1998) with Myron Kellner Rogers expanded on that work to show how organizations could be structured in more elegant, less cumbersome yet more sophisticated ways. *Turning To One Another* (2002) was a call to use dialogue as a means to integrate and unite communities. Interspersed with poems and photographs, these books were aesthetically pleasing as well as intellectually stimulating. They were useful for undergraduates, MBA students and practicing managers. The books explored different facets of organizational and social life through lenses that were unique, valuable and refreshing without being dogmatic or mechanical. The success and utility of Dr. Wheatley's previous books might lead one to believe that a compendium of her previous thoughts might be distilled into a compelling tome. Sadly, that is not the case.

Finding Our Way: Leadership for an Uncertain Time (2005) will be a major disappointment to Wheatley fans. It will do even less to inspire new readers to consider her ideas. The book is rife with conceptual, theoretical, and writing style flaws that hinder the readability of the book, dilute the message, and obfuscate the central tenets Wheatley would like the reader to embrace. Moreover, the collection of articles is disjointed, redundant, and extremely shallow despite the author's claim that much of the content was updated, revised, or substantially enhanced. The book reads like a series of wonderfully crafted introductory remarks but it fails to deliver much in the way of theoretical development or practical application that characterize her previous works.

Our primary concern with this book is conceptual. Margaret Wheatley wants her readers to believe that living systems are always growing, developing, and evolving into higher forms of themselves. Indeed, on page 96 she admonishes leaders "to forego any desire they have for repetition or sameness." This begs the question, "why does she spend 278 pages to basically reiterate everything she has written before?" Despite some cleverly placed introductory remarks, dedicated Wheatley readers will find that the content in this collection displays precious little variance from the original chapters and articles from which they were culled. Where is the evolution and growth in her writing and thinking? Likewise, she also wants the reader to believe that living systems work best when they are self-organizing. If that is the case, one has to ask, "why does she feel the need to write a prescriptive book that subtly and not so subtly argues that the only hope for the future is to embrace the world view she advocates?" Furthermore, if the reader takes seriously her assertions that: (a) it is impossible to impose anything on people (p. 105), (b) systems contain their own solutions (p. 106), (c) we each create our own interpretation of what is real (p. 91), or d) it is catastrophic to deliver changes without involving people in their creation (p. 89)—then, why does he/she really need Margaret Wheatley to help him/her "find the way?" Therefore, it is hard to make a case for why this book exists, when its tone, manner and content violate each of the principles the author claims to hold sacred. The conundrum inherent in Wheatley's approach is analogous to the manager who commands her employees to be empowered or the comedian who suggests that he takes humor very seriously. In short, this book appears to be a classic case of an author wanting the reader to do as she says rather than as she does. This error is magnified when the dedicated reader turns to page 296 to find that Dr. Wheatley has already produced a three DVD series which personally explores the critical issues in *Finding Our Way*. Dr. Wheatley sure has a lot of material for someone who supports the FAA official who said, "a lot of things are done intuitively, things that you can't write down in a textbook or you can't train somebody to do." Perhaps, instead of quoting this official, Dr. Wheatley should stop writing and allow managers to, "find their own way."

Another flaw in this book is the uncritical manner in which an open living systems biological model is presented as the primary metaphor by which to think about organizational life. While the metaphor is compelling, Wheatley completely ignores the idea that aside from being life affirming and creative, open living systems are also cold, cruel and violently dark places where death is not only a reality but a certainty. Failure to address this fundamental aspect of living systems is a Pollyanna view at best and at worst it is a gross misrepresentation of reality. Wheatley's approach creates false illusions of peaceful and prosperous relationships among living things that can't and probably should not be striven for or maintained. To focus solely on the creative, generative, and regenerative aspects of living systems denies the fundamental nature of the whole system. Managers who seek to create that which Wheatley advocates will soon be confronted with the shadow sides of the systems she describes and will have nowhere to turn for advice on how to deal with these aspects of organizational life. This could quickly render them frustrated, dispirited and burned out trying to create that which was impossible to create in the first place.

If the underspecified, underdeveloped and underrepresented aspects of a living systems approach do not frustrate the readers of this book, then a writing style flaw that will drive most readers crazy is the amount of redundancy it contains. Case in point is the story of the junior high school principal who used three rules to "lead" his school. It is told no less than three times in the first 93 pages of the book! Yet the reader is never specifically told how the principal enacted these principles, the obstacles and challenges the principal overcame to create this state, or the processes the principal used to maintain this enlightened way of being. While the story is enticing, by the third telling most readers will demand to know more about how this transformation occurred than Wheatley provides. Likewise, the phrase "In The Western World" or "Western Culture" is used as an ethnological indictment of inferiority with such frequency that one may wonder how the those of us in the West ever managed to launch and sustain a democracy, send a man to the moon, invent computers, or cure/prevent many of the diseases known to mankind. The ideological bias against Western styles of thought is so pervasive that Wheatley will likely end up alienating the very Western corporate executives and political leaders she so desperately wants to reach. While "artistic" and "ideological" redundancies can be forgiven, the flaw which can't be overlooked is the content redundancy. Wheatley repeatedly tells the reader: (1) the current command and control system doesn't work, (2) we need to emulate the principles found in living and open systems, (3) we are all interdependent and interconnected, (3) we cocreate reality, (4) participation is not optional, (5) we have to think long term, (6) life knows how to organize itself, (7) building trust and community are essential, (8) life must be free to create itself, (9) we can't plan or predict the future, (10) humans are inherently good and want to do better. Like the Bill Murray character who kept living the same day over and over and over again in the movie *Ground Hog Day*, readers of this collection will quickly begin to feel like Wheatley does nothing more than reiterate that which she has already reiterated. There are only so many ways to say the same thing and Wheatley seems determined to find them all, which is sad for an author who had so many original insights in her previous works.

The amount of redundancy in this book will create a very special problem for readers new to Margaret Wheatley. Namely, she never fully develops or explicates the ideas she espouses. Devoted Wheatley readers will love such turns of phrase and pithy one liners as, "you can't hate someone whose story you know" (p. 57), "the road is your footsteps, nothing else" (p. 43), "this god of science can only fail us" (p.125), "the problem is the problem" (p. 184), and "people can't be punished or paid into behavior" (p. 157). However, those lines are about as deep as it gets before the articles bounce to new ideas or rehash the same old ideas and stories. Readers who are not familiar with the logic and ideas that underlie her phrases will quickly find themselves asking such questions as "how" and "why?" Thus, while compelling "sound bytes" might be enough to satisfy those who are familiar with Dr. Wheatley's work they do not provide enough information to those who might be eager to contemplate, critique or implement the concepts about which she has written. Ultimately, this book is laden with too much of the wrong material and not enough of the thoughtful material which inspired and guided her previous work.

Finally, by her own admission, Wheatley writes that she likes to explore and think about organizations from the 50,000 foot perspective. However, as Henry Mintzberg is fond of saying—"knowing about something isn't the same as doing something." We applaud Wheatley's willingness to champion the idea that organizations are currently being managed in a toxic and dysfunctional manner that is harmful to the individuals who work for them, the stakeholders who interact with them and the larger environment. Nevertheless, saying the system is broken—over and over again—is not enough. In this regard, Wheatley offers painfully little in the way of hands on and practical advice for how those who are embedded in such organizations can actually change them. Pithy suggestions like "connect the community" (p. 174), "reclaim time to think" (p. 214), "prepare for the unknown" (p. 121), and "practice gratefulness" (p. 132) sound nice in theory but the working single mother manager or executive being pulled in a thousand directions is going to need a lot more help than catchy phrases. A person drowning in a lake doesn't need Margaret Wheatley standing on the shore chanting "embrace your inner child." At some point, we need all management authors—not just Margaret Wheatley—to descend from the clouds and mountain tops, roll up their sleeves and help us solve the problems they have exposed. Platitudes, parables, and poems are pretty shallow substitutes for the concrete actions plans, strategies and solutions we need our best management thinkers to devise and articulate. Mother Theresa, Pope John Paul, Martin Luther King, Gandhi, and the Dali Lama walked their talk and taught us all how to do the same. Margaret Wheatley would be well advised to stop writing or "rewriting" and start working on the very real problems that confront organizations, the people who comprise them and the societies in which they exist.

REFERENCES

Wheatley, M. J. (1993). *Leadership and the new science: Learning about organization from an orderly universe.* San Francisco: Berrett-Koehler.

Wheatley, M. J. (2002). *Turning to one another: Simple conversations to restore hope to the future.* San Francisco: Berrett-Koehler.

Wheatley, M. J. (2005). *Finding our way: Leadership for an uncertain time.* San Franscisco: Berrett-Koehler.

Wheatley. M. J., & Kellner-Rogers, M. (1996). *A simpler way.* San Francisco: Berrett-Koehler.

ABOUT THE AUTHORS

Terry Adler is currently an associate professor of management in the College of Business at New Mexico State University (NMSU). He received his PhD in strategy and information systems from the University of Cincinnati in 1996. Besides being widely published in the top academic business journals on such topics as trust, distrust, governance and project management issues, he was named the 2005 Donald C. Roush Professor of the Year at NMSU. Dr. Adler has made over 200 international presentations to organizations throughout the world.

Shawn Burkevich is currently a human resources generalist with Rockwell Collins. He received his MS in industrial/organizational psychology from the Florida Institute of Technology in 2006. His research interests include noncognitive assessment, training transfer, team dynamics, and employee engagement. Shawn advises the president of Simetrix Solutions, L.L.C. on training validation issues, and has previously served as a cook in the 2nd and 4th Infantry Divisions of the United States Army.

Phil Benson received his PhD in industrial/organizational psychology from Colorado State University in 1982, and teaches courses on human resources management at New Mexico State University in Las Cruces, NM. His primary interests are in the areas of staffing, compensation, and international HRM.

Danielle S. Beu, PhD, is an organizational development consultant with the American Heart Association. She earned her doctorate from the University of Oklahoma in 2001. She consults primarily on employee engagement, performance management, and leadership development. Her research is in human resource management with an emphasis on business ethics.

M. Ronald Buckley is the McCasland Foundation professor of american free enterprise, professor of management, and professor of psychology in the Michael F. Price College of Business at the University of Oklahoma. He received a PhD in industrial and organizational psychology at Auburn University. Dr. Buckley's research interests focus on the variables that influence the quality of employment relationships in terms of newcomer socialization, performance appraisal, and leader/follower interactions. His work has been published in such journals as *Academy of Management Review, Journal of Applied Psychology, Journal of Management,* and *Leadership Quarterly.*

Ingrid Campbell is a master of science student in psychology (I/O concentration) at Florida International University. She is a native of Jamaica, but received her baccalaureate degree while studying in Canada. Ingrid's research interests are broad, and cover selection, leadership, and organizational stress.

Thomas D. Carpenito is a recent graduate of the industrial/organizational psychology and human resource management program at Appalachian State University. Thomas received his undergraduate degree in psychology from Virginia Tech, where he worked under E. Scott Geller and Thomas Ollendick. Thomas is primarily interested in researching the intersection of personality psychometrics and managerial competencies within business executives. Thomas is from Kennett Square, Pennsylvania.

David Coghlan teaches organization development and action research at the University of Dublin, Trinity College. He has published widely in the area of organization development and action research. His books include, *The Dynamics of Organizational Levels* (with N. Rashford in the Addison-Wesley OD series, 1994), *Doing Action Research in Your Own Organization* (with T. Brannick, Sage, 2001, *Changing Healthcare Organisations* (with E. McAuliffe, Blackhall, 2003), and *Organizational Change and Strategy* (with N. Rashford, Routledge, 2006).

Deondra Conner (PhD, Florida State University) is an assistant professor of management at Alcorn State University. His research, which examines social influence processes, justice, and equity sensitivity, can be found in the *Journal of Applied Social Psychology, Personnel Review,* and the *Journal of Occupational and Organizational Psychology.*

Kristin L. Cullen graduated with a bachelor's degree in psychology and management from the University of Toronto. She is currently a graduate student in the industrial/ organization doctoral program at Auburn University. Her interests include training and skill-acquisition, organizational culture, and person-organization fit.

Loren Dyck is a doctoral candidate in the Organizational Behavior PhD program in the Weatherhead School of Management at Case Western Reserve University in Cleveland, Ohio. He also holds MBA and MA degrees from Hawaii Pacific University in Honolulu, Hawaii. Loren researches and teaches in the areas of emotional intelligence, human strengths, transformative cooperation, and organizational innovativeness. Loren also consults with and provides executive coaching to organizations in the private and public sectors

Viola Y. Fernandez, MS, is a graduate of the industrial/organizational psychology MS and the human resources/change management MSM programs at the University of Central Florida. Ms. Fernandez is currently enrolled in the human resources/change management MSM program at the same institution. She has presented her work at the Southeastern Psychological Association, and the Industrial/Organizational Psychology/ Organizational Behavior graduate student conferences. Her work has dealt with diversity issues in employment recruiting.

Barbara A. Fritzsche, PhD, is associate professor and director of the industrial/organizational psychology PhD program at the University of Central Florida. Dr. Fritzsche has coauthored over 80 papers, book chapters, presentations, and technical reports. Her research interests include decision making in job selection, e-learning, personality predictors of job performance, diversity in the workplace, and prosocial personality in the workplace.

Scott A. Goodman received his PhD in industrial/organizational psychology from The University of Akron. He currently is working at Shaker Consulting Group (a company he helped form) in the Cleveland, Ohio area. His interests cover a wide range of topics centered on increasing the value of clients' human capital by enhancing the performance and productivity of individuals, teams, and organizations.

Richard L. Griffith, PhD, is director of the industrial/organizational psychology program at the Florida Institute of Technology. His research examines personality issues in the workplace, specifically the faking of personality measures used in the selection context. His publications have examined the effect of faking on the measurement qualities of an instrument as well as the impact on rank order selection, in addition to a recently published edited volume on the topic of applicant faking. His recent work has focused on developing and testing a theoretical model of applicant faking behavior, and examining the job performance of those individuals identified as fakers.

Abhishek R. Gujar is currently a PhD candidate in industrial/organizational psychology at Florida Tech. His research interests include personality, response distortion, and the influence of cognition and affect on information processing. His current research focuses on computer-mediated communication and virtual teams.

Jonathon R. B. Halbesleben, PhD, is an assistant professor in the Department of Health Management and Informatics at the University of Missouri-Columbia. He received his PhD from the University of Oklahoma in 2003. His research interests include stress and burnout, organizational citizenship behavior, and health care management. His research has appeared in the *Journal of Applied Psychology, Journal of Management, Leadership Quarterly,* and the *Academy of Management Learning and Education.*

Jason Harkins is a PhD candidate in the Price College of Business at the University of Oklahoma in the area of Strategic Management. His research interests include strategic disclosure, top management team and entrepreneurial decision making, and understanding competitive advantage.

Wayne A. Hochwarter is a professor of management at Florida State University. He received a PhD in business administration from Florida State University, and has been on the faculties at Mississippi State University and the University of Alabama. His research interests include social influence processes in organizations, interpersonal effectiveness, accountability, and health consequences of stress at work. He has published articles in *Administrative Science Quarterly,* the *Journal of Applied Psychology,* the *Journal of Management, Organizational Behavior and Human Decision Processes,* and the *Journal of Vocational Behavior* on these topics.

Gregory R. Hyman, MS, graduated Florida International University in May 2005, with a Masters in Psychology (concentration in industrial/ organizational psychology). His interests include training and development, and leadership development.

Shannon Amerilda Irving, MS, is a doctoral student in the industrial/ organizational (I/O) psychology program at the University of Central Florida. She obtained her master's degree in I/O in 2005, and her interests include mentoring, gender differences, and computer-mediated communication.

Joshua A. Isaacson is currently a graduate student at Florida Institute of Technology studying toward a doctorate in industrial/organizational psychology. His main research interests are in the areas of personnel selection, group/team training, and issues dealing with technology in the workforce. His most recent work has dealt with the issues of personality and faking across cultures.

Claus Jacobs is a senior research fellow of the Institute of Management at University of St. Gallen, a visiting associate scholar of Templeton College at University of Oxford and a Fellow of Daimler Benz Foundation. His research focuses on discursive and episodic practices of strategizing and organizing that has been published in *Human Relations, Journal of Management Inquiry, Journal of Applied Behavioral Science* and *MIT Sloan Management Review* among others. He coedited also the Blackwell Strategic Management Society's volume on *Innovating Strategic Process*.

Matrecia S. L. James, PhD, is assistant professor of management at the Davis College of Business at Jacksonville University. She received her doctoral degree from the Florida State University in 2005. Her research interests include organizational cynicism, social influence, and spirituality in the workplace. She has published in the *Journal of Managerial Issues, Journal of Leadership and Organizational Studies, Journal of Applied Social Psychology,* and the *Journal of Applied Psychology*.

Andrew P. Kavulic is a graduate of the industrial/organizational human resource management program at Appalachian State University. Andrew's primary research interest is the fluctuation of stability in rater leniency, and is currently investigating longitudinal rater leniency trends. Other previous research includes behavior management through prompting and reinforcement, and the effects of stereotype threat on visual-spatial tasks. Andrew is from Atlanta, Georgia.

Diana Keith is a master of science student in psychology (I/O concentration) at Florida International University (FIU). Diana is in her final year at FIU. Her primary research interest is in the area of team effectiveness in applied settings, as well as multiparty decision making and negotiation. Diana's career has spanned 20 years in sales management and customer service. She has developed and managed successful teams in both business and nonprofit sectors. Diana is currently an executive coach in the areas of business development and work stress.

Dr. William Locander is the Davis Chair of leadership and director of the Davis Leadership Center at Jacksonville University. He can be contacted at the Davis College of Business, Jacksonville University, 2800 University Blvd. N., Jacksonville, Florida 32211.

Dr. David Luechauer is associate professor of leadership and associate director of the Davis Leadership Center at Jacksonville University. He can be contacted at the Davis College of Business, Jacksonville University, 2800 University Blvd. N., Jacksonville, Florida 32211.

Kevin T. Mahoney, PhD, is assistant professor of industrial/organizational psychology department at Louisiana Tech University. He received his PhD from the University of Akron in 2004. His research interests include individual differences and decision framing, and the history of psychological and management processes. His recent work has examined early innovations in survey research and the development of new methods to search and understand large collections of digitized documents. He has published in the *Journal of Vocational Behavior* and the *American Journal of Psychology*.

Elizabeth L. McChrystal, PhD, is director of human resources at Accent Technologies, Inc. She was the guest editor of this special issue. Her primary research interests are personnel selection, sexual harassment and EEO law compliance. Most of her recent work involves the legal perspectives of sexual harassment and personnel selection in small organizations.

Brian L. Perdomo graduated with a bachelor's degree in psychology from the University of Florida. He is currently a graduate student in the industrial/ organizational psychology doctoral program at Auburn University. He has annual conferences, including American Psychological Association and Association for Psychological Science. His interests include organizational socialization and person-organization fit.

Mitchell H. Peterson, MS, is pursuing his PhD in industrial/organizational psychology at the Florida Institute of Technology. His work has focused of personality measurement in the selection process. More specifically, his research has examined the motivational influences on faking behavior, as well as the impact of faking on hiring decisions and criterion-related validity. Mitchell also served as coeditor of a recently published edited volume on the topic of applicant faking.

Paul E. Pluta, MA, is an I/O psychology PhD candidate at Florida International University (FIU). He is currently employed as a human resources analyst with the County of Los Angeles, California. Paul's primary research interests focus on understanding and closing the gap between science and practice, particularly in the area of the attitudes of relevant stakeholders toward human resource programs. His recent work has focused on stakeholder reactions to structured employment interviews.

Bennett Price is a doctoral student in the industrial/organizational psychology program at Hofstra University. In 2005, he received his MS in I/O from Florida International University. His research interests include team decision making, performance evaluation, and individual and team effectiveness.

Kenneth R. Randall, MS, is a doctoral candidate in the industrial/organizational psychology program at Florida International University (FIU). His research interests include the effects of member cognitive ability and personality on team processes, performance, and adaptation to environmental turbulence. Kenneth has also conducted research in the areas of organizational culture, person-organization fit, and personnel selection.

Andrea Saravia received her master's degree in industrial/organizational psychology from Florida International University in 2005. Andrea is currently working in the human resources field.

Shannon A. Scielzo, MS, is a doctoral student in the industrial/organizational (I/O) psychology program at the University of Central Florida. She obtained her master's degree in I/O in 2005, and her interests include mentoring, gender differences, and computer-mediated communication.

Wesley A. Scroggins is an assistant professor of management at Missouri State University. He received his PhD in management from New Mexico State University. His current research interests include modeling employee fit perceptions and retention management. He has published in the *Journal of Health and Human Services Administration, Public Personnel Management,* and *Employee Responsibilities and Rights Journal.*

Kimberly A. Smith-Jentsch, PhD, is an assistant professor in the industrial/ organizational psychology program at the University of Central Florida. Dr. Smith-Jentsch is also the director of the Mentoring and Workforce Development Laboratory. Her research and publications focus on topics related to teams, performance measurement, training, and developmental relationships on-the-job.

Randolph Socin, Jr. is a doctoral student in industrial and organizational psychology at Florida Institute of Technology. He received his BA degree (2002) in psychology from Oakland University, Rochester. His primary research interests include personnel assessment and selection, applicant faking behavior on personality inventories, performance measurement, and test construction.

Jason Stoner is an assistant professor of management at Ohio University. He received his PhD from Florida State University. His primary research interests are in the areas of stress and identity. He has published in the *Journal of Occupational and Health Psychology, Journal of Vocational Behavior, Human Relations*, and *Leadership Quarterly*, as well as presented works at the Southern Management Association's annual conference, the Society for Industrial and Organizational Psychology's annual conference, and the national Academy of Management's annual conference. Jason is also a student affiliate of the Society of Industrial and Organizational Psychology, Southern Management Association, and the Academy of Management.

Daniel J. Svyantek received his degree from the University of Houston in 1987. He was a faculty member in the industrial/organizational psychology PhD program at The University of Akron from 1987 to 2003. He is currently a faculty member in the Psychology Department of Auburn University where he is program director of the industrial/ organizational psychology PhD program. He has published in journals such as the *Journal of Applied Psychology, Journal of Vocational Behavior, Journal of Applied Behavioral Sciences*, and *Human Relations*. He has consulted with several organizations on organizational change projects in the areas of problemsolving, compensation systems, and implementing work teams. He is particularly interested in the development of new evaluation methods for, and how the practical value of research is defined within, applied contexts.

Darren C. Treadway is an assistant professor of management at the University of Buffalo (SUNY). He received a PhD in organizational behavior and human resource management from Florida State University and an MBA from Virginia Tech. Treadway's research interests include the role of age in the workplace, social influence processes in organizations, performance appraisal, and social intelligence. His research has been published in *Journal of Management, Journal of Applied Social Psychology*, and

Research in Personnel and Human Resources Management. Prior to his academic career, Treadway worked as an operations and training manager for 8 years. His contact e-mail is: dtreadway@bus.olemiss.edu.

Peter D. Villanova is an assistant professor at Appalachian State University. He received his PhD degree in industrial psychology from Virginia Polytechnic and State University. His research interests include criterion problems, personnel selection, and performance measurement.

Melissa Weichert, MS, is a graduate of the University of Central Florida industrial/organizational psychology program and is currently an intern for the Learning and Development department of JetBlue Airways.

Michael M. Woodward, MS, is the president of Human Capital Integrated (HCI) a management and human resources consulting firm based in Miami, Florida. Mike is also a doctoral candidate in the industrial/organizational psychology program at Florida International University (FIU). Mike can be contacted at mwoodward_hci@yahoo.com.

Printed in the United States
110533LV00001B/30/A